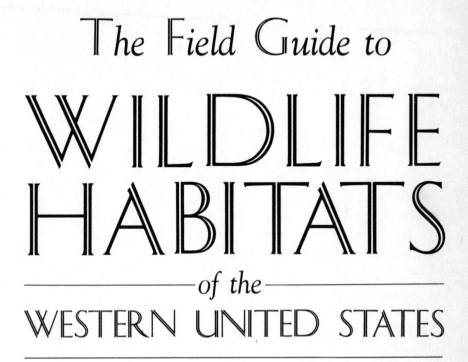

The Field Guide to WILDLIFE HABITATS of the WESTERN UNITED STATES

JANINE M. BENYUS

ILLUSTRATIONS BY GLENN WOLFF

A FIRESIDE BOOK
PUBLISHED BY SIMON & SCHUSTER INC.
NEW YORK   LONDON   TORONTO   SYDNEY   TOKYO

F

FIRESIDE
Simon & Schuster Building
Rockefeller Center
1230 Avenue of the Americas
New York, New York 10020

Copyright © 1989 by Janine M. Benyus
Illustrations copyright © 1989 by Glenn Wolff

DESIGNED BY BARBARA MARKS
Manufactured in the United States of America

10 9 8 7 6 5 4 3 2 1

Library of Congress Cataloging in Publication Data
Benyus, Janine M.
   The field guide to wildlife habitats of the western
United States / Janine M. Benyus : illustrations by
Glenn Wolff.
      p.   cm.
   "A Fireside book."
   Bibliography: p.
   Includes index.
   1. Habitat (Ecology)—United States. 2. Biotic
communities—United States.   I. Title.
QH104.B47   1989
574.5'0978—dc19   89-5975
                                                 CIP

ISBN 0-671-65909-X

IN LOVING MEMORY

OF MY MOTHER,

JOAN M. BENYUS,

WHO WATCHED

CAREFULLY AND

REMEMBERED ALL.

This book, like an aspen sprout, is connected to a vast network of underground roots generations older than itself. I am grateful to those researchers, past and present, whose insights illuminate these pages. Special thanks go to the Wildlife Biologists in the United States Forest Service, where I have worked for the past nine years.

I am also indebted to the professionals who were kind enough to review parts of the manuscript: Gary Brusca and Terry Roelofs, Humboldt State University; Kenneth Diem, University of Wyoming; Mark Dimmitt, Howard Lawler, and Peter Siminski, Arizona-Sonora Desert Museum; Richard Everett, Deborah Finch, Sarah Green, Raymond Ratliff, Leonard Ruggiero, Carolyn Hull Sieg, Daniel Vresk, and Jerry Verner, U.S. Forest Service Research; Dale Hein, Colorado State University; Michael Josselyn, San Francisco State University; Kimberly Smith, University of Arkansas; and Stephen Veirs, Jr., University of California.

A few people were particularly generous with their knowledge and their time: many thanks to the staff at Fireside; Diane Dabinski, Glacier National Park; Don DeSpain, Yellowstone National Park; Mike Hillis, Lolo National Forest; Glenn Wolff, an extraordinary illustrator; and most especially, Laura Merrill, U.S. Forest Service. For their help in the home stretch, I am grateful to Daniel Benyus, Mary Ann Hatton, Zoe Petersen, and Cynthia Robinson.

Lastly and most emphatically, I want to thank my family and friends who have been my living roots, nourishing me deep down while I wrote this book.

ABOUT THE AUTHOR

Janine M. Benyus has been exploring and writing about the natural world for fifteen years. Her publications include *The Wildlife Watcher's Guide to Habitats of the Northwoods,* which she wrote while working for the research branch of the U.S. Forest Service. She writes books and articles on natural history from her home in St. Paul, Minnesota.

ABOUT THE ILLUSTRATOR

Glenn Wolff is best known for his illustrations in the "Outdoors" column for the *New York Times.* His work has also appeared in numerous magazines and journals, including *Sports Illustrated* and *Audubon,* as well as many books for various publishers. He currently lives in northern Michigan with his wife and two children.

Contents

WILDLIFE/HABITAT PROFILES   47

Preface

I've always been comforted by the notion that somewhere out there, beyond the crime lights and the car horns, there are dark, dewy habitats humming with life. As I plan my escape to these havens, I take it for granted that they will be there when I arrive.

But lately, I've been wondering. I have a friend who works for the National Forestry Project in India. She keeps referring to this book as a historical document, a picture of something that may not exist a lifetime from now. In her country, so many of the forests have been stripped for fuel or fodder that only 12 percent of the land remains adequately covered by trees. A book describing India's habitats as they were even 30 years ago would be an archive piece today.

But could this kind of devastation happen in the United States? Actually, it's not that farfetched. The settlers who first saw this country could not have imagined that the "impenetrable" forest would one day be completely cleared away. Nor could they believe that the sun-blocking clouds of passenger pigeons would be reduced to a single stuffed specimen in a museum. Likewise, as we unwrap our fast-food hamburgers, we find it hard to believe that the beef was fattened at the expense of millions of acres of tropical rain forest. Half of all rain forests will be gone in a few years, and their loss could dramatically upset the world's climate. What would rising temperatures do to the robe of vegetation that clothes our continent?

Although we can't re-create habitats once they are gone, we can re-create our behavior before it is too late. Forty years ago, a naturalist named Aldo Leopold called for a land ethic that would have us treat the land—plants, animals, soil, etc.—as we would treat one another. Instead of appointing ourselves as conquerors, we would take our place as plain citizens of the natural world, expanding our circle of kinship to include all forms of life.

As a planet of people, we've already proven that we can enlarge our concept of social ethics. Consider, for example, that men and women were at one time enslaved as a matter of course. The sanctity of property eclipsed any consideration of human rights. Today, while slavery is still practiced in some parts of the world, most cultures view it as an atrocity. Perhaps someday, people will also view land abuse as a violent and antisocial act. In such a world, we wouldn't have to pay landowners to treat their land decently; the rewards of doing the right thing would be payment enough.

This kind of commitment to the land cannot be legislated. To endure, a social change of heart must be forged in the fires of personal change. As Leopold said, "We can be ethical only in relation to something we see, feel, understand, love, or otherwise have faith in." Visiting the places you read about in this book is the first step to seeing, feeling, and understanding them. The affection and faith will blossom in its own time.

In India, a small group of women began what is now a national conservation movement called Chipko, which means to hug or embrace. They began with the simple act of hugging trees to protest their removal. It is my hope that after reading this book you will also be filled with a desire to embrace the habitats of your own country, and keep them from falling into the hands of those who would abuse them.

How to Use This Book

Shhhh . . . What could that be?

Have you ever wondered what kind of animal might be rustling in the dark just outside your tent? Given the several hundred birds, mammals, amphibians, and reptiles found in the western United States, you could be flipping through field guides until your flashlight burns out. Unless, of course, you have a "search image" for that habitat—a mental laundry list of the wildlife you could expect to see there.

People who have lived or worked in the woods for a lifetime carry this sort of search image in their head. When they step into a habitat, they notice the kind of plants blooming underfoot and the type of trees spreading overhead. They have come to associate this vegetation with a certain community of animals. Under a ceiling of woodland oaks, for instance, they know to look for acorn woodpeckers, Anna's hummingbirds, plain titmice, western gray squirrels, and arboreal salamanders. They also know where in the habitat to look—on the ground for skunks, on the trunk for nuthatches, and in the canopy for warblers and squirrels.

If you haven't had the pleasure of living in the wild, take heart. This book puts the insiders' knowledge of wildlife habitats in your pack. With it, you can visit any woodland or waterway west of the 98th meridian and easily know which habitat you're in and what kinds of wildlife you're likely to see. More important, you'll find out why wildlife live in certain habitats, and what would happen to them (and to us) if these places suddenly disappeared.

You don't need technical training to use this book. The latest scientific studies have been transformed into simple stories that will stick with you. In your own wanderings, you'll uncover thousands of other stories enacted every day in the habitats around you. There are entire worlds to explore in every teaspoon of soil and every roothole full of rain—enough to feed your curiosity for years.

Before you go exploring, read the What Is a Habitat? section to find out why animals "choose" to live where they do. Knowing this, you'll be able to size up a habitat from an animal's perspective and predict which species would be likely to settle there. The Observation Tips section offers tricks of the trade that will better your chances of coming face to face with the wild residents. You'll learn how to think like an animal, how to lure, stalk, and hide from wildlife, and how to read their signs and signatures in the snow and mud. To help time your visits so you're out when the animals are, consult the Wildlife Events Calendar (see page 33).

Once you're outside, take a good look around. Are you in a forest, a woodland, a grassland, a desert, or a wetland? Are the trees broadleaf or needleleaf? Use the Habitat Key on p. 46 to narrow your choice to one of the 18 habitats. To verify your choice, compare the *habitat illustration* (there is one for each habitat) with what you see around you. The drawing includes characteristic leaves, flowers, and fruits, as well as wildlife and their signs you should be on the lookout for. A sampling of places where you can see the habitat (national parks, forests, and refuges) accompanies each illustration.

Now that you know where you are, read the *habitat profile* to find out why that habitat is unique, how it changes, and what it offers to wildlife. A checklist of indicator plants accompanies each habitat profile.

At the end of each habitat profile you'll find a Wildlife Locator Chart—a matrix that groups resident wildlife according to where they feed and nest. So, for instance, if a furry head pops up near your canoe in the rapids, you can turn to the mountain stream habitat, and look in the "Feeds in Water" column to find out which mammal it might be. Or if you spot a nest in the branches along shore, look in the row marked "Nests in Tree Canopy." Forty to fifty characteristic species are listed in each chart, giving you a complete "search image" for each habitat.

The habitat's most typical animals are illustrated above each chart. For more technical renderings, you may want to consult identification guides. This book is not meant to replace those guides, but rather to put a shelfful of information into a community context—the way you actually experience it in the field. In many cases, the illustrations you find here will be all you need to start enjoying the natural world around you.

After each chart, you'll find life history profiles of three key species—a bird, a mammal, and either a reptile or an amphibian—that are strongly associated with that habitat. You'll learn how each animal is adapted to its habitat and what to "look for," "smell for," and "listen for" to find it at different times of year. By learning how these animals excel in their environment, you'll also be learning about the community as a whole. Other animals that share the habitat will have many of the same survival adaptations.

Now you're on your way. You've learned the secrets of watching wild-life and you know how to identify the places where they live. If you'd like to know more, dip into the Resources for the Curious section at the back of the book. The Recommended Readings include some of my favorite sources, representing just a drop in the ocean of natural history literature. One of the great things about wildlife study is that amateur naturalists like you can add valuable information to our growing body of knowledge. If you'd like to be a part of the discovery, contact the groups listed in the Getting Involved section.

The deeper you delve into habitats, the more amazed you'll be. In each community, thousands of plants, animals, and microorganisms have evolved over eons to work together as one fantastic organism. I invite you to stand respectfully in their midst, and come to realize how much a part of them you are.

What Is a Habitat?

A PLACE TO LIVE

A habitat is an animal's home—the place where it finds what it needs to survive. A livable habitat should offer a tolerable climate, a varied terrain, ample space, and a dependable supply of food and water. It should have safe places for feeding, playing, hiding, resting, and raising young. A habitat, in effect, is the answer to an animal's everyday needs.

These needs may change throughout a year, or throughout the animal's life. Salamanders that swim in ponds during their early months may spend the rest of their lives crawling on the forest floor. Similarly, elk and mule deer migrate to cool mountain forests in summer, but head for the lowlands come winter. Even in the course of a day, an animal may visit more than one habitat to satisfy all its needs, just as you may work in one town and shop for groceries in another.

Very often, one of these habitats is the "preferred" one. This is the place where the animal spends most of its time, and gets most of its important needs fulfilled. Often, it is where it breeds and raises its young. In this book, animals are matched with their preferred habitats—where you'd be most likely to see them during spring, summer, and fall, when you're apt to be out looking.

The fact that you can predict where a species might spend its "working hours" is no coincidence. As you will see in the next section, an animal's preference for a certain habitat is the result of a long evolutionary journey.

WHY ANIMALS PREFER CERTAIN HABITATS

Animals are driven by the desire to eat, pass on their genes, and avoid being eaten. Through millions of years of trial and error, the survivors have become more efficient in their quest. They have developed physical traits and behaviors that help them get the most from their environment with the least amount of effort or risk. Naturally, animals gravitate toward places where their survival traits can really shine. In these preferred habitats, they have an edge over other animals that may not be as specialized to compete there.

You can predict where animals might live by looking for adaptations such as bill design, body size and color, skin or fur consistency, or even the kind of feet they have. The toes of treefrogs, for instance, have large round disks to help them hang onto the slick surface of leaves. In contrast, the toes of bullfrogs, ducks, and beavers are connected by webbing, which, though not particularly helpful in trees, is designed to give them a good push in the water. Tree-climbing squirrels, porcupines, and woodpeckers have sharp, bark-gripping claws, while the hooves of deer and moose are blunt and horny for pounding terra firma.

ADAPTIVE CHARACTERISTICS

Through the transforming power of natural selection, species develop traits that help them survive. Here are some of the physical and behavioral adaptations that link animals with their habitats.

In the Water:
Common Loon: heavy bones good for diving; webbed feet set far back for paddling power; can empty air sacs and push all air from feathers to sink straight down like a submarine; can shuttle oxygen to important organs when submerged for long periods.
Water Shrew: air bubbles under bristly feet allow shrew to run on top of water.

Beaver: special "goggle" layer over eyes; waterproof fur; webbed feet; valved nostrils; lips close behind teeth so it can dine without drowning.

River Otter: sleek shape; muscular body flexes up and down for speedy swimming; webbed feet.

Bullfrog: long kicking legs with webbed feet for "push"; eggs protected from cold temperatures by jelly mass; eyes placed on top of head so it can keep a low profile in water yet still see.

Spiny Softshell Turtle: can disappear under sandy river bottom by moving shell back and forth; long, sinuous neck allows it to keep nostrils above water while laying on the bottom.

In the Soil:

Common Snipe: long, probing bill "reads" the underground vibrations of earthworms; eyes set far back on head so it can keep watch when its bill is buried.

Pacific Mole: eyesight dim but unnecessary in dark habitat; broad forelimbs extend horizontally from body like flippers; clawed fingers are flattened like paddles; shoulder blades are enlarged; powerful chest muscles are the "hydraulics" of digging.

Thirteen-lined Ground Squirrel: elaborate burrows; can sense change in air pressure when burrows are invaded or caved in.

Northern Pocket Gopher: narrow hips ease tunnel transit; two-way

hair lays flat when backing up; touch-sensitive tail acts as rearview mirror; lips close behind teeth to keep dirt out of mouth when digging; fur-lined cheeks turn inside out for cleaning.

Western Hognose Snake: upturned snout helps it dig out prey; light sandy coloring for camouflage.

In the Snow:

Ruffed Grouse: grows combs between toes to keep from sinking into snow; dives into snowbank to sleep or escape predators.

Snowshoe Hare: extra fur creates "snowshoes" on long hind feet; winter coat is whitish with a slightly lighter underbelly to soften shadows under the rabbit and help it blend with backdrop of white.

Mice and Voles: build tunnels under the snow that are relatively warm, safe from predators, and close to food on the forest floor.

Ermine: coat turns white in winter; tail tip stays black to encourage predators to strike at the tail, not at the vulnerable torso.

Lynx: wide, floppy mops on paws help it float on top of snow; tufts on ears keep tips from freezing and may amplify sound.

In Tall Grasses:

American Bittern: vertical markings on chest look like reeds; behavior serves as camouflage too—stretches bill up to sky and sways when breeze moves the reeds.

Rails: vertically flattened bodies are "thin as a rail" to slip between grasses undetected.

Blackbirds: can perch between vertical stalks by balancing one foot on each of two stems.

Smooth Green Snake: bright green; when it straightens out, it looks like a fallen grass blade.

Leafy Forest Floor:

Ovenbird: plumage looks like fallen leaves; builds a leafy "Dutch oven" nest that is almost impossible to spot.

Yellow-pine Chipmunk: stripes blend with long, sharp shadows in open forests.

White-tailed Deer Fawns: speckled coats look like sunspecks on forest floor; odorless to elude keen-nosed predators.

Western Box Turtle: orange, black, and brown shell looks like dead leaves.

On Trunks or Limbs:

Woodpeckers: "grappling hook" claws for traction; stiff tail feathers for stability; reinforced skull bones for pounding. Extra-long tongue is stored in curved recesses of skull, then extended for remote-crevice probing. Tongue brushed with sticky barbs for pulling out insects.

Virginia Opossum: opposable "thumb" for clasping branches; tail can curl around branches.

Western Gray Squirrel: wide range of peripheral vision; memorizes routes through trees; tail acts as rudder; sensing hairs along body act as antennae.

Porcupine: backward-pointing quills dig into bark like spurs; strong thigh muscles clamp like a vise; paw pads roughened for a good grip.

Rat Snakes: belly scales adapted for climbing tree trunks; heart, lungs, and cells adapted to prevent swelling in lower body and speed blood back to head.

In the Leafy Canopy:

Wood Duck: narrow wings allow it to maneuver through the canopy at high speed; claws on webbed feet allow it to perch on branches.

Western Tanager: bright plumage blends with the sun filtering through leaves.

Treefrogs: enlarged, sticky toe pads "glue" them to leaves; tips of toes jointed to hook around twigs; body flattened to distribute weight; skin the color of leaves or bark.

Populations develop these special adaptations through the process of natural selection, colloquially known as "survival of the fittest." Natural selection favors the better-adapted individuals in a population. These individuals tend to live longer and produce more offspring than poorly adapted ones. As their adaptive genes are passed on again and again, the population as a whole begins to reflect an affinity for the habitat.

For some species, this affinity becomes very strong indeed. The animal that can satisfy all its needs in one habitat may never wander to another. It may become so specialized that it can't survive anywhere else. Many of our endangered species, such as the California clapper rails of salt marshes and the black-footed ferrets of the plains, fall into this restricted group. Their very existence depends on the health of one kind of habitat.

For other animals, habitat flexibility may be the key to survival. The ability to switch into new and different habitats allows species such as European starlings to multiply rapidly. These "jacks of all trades, masters of none" have parlayed their generalist tendencies into large populations.

HOW DO ANIMALS "CHOOSE" WHERE TO LIVE?

When an animal walks or flies through an area, how does it "know" whether this would be a good place to raise a family or find food? For some species, it's a simple matter of returning to where they were raised. Others must colonize new areas, relying on instinct to help them pick a good spot. Structure, patchiness, edge, size, special features, and other organisms are some of the factors that animals "consider" when choosing a habitat. There are, no doubt, more subtle clues that we don't yet understand. Next time you go into a habitat, try seeing it through an animal's eyes. Ask yourself the following questions to discover why an animal might "choose" to live there.

Structure. Are the plants the right shape, height, and leaf density for nesting, feeding, resting, and singing? How many vertical layers are there? Is the midstory open enough to fly from perches and catch insects? Are the understory and ground layer sparse or dense?

Bird researchers believe that birds key in on the structural "look and feel" of a habitat—the outlines and density of vegetation taken together. The species of plant is not as important as how it grows: whether it is a spreading shrub, flowering herb, vertical grass, or mature tree.

Each of these life forms (grass, herb, shrub, tree) represents a vertical layer in the forest profile. Each layer provides a place for nesting, hiding, or feeding that differs slightly from the site above or below it. Different heights in a forest canopy, for instance, have different temperatures, humidity levels, insect populations, and food resources. Over the span of evolutionary time, species have come to specialize in one or more of the layers, thus dividing up the resources the way newspaper reporters cover separate "beats."

The more layers there are in a habitat, the more opportunities there are for these specialists. That's why a dense, tangled forest has a longer role call of species than a simple, "clean" plantation.

Patchiness. Is the dense shade of the forest relieved by occasional openings, or is it just a monotonous, one-age, single-tree forest? Are there trees and shrubs of all ages, sizes, and conditions? Are there shrubs as well as midstory and upper-canopy trees? Are there grasses, succulent plants, and varying amounts of forest litter?

In addition to vertical zones, there are also different horizontal zones that can entice an animal to live in a habitat. A river, for instance, is made up of riffles, deep pools, and slow, wide stretches, all of which have different combinations of food, water, space, and cover that appeal to different species.

Natural disturbances such as windstorms, fires, insect infestations, and rockslides can create a gap in a large block of habitat and add a patch of an earlier stage of development. This mosaic effect gives wildlife a sunny field of berries, for instance, right in the middle of a dense, secure pine forest. A combination of patches allows animals to meet all their needs without traveling very far—a convenience factor that may mean the difference between life and death.

Edge. Are there zones of transition between two different types of habitat, such as field and forest, or marsh and shrub swamp? Is the contrast between the two sharp or gradual? How many miles of edge are there in this area? Are the perimeters of fields scalloped to provide more edge?

The junction between two different communities is one of the most

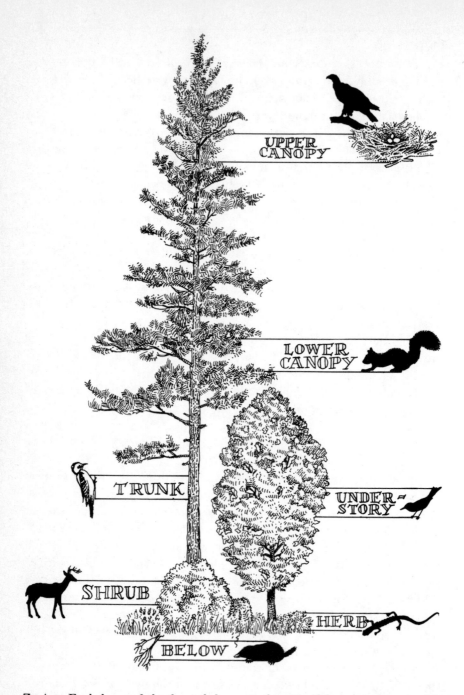

UPPER
CANOPY

LOWER
CANOPY

TRUNK

UNDER=
STORY

SHRUB

HERB

BELOW

Zoning: Each layer of the forest belongs to the animal best suited to survive there. By dividing up the forest's riches, animals can coexist while ensuring that none of the resources go to waste.

The edge, where two habitats meet, is one of your best bets for wildlife watching. You'll see residents of the forest and the field, as well as those specially adapted to live in this in-between zone.

heavily trafficked places in the outdoors, and consequently one of your best bets for wildlife watching. Here, animals from each community can be found together, along with "edge species" that specialize in this transition zone. The result is a community more diverse than either of the adjacent ones.

Habitats that are patchy have plenty of this edge environment. A gradual, shrubby transition between tall trees and short grasses will conceal wildlife as they are moving from one environment to the other. The vegetation along rivers (one long edge) also provides safe corridors that are essential for wildlife, especially when the river winds through miles of agricultural fields.

Size. Is the habitat large enough to roam in without having to cross roads or run into people? Is the center far enough away from the edges, where predators can enter?

Certain species of wildlife need large areas of unbroken terrain to roam in. Area-sensitive birds often build their nests deep in these extensive forests. If the center is too close to the edge, predators have easy access to these nests, and the birds may not be able to successfully raise their young. Grizzly bears need a wide range of feeding territory to support themselves. Gray wolves are especially sensitive to the intrusions of humans, and can be found only where wild lands stretch for miles.

Suburban sprawl has begun to chop up the once remote parts of our country. Biologists are concerned by this "forest fragmentation." They notice that there is a wider variety of species on large blocks of habitat, and a simpler, less varied clientele on small habitat "islands." When these islands are isolated in a sea of shopping centers and subdevelopments, there may be no way for new species to move in and replace those that die. The wildlife roster gets simpler and slimmer, until only a few people-adapted species (such as house sparrows and American robins) are left.

Special Features. Is the habitat close to water? Are there enough old trees to form cavities for nests? Are there perches for singing? Is the soil loose enough for easy digging?

A habitat may seem ideal, but if it doesn't provide a particular ingredient essential to the lifestyle of an animal, the species can't survive there for long. If the soil is too hard for the common snipe to probe, or the trees too young for nest cavities to form, or the water too stagnant for the Pacific giant salamander to breathe in, they must move on. When you read the life histories of wildlife, keep their special requirements in mind. This will help you narrow down the habitats you can find them in.

Other Organisms. Will competition from similar species be too stiff? Will predators be too abundant to travel safely? Will there be enough of the right foods to eat? Will parasites plague the young nestlings?

No organism is an island; each lives in an environment that is influenced and changed by other organisms that share the space. Bluebirds, which have bills too weak to peck out their own homes, depend heavily on the advance work of woodpeckers. Black-tailed prairie dogs do the advance work on the plains, supplying burrowing owls, rattlesnakes, and other creatures with "free" accommodations. Relationships are sometimes negative, however, and pressure from competitors, predators, disease organisms, and parasites can make an otherwise ideal site inhospitable.

WHAT HAPPENS WHEN A HABITAT CHANGES?

Once animals have settled into the habitat they are best suited to, what happens when it changes? Natural communities are in a constant state of flux, changing and transforming in a process called "succession." In succession, communities succeed one another, each one better adapted to the conditions of the site.

Consider the slow parade from bare ground to dark forest, for instance.

Annual weeds grow from seeds and make the soil fertile enough for grasses and perennial plants to get started. These stabilize and enrich the soil so that shrubs can break in. The shrubs shade the grasses and make room for tree seedlings, which finally shade out the shrubs. Even these sun-loving trees are not fated to remain for long, however. As they mature, an understory of shade-tolerant trees rises and eventually overtops the pioneers. Although this "climax" community is more stable than most, it is far from static. One lightning strike on a dry day can start the process all over again.

Each of the plant communities has its associated animal communities that wax and wane along with it. The ousted species survive by moving to another habitat that meets their needs. If there is one.

When humans alter habitats, it doesn't necessarily signal the beginning of a natural change. By pouring concrete, dumping wastes, introducing exotic pests, draining wetlands, or spraying chemicals, we often trigger an irreversible change. If the change affects a large area, there may be nowhere for sensitive species to turn. Other habitats may already be occupied or may lack elements that are critical for survival. Crowding animals into less-than-ideal habitats will diminish their populations, until, on a local level, they may become extinct.

When we lose a species, we also lose the free service that it performs in the ecosystem. Perhaps the lost species was a soil burrower, creating tunnels that rodents, toads, or insects used for shelter. Or perhaps by burying its food, it inadvertently "planted" acorns that grew into oaks. If it was a predator, its prey may suddenly explode in numbers, stripping large swathes of food plants from the area, forcing other species to seek new habitats.

EXTINCTION IS FOREVER

When extinction occurs on a worldwide level, the loss is even more profound. Species are the unique result of millions upon millions of years of genetic improvement. Once this carefully crafted template is lost, it can never be re-created. On a purely selfish level, we humans have much to lose when a species fades to extinction. Nearly half of our medicines come from plants and animals, yet only 2 percent of all species have been tested for their usefulness. If extinction rates continue as they have, nearly one-fifth of the species on earth today will be gone by the end of the century.

Forfeiting the opportunity for breakthroughs in medicine, agriculture, pest control, and environmental monitoring is actually one of the lesser dangers of extinction. The real menace is the tear in the intricate fabric of the worldwide ecosystem. A tear that starts small tends to run, and the fabric no longer covers or insulates as well as it once did. By weakening the ecosystem, we sabotage its power to heal, nurture, and replenish all life, including human life.

It's important to make a distinction here between natural extinction, which has been occurring for eons, and the relatively recent cases of human-caused extinction. In the past, as one species succumbed to a slowly changing environment, a better-adapted species evolved to take its place. This changing of the guard took place gradually, and for the most part, there were more new species than there were species going extinct. The result was a slowly growing pool of organisms.

Ecologists Anne and Paul Ehrlich compare this process to a faucet running new species into a sink, while extinction drains them away. As we overexploit organisms and whittle away at their habitats, we are actually widening the drain, and allowing species to go extinct more rapidly. At the same time, we are clogging the faucet up above, interfering with the ecosystem's ability to produce new heirs. By some conservative estimates, we are now losing one species a day, and that rate may increase to one an hour by the year 2000. At that rate, new species cannot possibly evolve fast enough to keep the level of the pool from sinking.

Extinction is the drain through which we lose unique, irreplaceable organisms like those in the margin. Human pressure on habitats has so widened this drain that new species cannot evolve fast enough to keep pace with extinction.

OUR NEW RESPONSIBILITY

Humans are changing the face of the earth. Armed with superhuman technology and a snowballing appetite for resources, we could conceivably make changes that would rival the ice age glaciers in their violence and scope. With this capacity comes a heavy burden of responsibility. Restraint

Most animals depend on a variety of habitat types to meet their daily needs. The best of all worlds is an area that has patches of old and young trees, both needleleaf and broadleaf, relieved occasionally by clearings and sources of clean water. This kind of diversity is healthy for the whole ecosystem. A diverse habitat, like a diversified economy, is less likely to crash when one element fails.

and wisdom are the emblems of an ecological conscience that we are finally beginning to form.

It is too late for us to step away from land management and simply "leave the land alone." We've made an indelible mark on the raw wilderness that was once the western United States. Some parcels of wilderness have, thankfully, been set aside as living laboratories, examples against which we can assess the health of our populated lands. But that is not to say that we can't live respectfully on settled lands.

National forests are "working" forests; they are professionally managed to provide wood, water, forage, recreation, and wildlife on a continuing and renewable basis. Each forest charts its future activities in a document called a "forest plan," which is subject to public review and comment. Your suggestions and objections must be considered before a single tree is felled or a foot of pipeline laid. In the same way, your city, county, and state lands are also managed with your tax dollars, and therefore can be influenced by your voice.

Although we can't go backward and make the West what it once was, we can at least try to maintain all the habitats that we now have. As Aldo Leopold reminded us, the first rule of intelligent tinkering is to save all the cogs and wheels, assuming each is important in its own way. On a planet as small and as fragile as ours, this simple respect for the land is much more than a courtesy; it's a matter of survival.

Observation Tips

THE WILDLIFE ARE WATCHING

It's the sleepy end of a long day in the outdoors, and your campfire is crumbling into embers. Suddenly, you get the feeling you're being watched by a tiny pair of eyes just beyond the ring of light. Chances are it's not just your imagination. After all, you've been under observation all day!

Wildlife are the world's most astute wildlife watchers. Whether they are hunting or trying to avoid being hunted, animals keep their ears pricked and their eyes peeled. They sniff the air for strange scents, and even use their tongue and whiskers to investigate their world. To outfox their enemies, they have also become masters of evasion. Their coat, feathers, scales, and skin are patterned to help them blend into their habitat, and their every move is calculated to keep them from being seen.

Into all this cleverness, we humans come, with our eager intellects and our average set of senses. The wild disguises tend to work on us, especially if we are not accustomed to watching wildlife. As a result of our "training," we are more apt to see an approaching car than we are to see a bat fluttering by. But like athletes who learn to sense a ricocheting racquetball behind them, we can train ourselves to see "invisible" wildlife in the woods. The first part is simple: be where the action is when the action is most likely to occur.

LOOK IN THE RIGHT PLACE

Animals tend to spend most of their time in areas where all their needs can be conveniently met. The animals you'll meet in the wildlife profiles were chosen for their special affinity to that habitat. Be aware, though, that habitat needs change from winter to summer as well as during different phases of the animal's life. For instance, many ducks that you'd normally look for on open water will take to the densest parts of marshes during the late summer when they shed their flight feathers and are suddenly vulnerable. Again, a look at the life history of the species will help you know where to look for it in any season.

It also pays to look up, down, and all around. Hikers who only watch the trail before them will tend to miss the owls roosting overhead, the martens chasing red squirrels in the branches, the woodpeckers poking out of tree holes, or even the warblers nesting at eye level just off the trail. Each of the layers in a community is occupied by animals that are specially suited to find food or cover at that level. Knowing which "piece of the pie" the animal specializes in can help you direct your search and spot the animal more easily. To find out where certain animals nest or feed—underground, on the ground, in shrubs, in the upper canopy, or in the air—consult the Wildlife Locator Chart for each habitat.

LOOK AT THE RIGHT TIME OF YEAR

Wildlife use different parts of their habitat at different times of year. If you know what critters are likely to be doing in any one season, you'll be more likely to find them. The calendar below can help you plan your outings to coincide with those peak periods.

Spring: Migrants return north to breed. Hibernators wake. **Summer:** With life in full bloom, summer is a season-long feast—a good time to raise a family. **Fall:** Migrants head south for warmer climes. Overwintering animals store food for the long haul. **Winter:** Some animals hole up for the winter. Predators feed on animals weakened by winter hardships.

Wildlife Events Calendar—Spring

Birds:

Migrating birds begin to return in waves, each week bringing a new species to paint the branches with color. They are in full breeding plumage—singing and performing conspicuous displays in hopes of being noticed by a potential mate. This may be their most vocal and viewable time of the year (especially before the leaves pop out).

Mammals:

Hungry mammals are browsing on succulent buds, shoots, and grasses, especially along roadsides and openings where the snow melts first. Moose and deer, starved for sodium after their spartan winter diets, often head for ponds where salt-rich aquatic plants grow. Hibernators such as black bears, weasels, and chipmunks are down to only a fraction of their normal weight. Once they regain their strength, the yearlings shove off to find new territories and the adults begin to breed.

Amphibians and Reptiles:

Amphibians are moving en masse from their hibernating spots to ponds for breeding. Many wind up flattened on highways that lay between their winter home and their breeding pond. The frogs and toads that reach the ponds fill the air with impressive trills in an effort to attract a mate. Meanwhile, salamanders, the quiet amphibians, are mating on the bottom of ponds, and hanging their eggs under logs, roots, or in the water.

Snakes tend to be rather groggy when they first emerge from their rock-crevice hibernacula. It takes a few days of basking in the sun to warm their temperature back up to the point where they can be fully active. Look for them on rocky, southwest-facing slopes, in the dust of unused forest roads, or on sunny logs. After they warm up and mate, they will move off into the woods or fields for the summer. Water turtles bask on half-submerged logs to warm themselves, sometimes piling on top of one another.

HOODED
MERGANSER

Wildlife Events Calendar—Summer

Birds:

In the North, late-arriving birds begin to nest, taking advantage of the fuller leaf cover. After one or more broods, they spend the summer foraging, becoming noticeably quieter. In late summer, some waterfowl shed their flight feathers and retreat to dense marshes where they can hide from predators. Early migrants begin to stage together in late summer, fueling up for the long journey south. Their restlessness at this time of year is called "zugunruhe," which means travel urge.

Mammals:

Young mammals are being raised and taught to fend for themselves. Summer is a good time to see family groups traveling together. Autumn breeders such as deer are feeding heavily in bushy openings in preparation for breeding season (called the rut).

Amphibians and Reptiles:

Many amphibian adults leave their breeding pond and disperse into woods and fields, most of them sticking to moist, humid places where they can keep their permeable skin moist for breathing. Young salamanders (newts) and tadpoles spend several weeks in the water, metamorphosing into adults that will seek land later in the summer. Watch the highways during warm summer rains; the moisture encourages frogs and salamanders to go out foraging.

Snakes spend the summer eating, shedding skin, basking, and avoiding predators. Land snakes may seek deep shade or burrows during the hottest part of the day. Turtles that grow too warm atop their basking logs simply slide into the water to cool down.

VIRGINIA OPOSSUM

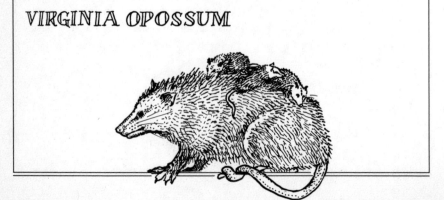

Wildlife Events Calendar—Fall

Birds:

As early frosts begin to kill insects and brown up the vegetation, many birds start to wing their way south, where food resources are still plentiful. Noisy flocks of migrants may descend on your area to feast on wild berries and grain for a few days. One morning when you wake, they will be gone. Wetlands along traditional flyways are great viewing spots, offering food and rest to hundreds of thousands of ducks, geese, and swans.

Mammals:

Hibernators are busy gorging on the fall crop of nuts and berries, gaining fat that they will live on for the next several months. Squirrels, beavers, and chipmunks are stockpiling enough to get them through the coldest days. Male deer and moose, full of the sap of the rut, are pawing and snorting through the woods, necks engorged and antlers itchy with velvet. Once their racks harden, they may lock horns with other males over the right to mate with a doe.

Amphibians and Reptiles:

Frogs and salamanders can be seen moving overland and across roads, heading for their winter quarters (hibernacula). They burrow beneath roots, rocks, or in the mud at the bottom of ponds—deep enough so that frost doesn't reach them and they can keep ice from forming in their tissues. Turtles burrow under ponds and in the soil, while snakes crawl into rock crevices and ant mounds.

TIGER RATTLESNAKE

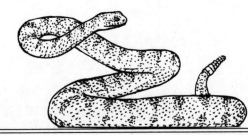

Wildlife Events Calendar—Winter

Birds:

The southern United States is a balmy winter home to many of the birds that northerners call "theirs." Some birds remain up north, however, adding color (northern cardinals), sound (woodpeckers), and vivaciousness (chickadees) to snow-muffled forests. When food supplies in Canada fail, irruptions of boreal species such as the great gray owl make for exciting birding.

Mammals:

Deep snow sends deer and moose to wind-shielded evergreen swamps, where they tromp down a network of trails for easy travel. Other mammals are curled tail-to-nose in their dens, breathing and metabolizing at a fraction of their normal rates. Look for plumes of water vapor rising like smoke signals from the chimneys of muskrat and beaver lodges. Under the snow, chambers open as the frozen crystals give up their water and begin to shrink. In this subnivean world, moles and shrews scurry along runways, feeding on seeds and paralyzed insects. On the surface, lynx chase hares, both running on "snowshoes" of extra fur that grows on their paws.

Amphibians and Reptiles:

Frogs are waiting out winter beneath the ground, breathing through their skin. Those at the bottom of ponds breathe a sort of muddy oxygen. Snakes are hibernating, sometimes in large groups of many kinds of species. Turtles under the ice breathe through their skin and through an all-purpose opening called the cloaca. A lining of sensitive tissues acts like a gill, filtering oxygen out of the muddy water and into their blood.

SNOWSHOE
HARE
(winter)

There are several "shifts" in the wildlife workday. Activity peaks at dawn and dusk, when the "changing of the guard" brings daytime animals in contact with those of the night.

LOOK AT THE RIGHT TIME OF DAY

Daytime. Early and late in the day are the best times to look for wildlife in the summer. High noon is usually too hot for most activity, and many animals are in day beds at this time. This may change in the winter, when some animals shift their activity to the warmest, middle part of the day.

Dusk and Dawn. Activity usually peaks in the twilight hours. Songbirds greet the dawn as night hunters catch one last meal. At this changing of the guard, animals of the daytime and nighttime mingle with those that are active only at sunrise and sunset. Tracks are fresh, winds are still, and sounds are likely to carry far at this time of day.

Nighttime. A whole world comes alive behind the mask of night. Owls and flying squirrels with their huge, light-gathering eyes are deftly sailing through the air. Four-footed carnivores are zigzagging back and forth, noses pressed to the trail of some hapless prey. Nights with a full moon are especially active. Use the moon as a searchlight or as a backdrop against which you can watch the silhouettes of high-flying migrant flocks.

HOW TO LOOK — NEW WAYS OF SEEING

Once you've mastered the wheres and whens, the real challenge of wildlife watching begins. Now you must learn *how* to look—how to see things beyond your normal set of experiences. In this quest, it's important to use not only your eyes, ears, nose, mouth, and fingertips, but also your imagination. As successful wildlife watchers will tell you: to find an animal, it helps to think like one.

Putting on the Skin of an Animal. Indian hunters used to dress in the skin of the animal they were stalking in order to get close to it. In the same way, you can crawl into an animal's mind to predict how it might behave. What would your day be like if you were a frog or a weasel or a hummingbird? Imagine how you would elude your enemies, stalk prey, find a place to sleep, and protect your young from the elements. Where would you run for shelter? Where would you bury food to last you through the winter? What would you do if a human entered your territory? To help answer these questions, find out as much as you can about an animal's lifestyle—the role it plays in its habitat and what it needs in order to survive. Books like this one are a good place to start, but better yet, get outside and watch animals being themselves in habitats near you.

See the Forest, Not Just the Trees. Watching wildlife is sometimes like being at a three-ring circus. So as not to miss any action, focus on the center ring attraction for a few minutes, then scan the surroundings to get a sense of context. Focusing and expanding every few minutes will enable you to see the whole show, not just a part of it.

What's Wrong with This Picture? Wildlife are intimately familiar with every stick and stone in their territory, and will easily notice something out of place, just as you might notice if someone moved a lamp in your living room. Try to see their world as they do; memorize the backdrop so anything new stands out. Watching how fast leaves fall on a breezy autumn day, for instance, can help you discern something moving at a different speed.

Use Peripheral Vision. Quick. How much of your surroundings can you see without turning your head? Using your peripheral vision outdoors will allow you to notice more, while actually getting you closer to wildlife. Animals are often threatened by a head-on stare, since this gesture signals aggression in most wild codes. Keeping your gaze averted may cause animals to relax or even approach you. To help strengthen your powers of sideways vision, practice seeing colors and distinguishing shapes at the very edge of your sight.

Extend Your Senses. In the early days of natural history study, if you wanted to identify a bird flying by, you would simply shoot the specimen. Today, thank goodness, you can get a close look at a living animal, even if it's way across the lake. Technology allows us to see like a hawk, hear what a bat hears, and find our way in the dark like an owl. Here are a few ways to improve on your natural equipment:

Sharper Eyes

Use binoculars, a tripod-mounted spotting scope, or the zoom lens on your camera to bring a distant speck into sharp focus. Most birders use a 7 × 35 or an 8 × 40 power binocular with a central focusing mechanism. The trick to getting a bird in your sights is to (1) find it with your unaided eye, (2) keep watching it as you raise the binoculars to a spot just below your eyes, (3) sight the bird over the top of the barrels, and, (4) without moving your head, bring the binoculars to your eyes.

Use a tilting mirror mounted on a telescoping pole to see the canopy world above you. Be careful not to disturb birds in their nests. Nest snooping is especially hazardous to rare or endangered species!

Better Ears

Use a parabolic reflector and headphones to pick up faint sounds. A tape recorder can capture them so you can bring the sounds of the outdoors indoors.

Keener Nose

Train your dog to follow scent trails and point out animals you may not be able to see.

In the Dark

Cover the end of your flashlight with a red filter (theatrical supply houses often have red gels that work well). Many animals see red as black and will go about their business without noticing your light.

Sprinkle fluorescent powders on the ground along wildlife trails. The tracks animals leave with every footfall will show up brightly under a black light.

Underwater

Strap on a mask, snorkle, flippers, or even scuba equipment to get eye-to-eye with aquatic wildlife.

GETTING WILDLIFE TO COME TO YOU

Get a Front Row Seat. Like us, wildlife are creatures of habit. They often use the same trails day after day, and fall into a routine that you can almost set your clock to. Water borders, trail intersections, raised knolls, natural springs, scent stations (where they leave droppings or scent marks), and den sites are likely to be high-traffic areas. Another good place to watch and wait is near the carcass of a large animal. Sit facing an area you haven't walked through; if it is upwind, wildlife may not yet be aware of your presence. Make sure there are shrubs or thick grasses for safe travel; wildlife won't cross unsafe, open areas to get to you. Sit with the sun at your back so the animal has to squint to see you (you'll also get a better photo this way).

Try to Blend In. Remember that wildlife are sensitive to anything new in their surroundings. To minimize your strangeness, dress in natural colors, cover your face and hands (with camouflage netting, gloves, or face paint), and make only slow, measured movements. Be aware that your eyeglasses can glint like a beacon in the sun; cover them somehow or leave them at home. Mask your scent by storing your clothes with a sachet of pine and bayberry (or better yet, natural fragrances from that particular habitat), and avoid scented soap and shampoo. If you sit out in the open to wait, flatten yourself against a rock or a tree so your outline is not so obvious. If you stand, make sure a long shadow or your reflection in the water won't betray your presence.

Use the Habitat to Hide You. Find something large enough to hide behind: upturned roots, downed logs, cattail clumps, boulders, etc. To see wetland animals, try wading into a marsh with cattails and other water plants tied onto your clothes. Or, camouflague yourself with leaves and go out on a limb to see warblers, kinglets, vireos, and other canopy birds.

Build a Blind with a View. Once you find a rewarding observation site, try rigging an artificial blind that you can use for the whole season. Place it out at least ten days before you first use it so wildlife will have time to get used to it. When you finally go in, have a friend accompany you. While you duck in, have your friend keep on walking. Wildlife can't count, and if they believe the human presence has passed, they may venture out sooner. A blind up in a tree may give you a good vantage point for watching larger animals that rarely look up for danger.

Do Animal Impersonations. If you don't have a blind, train yourself to sit comfortably, with eyes averted and muscles relaxed. Try "grooming" or "preening" as other large animals do. This "behavioral blind" technique has allowed many large-animal researchers to be accepted as one of the herd. You can also impersonate the call of a bird, and if you're good enough, the bird will respond in kind. It sings to let you (who it thinks is an intruding bird) know that this is its territory. With a baleful enough wail, you might even get a wolf pack to respond. You can also get frogs to chorus by imitating their voices. Tape recordings of animal calls can also be used, but require some caution (see Good Manners Are Good Form, page 42).

Sound the Alarm. Try imitating the alarm call of songbirds by saying the word "pish" a few times through clenched teeth. Curious birds may come to investigate the cry, especially if it's during breeding season when males are quick to defend their territories. Pishing works best when the birds are already giving chip calls, signaling their concern over your presence. Predators such as owls, hawks, foxes, raccoons, coyotes, and bobcats, may come running if you imitate the squeaks and squeals of a rodent in its death throes. Kissing or sucking the back of your hand may be just as effective as a store-bought caller. You're liable to get the most response in April, May, and August during the three hours before dark.

Rattle Up a Buck. You'll need a set of deer antlers for this one. Rattle the tines of the antlers together, scrape in the litter, and beat the bushes to imitate the sounds of two bucks fighting for a doe. During the autumn rut, you might get a curious buck to respond to your rattle.

Wave Something Colorful. Animals such as bobcats, ground squirrels, minks, and gray jays are incurably curious. Keeping yourself well hidden, try waving a scrap of colored cloth or a piece of aluminum to lure them into view.

STALKING WILDLIFE

1. Follow in Their Footsteps. Look for wildlife "highways" of all sizes, from vole-sized runways chewed in the grass to well-rutted deer paths. On dewy mornings, look for a dry trail in the grasses. Following these might take you to a favorite feeding ground, a watering hole, or a den.

2. Keep the Wind in Your Face. Smells will be fanned out behind you, rather than into the keen nose of the animal you are walking toward.

3. Keep the Sun at Your Back. The animal will have to squint to see you. If the sun is in your eyes, you may not be able to pick out shapes and colors as easily.

4. Play "Red Light, Green Light." Like the backyard game, wait to move until the signal is green, that is, when the animal is busily engaged in grooming, eating, etc. At the slightest sign that it is listening—tensing,

The numbers in the illustration correspond to the stalking tips in the text. Try using these techniques to get close to wildlife without alarming them.

ear twitching, raising its head—you should freeze. When it goes back to its task, you can advance again. You may be able to get within a few feet of a drumming ruffed grouse this way.

5. Move from Hiding Place to Hiding Place. When you do move, keep vegetation between you and the animal so it doesn't see your silhouette. If you take a peek, look around and not over the bush or boulder. Slink low to the ground when on hilltops.

6. Be the Creature from the Black Lagoon. Wildlife won't expect you to be coming from the water (not a typical human habitat). Try floating like a turtle, with just your head above the waterline, to get up close to animals on shore.

READING THE TRACES OF WILD LIVES

Wildlife stories are full of drama—hair-raising tales of chase and capture, braving the elements, and defending their young against all odds. These stories are recorded not only in books but also in the habitats that wildlife visit. The inscriptions are subtle—a shed antler, a drop of blood, the panicky imprint of a wing in the snow. These signs and signatures literally fill forests and meadows, and can tell you much about the sequestered lives around you.

The size, depth, and condition of tracks, for instance, can tell you how large the track-maker was, whether it was limping or running, and if it was alone or in a group. Claw marks and scrapes on the ground are "bulletin boards" where wildlife post messages to one another. Cast-off body parts such as snake skins or antlers tell you something about the age and condition of the animal. Animal droppings can reveal what they've been living on. Soft summer "cowpies" reflect a diet of berries and fruits, while a meat diet will produce droppings filled with hair and bones.

Try piecing together the comings and goings of the wildlife community by looking for the types of clues in the Wildlife Sign Chart.

GOOD MANNERS ARE GOOD FORM

There's a fine line between just observing wildlife and being intrusive. Even well-intentioned wildlife watchers like you can cross that line without meaning to. Here are some tips to help you admire wild animals without alarming them.

Don't Bankrupt an Animal's Energy. Most animals perceive you as a possible threat. They are willing to let you get just so close before they feel

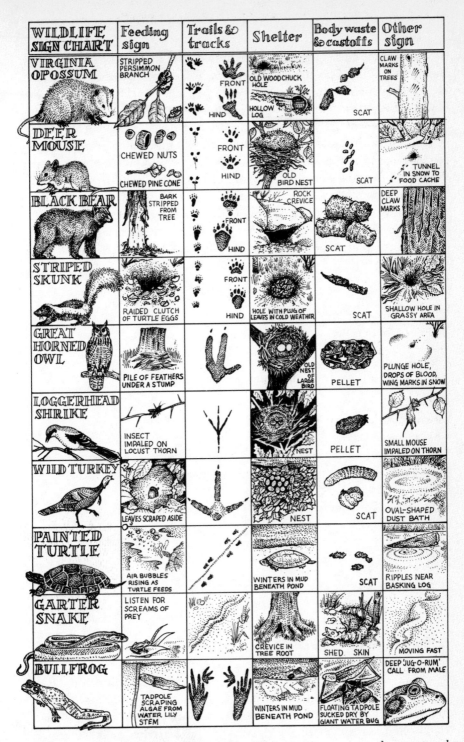

WILDLIFE SIGN CHART	Feeding sign	Trails & tracks	Shelter	Body waste & castoffs	Other sign
VIRGINIA OPOSSUM	STRIPPED PERSIMMON BRANCH	FRONT / HIND	OLD WOODCHUCK HOLE / HOLLOW LOG	SCAT	CLAW MARKS ON TREES
DEER MOUSE	CHEWED NUTS / CHEWED PINE CONE	FRONT / HIND	OLD BIRD NEST	SCAT	TUNNEL IN SNOW TO FOOD CACHE
BLACK BEAR	BARK STRIPPED FROM TREE	FRONT / HIND	ROCK CREVICE	SCAT	DEEP CLAW MARKS
STRIPED SKUNK	RAIDED CLUTCH OF TURTLE EGGS	FRONT / HIND	HOLE WITH PLUG OF LEAVES IN COLD WEATHER	SCAT	SHALLOW HOLE IN GRASSY AREA
GREAT HORNED OWL	PILE OF FEATHERS UNDER A STUMP		OLD NEST OF LARGE BIRD	PELLET	PLUNGE HOLE, DROPS OF BLOOD, WING MARKS IN SNOW
LOGGERHEAD SHRIKE	INSECT IMPALED ON LOCUST THORN		NEST	PELLET	SMALL MOUSE IMPALED ON THORN
WILD TURKEY	LEAVES SCRAPED ASIDE		NEST	SCAT	OVAL-SHAPED DUST BATH
PAINTED TURTLE	AIR BUBBLES RISING AS TURTLE FEEDS		WINTERS IN MUD BENEATH POND	SCAT	RIPPLES NEAR BASKING LOG
GARTER SNAKE	LISTEN FOR SCREAMS OF PREY		CREVICE IN TREE ROOT	SHED SKIN	MOVING FAST
BULLFROG	TADPOLE SCRAPING ALGAE FROM WATER LILY STEM		WINTERS IN MUD BENEATH POND	FLOATING TADPOLE SUCKED DRY BY GIANT WATER BUG	DEEP 'JUG-O-RUM' CALL FROM MALE

Here are some telltale signs of wildlife. With practice, you can learn to read them like calling cards to know which animals are at large in the habitat.

they must take action to defend themselves. Even the simple act of freezing and listening can be taxing. Their heart beats faster, they use up their food faster, and while they are watching you, they lose valuable foraging time. If you get too close for comfort, they will have to flee, which can burn up quite a bit of energy. One disturbance won't harm them, but repeated episodes might begin to cut into energy reserves that they need for raising young or keeping themselves warm. You can help by making your visits short and observing the animals from a distance they consider safe.

Keep Your Distance. How close is too close? If the animal shows the following signs (in ascending order of irritation), you are in the "disturbance range" and should sit quietly or slowly back away. Remember that binoculars and spotting scopes can bridge the distance between the two of you without unnerving the animal.

Birds
• Head raised, looking at you.
• Skittishness.
• Excessive preening, bill wiping, or pecking at food.
• Alarm calls, repeated chirping and chipping.
• Distraction display, e.g., dragging broken wing or spreading tail.

Mammals
• Head raised, ears swiveled toward you.
• Skittishness.
• Moving away or lowering its head, with ears back in preparation for a charge. Hairs on its neck and shoulders may stand up.
• Playing dead.
• Aggressive behavior, e.g., baring its teeth, charging, snorting, or slapping the ground with its paw.

Reptiles
• Hissing or rattling.
• Playing dead.
• Snakes raise their upper body, open their mouth.
• Striking.

Tiptoe Around Nurseries. Nesting animals are especially sensitive to disturbance. As you admire the nest, parents may be hanging back, while eggs chill or nestlings become dangerously hungry. If disturbed often enough, parents may abandon the nest, or young animals may leave before they are ready to fend for themselves. Remember also that predators may be following your scent trail, which takes them to nests they might otherwise have overlooked.

Before approaching a nest, always scan the area with your binoculars to see if the female is around. Use stalking techniques to keep her from being alarmed. If you are taking pictures, don't be tempted to trim back vegetation to get a better shot. The foliage you remove might have been shading the nest or screening it from winged predators. Better to leave the vegetation in place and limit your stay to no more than fifteen minutes.

Turn Rocks and Logs Back Over. When uncovering reptiles and amphibians, be sure to replace the debris you turn over. You're lifting the roof off their home! Leaving them exposed will subject the residents to the elements and predators.

Keep an Eye on Pets. A rambunctious dog or cat can do much damage by chasing wildlife or digging up their eggs, food stores, or burrows.

Cut Motorboat Speed Near Shore. Besides frightening wildlife, a speeding boat can cause serious erosion on shore. Boat wakes are tidal waves to breeding snakes, turtles, salamanders, frogs, emerging hibernators, and wading shorebirds. A whole raft of eggs may be washed away in one crest.

Don't Tempt Wildlife with Food. Bears and other so-called dangerous animals are rarely interested in fighting with you, but they are interested in your food. Never bring it into your tent with you, and before turning in, tie it up between two trees, well out of their reach. Making wildlife dependent on handouts does them no favors, and may lead to their untimely death. What if the next person they approach has a gun instead of a piece of bread?

Don't Be a Hero. There may come a time when you inadvertently get between a mother and its young, or a hungry animal and its dinner. Naturally, this will be seen as a threat. Don't run, and don't stare directly at the animal, as this can be interpreted as aggression on your part. Instead, avert your eyes and back away slowly—the wildland equivalent of "crying uncle."

Respect the Rights of Your Own Species. Many landowners will gladly waive their no trespassing policy if you let them know why you're there. Keep relations smooth by walking the edges of fields rather than through crops. And if you run into other rapt observers, stay still so you don't spook the wildlife they are watching.

HABITAT KEY

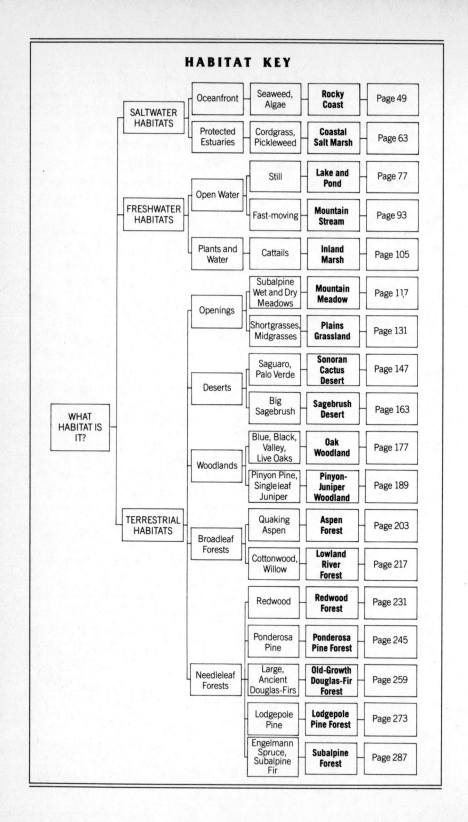

SALTWATER HABITATS	Oceanfront	Seaweed, Algae	**Rocky Coast** — Page 49
	Protected Estuaries	Cordgrass, Pickleweed	**Coastal Salt Marsh** — Page 63
FRESHWATER HABITATS	Open Water	Still	**Lake and Pond** — Page 77
		Fast-moving	**Mountain Stream** — Page 93
	Plants and Water	Cattails	**Inland Marsh** — Page 105
TERRESTRIAL HABITATS	Openings	Subalpine Wet and Dry Meadows	**Mountain Meadow** — Page 117
		Shortgrasses, Midgrasses	**Plains Grassland** — Page 131
	Deserts	Saguaro, Palo Verde	**Sonoran Cactus Desert** — Page 147
		Big Sagebrush	**Sagebrush Desert** — Page 163
	Woodlands	Blue, Black, Valley, Live Oaks	**Oak Woodland** — Page 177
		Pinyon Pine, Singleleaf Juniper	**Pinyon-Juniper Woodland** — Page 189
	Broadleaf Forests	Quaking Aspen	**Aspen Forest** — Page 203
		Cottonwood, Willow	**Lowland River Forest** — Page 217
	Needleleaf Forests	Redwood	**Redwood Forest** — Page 231
		Ponderosa Pine	**Ponderosa Pine Forest** — Page 245
		Large, Ancient Douglas-Firs	**Old-Growth Douglas-Fir Forest** — Page 259
		Lodgepole Pine	**Lodgepole Pine Forest** — Page 273
		Engelmann Spruce, Subalpine Fir	**Subalpine Forest** — Page 287

WHAT HABITAT IS IT?

WILDLIFE HABITAT PROFILES

DAYTIME   DUSK · DAWN   NIGHT

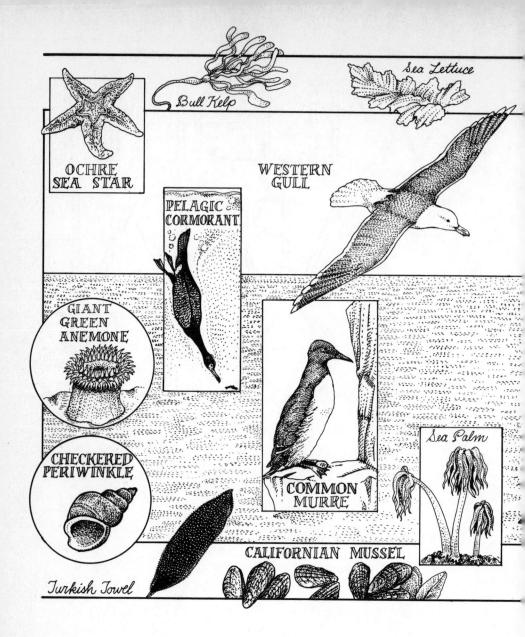

Bull Kelp

Sea Lettuce

OCHRE
SEA STAR

WESTERN
GULL

PELAGIC
CORMORANT

GIANT
GREEN
ANEMONE

CHECKERED
PERIWINKLE

COMMON
MURRE

Sea Palm

CALIFORNIAN MUSSEL

Turkish Towel

LEACH'S STORM-PETREL

TUFTED PUFFIN

AMERICAN BLACK OYSTERCATCHER

black zone
periwinkles
barnacles
rockweeds
mussels
kelp

CALIFORNIA SEA LION

ACORN BARNACLE

Surf Grass

Rockweed

Rocky Coast

WHERE TO SEE THIS HABITAT:

California: Cabrillo National Monument; Channel Islands, North Cascades, and Redwood national parks; Farallon Islands National Wildlife Refuge; King Range National Conservation Area; Point Reyes National Seashore
Oregon: Cape Meares, Oregon Islands, and Three Arch Rocks national wildlife refuges; Taquina Head National Area
Washington: Copalis, San Juan Islands, and Willapa national wildlife refuges; Olympic National Park

Rocky Coast

BEGINNINGS

You can see them way out there. Long, rolling swells that have traveled thousands of miles across open water, powered by a storm that ended days ago. Crowded now by the rising ocean bottom, they buckle up and crest, heaving their full force against the weathered bedrock of the continent.

Each wave that crashes compresses air into tiny crevices and weaknesses in the rock, causing the crevices to widen bit by bit. Storm-lashed waves are powerful enough to tear out whole pieces of the rock and hurl them back against the cliff, thus undercutting it at its base. Once this horizontal cave cuts deep enough, the overhanging lip of rock collapses or "calves," leaving a pile of rubble at the base of the cliff. The constant force of water rolls these bigger boulders back and forth, slowly grinding them into smaller pieces that will be whisked away, leaving the cliff face vulnerable once again to the waves.

The scalloped look of our shoreline is due to the varying degrees of resistance to this sort of erosion. The headlands that you see forging out into the sea like the prow of a boat are composed of resistant rocks such as granite or basalt. The rocky "seastacks" that remain just offshore are stubborn leftovers from the last shoreline. The coves that finger inland between two headlands may have been faults in the rock composed of softer material. In these protected coves, the water slows down enough to drop the "trailings" of cliffside mining, creating crescent beaches of sand.

Believe it or not, life does manage to take hold along the rugged, rocky coast. The degree of wave shock, along with the daily and fortnightly cycle of high and low tides, ordains where certain kinds of life can be found.

Dry land begins above the line of highest tides, while the deep sea begins below the line of lowest tides. Between these two lines is the intertidal zone—a habitat that at certain times of the day or season may be covered by seawater or exposed by low tide. Life on the higher rocks must endure the hazards of being exposed—including the blistering sun, land predators, drying out, and rainwater. Those lower on the rocks spend more of their day submerged, coping with attacks from sea creatures, relentless wave action, and constant saltiness. How well an organism responds to these hazards will determine where on the rocks it will take up residence. Learning the "seating assignments" will increase your appreciation of the rocky coast habitat.

LIFE BETWEEN THE TIDES

The official meeting of land and sea, be it in Australia, Africa, or Argentina, is marked by the "black zone"—a band of lichens (*Verrucaria* spp.) and blue-green algae that is soaked by the sea only during the two highest tides of each month ("spring tides"). Some of these algae are covered by a gelatinous coat that keeps them from drying out, but makes for treacherous footing. Tiny, spiral-shelled periwinkle snails move slowly across the black zone, scraping off the algae with their "radula"—a fleshy conveyor belt studded with tiny teeth (3,500 in the common periwinkle). These teeth abrade bits of rock along with the algae, and as they wear out, a new row of teeth is "rolled" up to take their place.

Farther down is the barnacle zone, so tightly packed with the flinty white cones that the rocks may appear white from a distance. Each acorn barnacle is a wonder to behold. The barnacle's shell consists of six neat-fitting plates, sloped in the shape of a cone so that waves break over them without resistance. Atop the cone is a "sunroof" of four plates that the barnacle can close to keep from drying out between tides. Next time the water rolls in, wade over and find out what lurks inside the bony shell. In the right light, you can see just the faintest shadow flickering at the top of each cone. These are the appendages of the barnacle kicking food down into the shell, where its hungry mouth waits. When this upside-down architect dies, its shell, still cemented to the rocks, is used by the tiny young of periwinkles, shrimps, and others for shelter. Scattered among the barnacles are limpets—snails with flattened, volcano-shaped shells that also divert water easily. Some kinds of limpets rasp away the rock to form a small depression or "home" to which they faithfully return after a day of algal grazing.

Below the barnacles are the gardens of rockweeds, a group of brown algae with swollen bags of reproductive cells at the tips of their branches. When the tide is in, these plants are buoyed up straight like tiny forest trees. When the tide slacks, the rockweeds lay down in overlapping curtains, trapping and holding moisture beneath them. Many creatures live within this temporary haven, protected from the sun and dry air by the rubbery fronds.

Below the rockweeds, thousands of upright Californian mussels open their shells so they can strain microorganisms from the incoming seawater. They attach to the rock via "byssus" threads, thin streams of liquid that flow from their fleshy foot and harden into threads of steellike strength. These byssus threads intercept sediments and create another protected microhabitat for small organisms. Intertwined with the mussels you may see beds of a carpetlike red algae called Turkish towel, along with raised clumps of goose barnacles, or patches of sea palm where the surf is strong.

Sea palm, a seaweed that looks like a miniature palm tree, anchors itself among the mussels with clawing holdfasts that resemble tree roots. When the beds are packed to capacity, the sea palm ingeniously attaches

CHARACTERISTIC PLANTS:

Trees and Shrubs:
salal
thimbleberry

Algae and Seaweeds:
agar weed
algae
black pine
boas
bull kelp
corraline algae
encrusting coral
enteromorpha green
  algae
feather boa
fir needle
giant perennial kelp
green algae
harebell
hummingbird's trum-
  pet
iridescent seaweed
laver
lichens
little rockweed
nail brush
nootka rose

nori
red fescue
rockweed
roseroot
sea lettuce
sea palm
sea sack
sea staghorn
seaside plantain
sugar wrack
surf grass
tar spot
thrifts
Turkish towel
vetches
wild thrift
winged kelp

Sea Palm

itself to a mussel instead of the rockbed. When a storm unseats the sea palm, it rips the mussel up with it, freeing up a prime plot of rockbed. The sea palm's spores, which have been "waiting" for just such an opportunity, quickly colonize the gap.

At the lowest limits of the intertidal zone are the broad, frilled streamers of large kelps. If they look somewhat ragged, it's by evolutionary design. The leaves are built to split, tear, and "give" under the force of the waves so that the holdfasts are spared the strain. Starfish such as the ochre sea star are among the many organisms that seek refuge within the tangle of holdfasts during low tide. When the tide rises, the starfish creep up to the mussel beds to feast. To disarm a mussel, the starfish humps its body over the closed shell and pulls the valves apart. It then turns its stomach inside out and slides it into the crevice, thus digesting the fleshy creature within.

Lurking in the mirrorlike tide pools among the rocks is a bright green animal that looks like a plant in bloom. The "blossom" of the giant green anemone is actually a ring of stinging tentacles that paralyze small animals that wander too close. The exploding darts within the tentacles are harmless to humans, unless they come in contact with a thin-skinned area, such as your tongue.

Just a note of caution about exploring the tide pools at the water's edge: keep your eye on the tide and on the size of the swells. If a rogue wave catches you, spread your body like a starfish, flat against the rock, and hold on so you're not swept away. Also, be careful to replace any rocks you turn over, and to leave the peculiar animals you find in their natural homes.

WHAT'S IN IT FOR WILDLIFE?

The surf crashes, the spray flies, and the gulls and surfbirds rise and settle, rise and settle, at one with the breathing of the waves. They may lounge at the spray zone for hours, biding their time until the tide rolls out and exposes the banquet of sea life stranded on the intertidal rocks.

In the meantime, the high water has buoyed the beds of kelp and created an underwater forest populated by herrings, sand lances, sculpins, blennies, and other fish. From the sky, gulls, pelicans, and terns dive headfirst, emerging from the spray with a finny meal in their beaks. The winter flocks of red-breasted mergansers, harlequin ducks, surf scoters, and western, red-necked, and horned grebes paddle on the surface, diving under occasionally to harvest the riches. Cormorants dive deep, powered by their large, webbed feet. Auklets, murres, murrelets, guillemots, and puffins "fly" underwater, using their short wings to propel them. Storm-petrels hover

over the water, pattering their feet along the surface, and filling their bills with "zooplankton"—clouds of tiny animals that drift freely in the sea.

After feeding, many of the birds indulge in a cold-water bath. With a dipping and scooping motion of their head, they throw droplets over their back and hold their feathers open so the water soaks through to the down-covered skin. Like scratching and yawning in humans, these preening actions are contagious and will ripple through the flock. This phenomenon has survival advantages for birds that make their living in the water because preening keeps their feathers well oiled, and thus keeps their bodies well insulated.

When the tide falls, battalions of birds fan out over the rocks in search of mussels, limpets, crabs, and other crustaceans. The surfbirds, black turnstones, wandering tattlers, and rock sandpipers are all outfitted with dark gray plumage that blends well with the color of wet rocks. Black turnstones flip small rocks and seaweed with their bill, exposing surprised crabs and other creatures. Black oystercatchers, with even darker black plumage, use their long red bill to pry into or smash open shellfish. Extremely low tides expose an even richer larder of foods. Gulls and crows wander down to pick apart the strands of kelp and to poke for animals caught among the holdfasts.

If you're lucky, you'll find a rocky ledge remote enough to entice harbor seals and California and northern sea lions to "haul out" for a snooze or to rear their pups. Be sure to watch the waters in front of the rocky shoal for the gleaming heads of sea otters, seals, or sea lions cavorting, courting, or fishing in the swells. At night, land mammals such as minks, raccoons, and foxes are known to pick their way along the rocky beaches, searching for casualties of the low tide—dead fish, birds, or other sea life. In the higher, drier headlands, mule deer, Townsend's moles, or vagrant shrews may be found in the rare pockets of vegetation.

For the most part, however, rocky cliffs facing the sea are notably free of mammalian predators. This is one of the reasons why so many birds build their nests on these promontories. Closest to the spray zone, you'll find the nests of black oystercatchers (little more than an egg on the rocks) and of pelagic cormorants (a little seaweed on a ledge near the water). Pigeon guillemots pack themselves in dense rows on narrow ledges a little higher up from the spray zone. Sometimes the ledges are so narrow that the guillemots have no room to turn around after landing; they actually have to take off facing the cliff! Brandt's cormorants usually select a gentler slope, while the double-crested cormorants place their nests on the tops of cliffs along with burrow-nesting tufted puffins. You can see the droll-faced puffins loitering outside their nest holes in early morning, in late evening, or on foggy days. Also look for rafts of puffins swimming in the water near their nesting islands. Other seabirds that nest in cliff-face colonies are

XANTUS' MURRELET BROWN PELICAN NORTHERN SEA LION SEA OTTER HARBOR SEAL GRAY FOX ROCK SANDPIPER

WILDLIFE LOCATOR CHART—ROCKY COAST

	Feeds from Air	Feeds on Ground	Feeds in Shallow Water (Wades or Dabbles)	Feeds Underwater (Dives or Dips)
Nests in Tree Canopy	Brown Pelican	American Crow	Great Blue Heron	Marbled Murrelet
Nests on Ground	Peregrine Falcon Elegant Tern Black Swift	Snowy Plover, American Black Oystercatcher, Wandering Tattler, Black Turnstone, Surfbird, Rock Sandpiper, Western Gull, Glaucous-winged Gull, Mule Deer	American Wigeon	Brandt's Cormorant, Pelagic Cormorant, Harlequin Duck, Surf Scoter, Red-breasted Merganser, Common Murre, Pigeon Guillemot, Xantus' Murrelet, Northern Sea Lion, California Sea Lion, Harbor Seal
Nests Beneath Ground or Debris	Fork-tailed Storm-Petrel Leach's Storm-Petrel Ashy Storm-Petrel	Townsend's Mole, Gray Fox, Island Night Lizard		Cassin's Auklet, Rhinoceros Auklet, Tufted Puffin, River Otter
Nests on Water				Horned Grebe
Nests in Water				Sea Otter

common murres, glaucous-winged gulls, and four burrowing nesters that are active only at night—Cassin's and rhinoceros auklets and fork-tailed and Leach's storm-petrels.

The rule of thumb when visiting these rocky nurseries is to admire from a distance. Although you may mean well, your footsteps may crush a well-camouflaged oystercatcher egg or cave in the burrow of a puffin. Your very presence may cause the birds to flush from their nests and leave their eggs or young exposed to marauding western gulls, glaucous-winged gulls, American crows, and common ravens that are always on hand to take advantage of such an opportunity. The best view of a busy colony is through the lenses of binoculars.

Common Murre

The best way to get to know the murres is to bob in a boat all day within binocular range of one of their "loomeries," or breeding colonies. On Farallon Islands in California, there are three-quarters of a million murres nesting in every available square inch of ledge and clifftop. It's literally standing room only, with the brooding females packed in shoulder to shoulder, each one balancing a single large, pear-shaped egg on top of her feet. Whatever discomfort there may be in this extremely high-density living is offset by the security it provides. When a predator such as a gull, skua, jaeger, or osprey approaches the colony, it is greeted by a fortress of sharp, upraised bills, loud squawks, and flapping wings. If the birds were in smaller or looser colonies, they couldn't mount such an effective defense, and might easily lose their young to predators.

Living this closely becomes complicated by the fact that each bird, although touching its neighbor, is also actively defending the tiny territory it occupies. The only reason the loomery is not in total pandemonium is that the murres have developed a complex "language." By using vocal and physical gestures, an interaction that has the potential of being violent usually fizzles into mutual tolerance. The owner of a territory first threatens an intruder by flapping its wings and crying. The intruder responds with a series of appeasement gestures that say, basically, "I don't want to fight." These gestures include turning or stretching away, sky-pointing with the bill, and side preening. Similarly, when a bird walks through the flock, it usually keeps its wings outstretched in a position that means "I'm not a threat." Young and adult birds also have a special vocabulary that helps them keep track of one another in the crowded nursery.

When it comes time for the young to leave the nest, they usually walk back and forth on the ledge for a few days, calling out to the adults below, as if for reassurance. The adults respond to the young with growling calls that seem to say "come on." Eventually, the young birds get the gumption to jump, sometimes falling more than 1,000 feet. Their baby fat and small size help them land unharmed on the rocks or in the sea below. This "early out program" is part of the murre's survival strategy; the earlier the young can leave land, the less chance they have of being attacked by land predators. The adults then convoy them out to the sea, where one adult, usually a male, teaches them how to dive for fish.

Common murres are among the best divers of all the auks (a family of seabirds that also includes puffins and murrelets). Like penguins, they use their short wings to "fly" through the water, diving to depths that would put the "squeeze" on most other birds. In murres, the reinforced ribs, breastbone, and spine form a rigid box that keeps the heart and lungs from collapsing under the pressure.

One hazard that murres have yet to evolve a response to is the danger of oil spills. Because they spend so much time in the sea, and because they have only one or two eggs a year (after three or four early nonbreeding years), murres are particularly vulnerable to pollution. If a catastrophic oil spill wiped out 50 percent of their population, it might take twenty years for the population to bounce back.

Look for common murres—standing on wide ledges and on top of cliffs. From the front, they look like they are wearing white turtleneck sweaters, but their heads and backs are black. They can sometimes be seen landing at their colonies in midwinter. Look for groups below the nest sites performing flying displays on calm winter afternoons.

Length: 16–17½ inches.

Look for nests—which are simply an egg laid on a bare piece of ground. The eggs are pear-shaped, perhaps to keep errant eggs from falling over the ledge (they roll in a circle instead). The pear shape may also help during incubation; as the bird holds the egg on top of its feet, the widest part of the egg is warmed by a bare spot on the bird's belly.

Look for whitewashed cliffs—that mark a well-used loomery. Their guano (excrement), a source of potash, is important to the growth and abundance of marine life in the oceans around their cliffs.

Listen for—soft purring noises, as well as croaks, growls, and moans around the nesting colony. The alarm calls are loud, trumpeting squawks, which intensify when taken up by many birds at once. Adults and young get to know each other's voices during the 1–5 days it takes the crying chick to peck its way out of the egg. In a crowded nursery, this sound-print is an important means of identification.

American Black Oystercatcher

Nature writer Philip Kopper wrote that an "oystercatcher on the beach stands out more than a clown at a Quaker meeting." Their ink-black plumage, which blends well with the wet rocks of their habitat, is offset by jaunty accessories: pink legs and feet, orange pupils, and a bright red bill that is twice as long as the bird's head.

The oystercatcher's bill could well have been the inspiration for the double-bladed knife used by commercial oyster gatherers. It is laterally flattened, with sharp edges on top and bottom, and a blunt tip for prying shellfish off the rocks. If the mussels have their shells ajar, the oystercatcher quickly inserts its bill and cuts the adductor muscle so the shellfish can't "clam up." To feast on a closed bivalve or limpet, it "jackhammers" through the shell, then picks out the soft edible portion. The bill can also be used to probe beneath mud and sand for hidden morsels.

Individual oystercatchers tend to perfect a particular style of feeding, and then specialize on items such as mussels, clams, chitons, limpets, barnacles, oysters, crabs, worms, or other invertebrates. Young oystercatchers, initially dependent on their parents for handouts, will eventually perfect their own style, which usually includes some of their parents' tricks.

Throughout the year you are likely to see these gregarious birds in twos, fours, or even larger flocks. At breeding season, the flocks disperse and territories are vigorously defended. The male birds take a stance along their invisible fences and perform a ritualized "piping display" in which they arch their neck, point their bill downward, and utter a succession of piping notes. The display tends to attract neighboring territory holders, until a convention of ten pairs of piping birds may be seen rushing up and down their boundaries. The display can also be given in the air, and is usually the first greeting an intruder receives.

Look for American black oystercatchers—walking with sedate, but jerky movements along rocky ledges exposed by the retreating tides. They seem to be a bit encumbered when they walk, but can break into a run if need be. They may also wade belly deep in water to find prey. Favored flocking sites along the shore may attract thousands of birds.

Length: 17–17½ inches.

Look for nests—in shallow scrapes on a rocky ledge or a gravel beach. The female lays 1–4 eggs in May or June, and because of the high rate of predation, she may have to renest in order to pass on her genes. Both males and females take care of the eggs.

Listen for—a sharp "whick, whick" when startled, or a soft "phee-ah" when flying.

Sea Lion

The performing "seals" of circus fame are actually California sea lions, one of two species that are commonly seen along the Pacific coast. The larger species are called northern sea lions. The sea lions differ from seals in that they have small, furled ears on the outside of their head, and flipperlike hind feet that can swing up under their body to help them scrabble about on land. Unlike the whales and porpoises, which have severed their ties to the land, sea lions are somewhere in between landlubbers and pure sea creatures. Although they catch all their food in the water, they do haul out on the rocks to rest, breed, and raise their young.

The bulls (males) climb up onto the shores of "rookeries" early in May and begin dividing the real estate into exclusive territories. Only the bulls that win their "fight" will have the privilege of breeding, a mechanism that ensures that the fittest bulls will sire the most pups. Property lines are drawn by mock battles—usually a series of bluffs and bellowing threats issued face-to-face by vying bulls. These encounters rarely escalate into physical fights, however (another built-in survival tactic for the species).

It was once believed that the groups of northern sea lion females in each territory were "harems" held together by the male. Then observers noticed that the "harem" personnel changed daily as females wandered at will across territory lines. Now it is believed that females simply tend to cluster with one another, showing no particular allegiance to a male. They may breed with one male, then raise their young in another male's territory. The pups spend up to three months playing and learning to swim in the tidal pools among the rocks. Finally weaned from the mother's rich milk, they are able to catch fish on their own.

When sea lions enter the water, they seem to be imminently more at home than they are on land. The 2,200-pound bulls, ponderous and plodding on land, are suddenly graceful and supple, even in heavy seas. Their mammalian characteristics have been streamlined for water life. Their ears have been reduced, and their leg bones have been shortened and drawn into their trunk until only the flipperlike feet are left. They swim with simultaneous strokes of their leathery fore-paddles, using their hind flippers as rudders.

Internally, they are efficient diving machines. As they descend to depths of up to 600 feet, where the pressure can be life-threatening for humans, their trachea and lungs are built to collapse without harm. They are also able to stay submerged because of numerous oxygen-saving mechanisms, such as a slowing of the heart each time they hold their breath.

As incongruous as it may seem for a buoyant creature, sea lions have a habit of swallowing rocks, accumulating as many as ten at a time in their stomach. Possible explanations abound; perhaps they use the weight as ballast in diving, or maybe as a millstone for grinding up large pieces of food. Other researchers seem to believe that the rocks distend the sea lions' stomach, helping them to stave off hunger pangs during the long fasts they often endure. Female sea lions fast for the first two weeks after giving birth, for instance, and breeding bulls may abstain for as long as two months while they are defending their real estate.

When they finally do go searching for food, they are well equipped for the task. As they swim, they send out high-pitched sounds and then read the echoes bouncing back from objects such as fish. This is the same sort of sonar system that bats and porpoises (and air traffic controllers) use. Unfortunately, their habit of keying in on fishing nets has earned them a reputation as competitors for commercial fish. Before the theory was actually tested, fishery personnel in British Columbia gunned down thousands of northern sea lions on their breeding grounds, wiping out half the population in only five years. Later, researchers found that although sea lions partake during salmon runs, they are not a year-round threat to commercial fisheries. In fact, their preferred foods are "junk" species, as well as squid, octopus, and herring. Luckily, the routine slaughter of the sea lions has been slowed by protective legislation. Although a few bullet-peppered animals still wash up on the shores, their populations are beginning to recoup.

Look for sea lions—hauled out on intertidal rocks or cavorting in groups of several hundred offshore. They dive and surface as a group when they hunt, presumably so that the random movements of one animal won't spook the fish for the rest of the herd. They are occasionally seen in harbors and river mouths along the coast. You can tell the two western sea lions apart by their color and size: the California species is darker and smaller and has a crest on its head, while the northern sea lions are large and tawny, with a pelt that looks white when wet.

Length: California sea lion, 5½–8 feet; northern sea lion, 8–10½ feet.

Look for rookeries—offshore on wave-beaten rocks. Ask local naturalists where to see sea lions. Use extreme caution when sightseeing from a boat so as not to disturb the breeding herd. A mass exit off the rocks has sometimes left many squashed pups.

Listen for—the higher "honking" sound of California sea lions, or the belching, throaty bellow of the northern sea lions.

BLACK TURNSTONE

CASSIN'S AUKLET

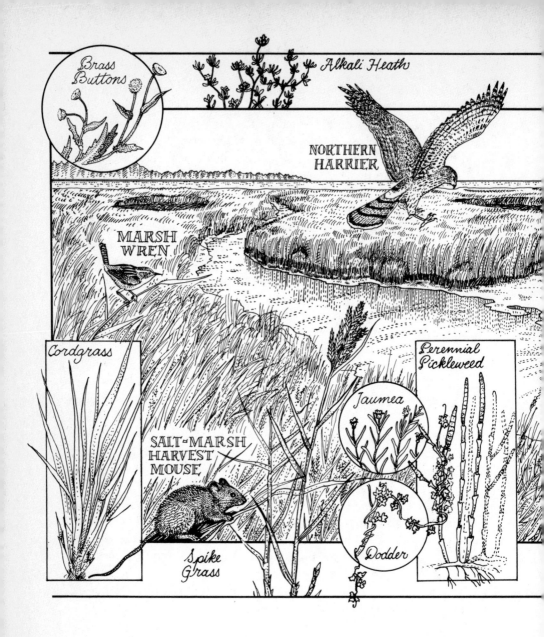

Brass
Buttons

Alkali Heath

NORTHERN
HARRIER

MARSH
WREN

Cordgrass

Perennial
Pickleweed

Jaumea

SALT-MARSH
HARVEST
MOUSE

Dodder

Spike
Grass

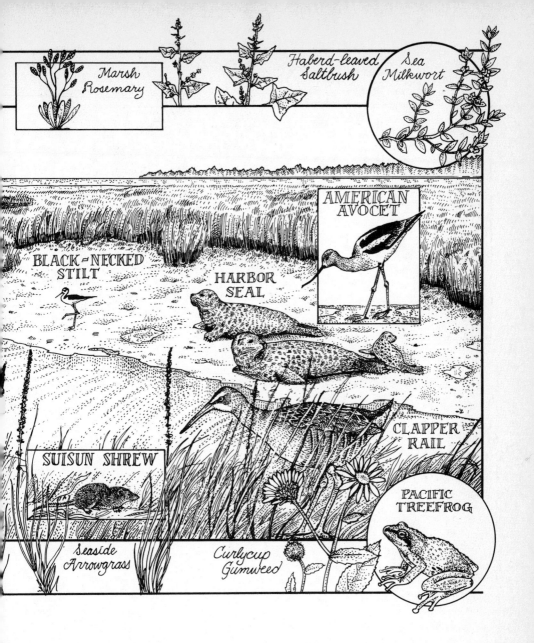

Marsh Rosemary

Haberd-leaved Saltbrush

Sea Milkwort

AMERICAN AVOCET

BLACK~NECKED STILT

HARBOR SEAL

CLAPPER RAIL

SUISUN SHREW

PACIFIC TREEFROG

Seaside Arrowgrass

Curlycup Gumweed

Coastal Salt Marsh

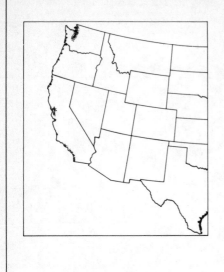

WHERE TO SEE THIS HABITAT:

California: Elkhorn Slough Estuarine Sanctuary; Salinas River Wildlife Management Area; San Francisco Bay and San Pablo Bay national wildlife refuges
Oregon: South Slough Estuarine Sanctuary
Washington: Dungeness, Nisqually, and Willapa national wildlife refuges

Coastal Salt Marsh

BEGINNINGS

Most rivers along the Pacific coast don't pour directly into the crashing waves of the sea. Instead, they fan out into bell-shaped, inland bays called estuaries—the halfway houses between salt and fresh water. These estuaries were formed over the past 10,000 years, as rising sea levels submerged the coast and drowned the mouth of many river valleys. Over the years, mud and sediment from both the sea and the rivers have settled to the bottom of these relatively quiet holding tanks. Along the edges, the sloping mud shores support acres of a special class of plant called "halophytes"—those that can tolerate salty conditions.

The part of the shore closest to the water is colonized by Pacific cordgrass. This plant is tall enough to be able to collect the rays of the sun, even when it is inundated by two high tides a day. Its stems are filled with large air-shuttling cells to help the waterlogged roots get oxygen from the blades. These blades are adapted to curl into a long tubular shape when the tide retreats, thus protecting the breathing pores from drying winds. Beyond the high-tide line, the cordgrass gives way to pickleweed, a lower-growing plant with a woody stem and water-storing leaves. Many other plants round out the community. Jaumea and seaside arrowgrass grow in patches within the pickleweed, along with the bright orange threads of dodder, a parasitic plant that may completely cover pickleweed. Marsh gum-plant and spike grass are often found on natural rises within pickleweed or along the upland edge of the marsh. When wrack material (old seaweed, egg cases, crab shells, and other floating riffraff) is washed up by high tides, it may smother the pickleweed and form a patchy depression that is then colonized by alkali heath and saltbush. Other disturbed-site colonizers are salt marsh sand spurry and brass buttons. Marsh rosemary is one of the plants that forms the upper boundary of the marsh.

Channels dissect the marsh, bringing nutrient-rich tidal water in, and then flushing organic "exports" out. On the higher parts of the marsh, these channels are steep and incised into the mud. Channels that are wider than they are deep are called sloughs. Very high tides may fill shallow depressions in the high marsh, which then evaporate, leaving bare, salt-encrusted areas called salt pans. In the lower marsh, channels tend to meander as they flood and then drain the shallow beds of cordgrass. With each retreat of the tide, juicy mud flats are uncovered. Each of these subhabitats provides a different regime of saltiness, inundation, exposure, light, heat, or cold. These conditions separate organisms into various zones, according to what they can handle, or what they prefer.

THE GREAT SALT TEST

Of all the challenges a salt marsh organism faces, salinity may be its greatest test. To appreciate just how tricky it is to live in a salty environment, it

CHARACTERISTIC PLANTS:

Herbaceous Plants:
alkali heath
annual pickleweed
Baltic rush
bear sedge
brass buttons
Canadian sand spurry
cow clover
coyote bush
creeping alkali grass
curlycup gumweed
devilsclub
ditch grass
dodder
dwarf spikesedge

haberd-leaved salt-
   bush
hairgrasses
jaumea
least mouse-tail
low bulrush
Lyngby's sedge
marsh bird's beak
marsh gum-plant
marsh rosemary
meadow barley
northern starworts
Pacific cordgrass
Pacific silverweed
perennial pickleweed
redtop

salt marsh sand
   spurry
saltmarsh bulrush
salt rush
seacoast bulrush
sea milkwort
seaside arrowgrass
seaside plantain
sedges
soft bird's beak
spike grass
three-square bulrush
tufted hairgrass
tule
western dock

helps to know something about the way plants draw water into their roots.

The system, based on osmosis, is elegantly simple. The starchy, nutrient "soup" on the inside of the root cell is more concentrated than the fresh water in the soil. The fresh water moves into the root cell in an attempt to dilute the more concentrated solution and bring the two to equilibrium. When a root cell is immersed in salt water, however, the roles are reversed. The root cell now has the weaker solution, and water flows out of the roots in an attempt to dilute the salty sea. Some halophytes counteract this by hoarding salt until their root cells are even saltier than the sea. The now weaker seawater rushes into the roots to try to dilute them!

To rid itself of excess salt, cordgrass excretes it through special glands in its leaves. Look for the shimmer of white crystals drying on its leaves at low tide. Pickleweed tries a different approach. Instead of glands that exude salt crystals, pickleweed collects them in vacuoles. As certain plant parts accumulate too much salt, they are sloughed off, usually in fall and winter when the rest of the plant turns red.

Marsh animals must also rid themselves of this salt before it builds up in their body and poisons them. Some sea birds have special nasal glands through which they "blow brine." Salty drops flow down grooves to the end of their beak, and are then whisked away in the characteristic "head-shake." Turtles "cry" out the salt through special tear glands. Lacking special glands, the savannah sparrow simply concentrates salt in its urine, tolerating levels that are five times higher than those in its blood.

WHAT'S IN IT FOR WILDLIFE?

Despite the challenges of salt and tides, salt marshes are among the most productive ecosystems on the planet. Without one ounce of fertilizer or pesticide, salt marshes raise a crop tilled only by the tides. They produce twenty times more food than an equal area of the open sea, and twice as much food as our cornfields do. Some of the green plants are eaten directly by insects, crabs, and other organisms, but most are eaten after they die. Fungi and bacteria break the grasses down into smaller pieces called detritus, which are then exported out to the estuary with each tide. Literally millions of saltwater creatures depend on this floating food source. In addition, many ocean animals spend the early part of their lives in estuaries, including half of all the seafood we harvest off the Pacific coast.

Our marshes also have international significance in that millions of birds migrating along the Pacific flyway from Alaska to Antarctica stop here to rest and refuel. This pitstop makes for some unbeatable wildlife watching. High tide brings fish up the channels of the marsh and provides flooded expanses for northern pintails, geese, and swans to paddle in. In the mud of the marsh are juicy burrowers such as Baltic clams, ribbed mussels, and many insects. Under the cover of plants, there are scurrying yellow shore crabs, snails, and many other edibles.

The real feast starts when the tide subsides. Fish are then concentrated in sloughs or shallow ponds. Fish-eating birds such as herons and egrets stand poised at the water's edge, making rapid stabs at the darting shadows. Cormorants dive from the surface, and terns plunge from the air, also in pursuit of fish. A chorus line of shorebirds that have been perched on high spots during the flood tide can now line up along the retreating water's edge, feeding on the newly exposed mud flat and open areas of the marsh. The more common species include American avocet, long-billed dowitcher, dunlin, marbled godwit, semipalmated plover, willet, black-necked stilt, and various sandpiper species. Most are migratory; only the American avocet, black-necked stilt, and snowy plover stay behind to nest in this region.

Each shorebird specializes in a certain kind of food, and hunts for it in a unique way so that the competition between species is reduced. Avocets sweep the surface of the flat with their bill, searching for small mussels. Semipalmated plovers rapidly peck the surface while western sandpipers peck just underneath, reaching a different layer of prey items. Willets probe for small bivalves 2 inches below the surface, while dowitchers and marbled godwits, with their longer bills, probe 3 inches and 6 inches below the surface.

Resident species such as rails also use the tidal sloughs as foraging habitat. Their nests, which are secreted in the cordgrasses close to the water, are often threatened with flooding. The light-footed clapper rail's solution is to build a platform nest of dead cordgrass stems that will float up and down with the rising tide.

Black rails nest in pickleweed along with song sparrows and savannah sparrows. Look for great blue heron and black-shouldered kite nests at the top of coyote bushes, thick-leaved shrubs that bloom white in the fall. The secretive rails and sparrows are sometimes best seen when high tides flush them to the higher ground of the marsh. Here, they become quite vulnerable to predators such as ospreys and hawks. At this time, the taller vegetation of the transition zone is extremely important for their protection.

Mammals also use brackish marshes (which are less salty than salt marshes) as a foraging and nesting area. Muskrats often bring mussels up on the banks to eat before returning to their lodges or bank burrows. Minks prowl the banks at night, ducking in occasionally for a fish or muskrat meal. Raccoons, skunks, and foxes may wander down from the uplands to feed on aquatic washups as well as on the populations of mice, voles, and ground squirrels that make their homes here.

Two species of rodents actually choose to live in the salty portions of the marsh: Suisun shrew and salt-marsh harvest mouse. Salt-marsh harvest mice spend most of their time in the pickleweed plots, feeding on the green vegetation and seeds. They must swim or retreat to higher ground during high tides, always choosing areas of good plant cover to screen them from their aerial enemies. Short-eared owls and northern harriers ply the skies night and day (respectively), looking for mice that are unable to find such cover.

Occasionally, harbor seals use the waters around a marsh as a place to raise young, and can be spotted hauling out on the pickleweed and spike grass at high tide or on the mud flats at low tide. Reptiles and amphibians have a somewhat harder time finding a home on the marsh. Reptiles need an underground refuge and egg-laying sites that are above the high-tide line. Because the compacted soils of the upper marsh are hard for them to burrow into, they must depend on the prep work of other burrowing animals. Amphibians such as frogs need fresh water in which to lay their eggs and develop. Although they may not be able to actually reside here, many species come down from the uplands to prowl for insects and spiders. Keep your eyes peeled for gopher snakes, Pacific treefrogs, southern alligator lizards, and western fence lizards.

The salt marsh is a nursery to some species, a lifelong home to others, and a water purifier for the entire coast. Unfortunately, many people don't appreciate the gifts of the marsh. They see these wetlands as smelly, mosquito-breeding wastelands that might be better used as airports or dumping grounds. The San Francisco Bay was once ringed by the largest continuous tidal marsh system anywhere on the Pacific coast. Fresh water from the huge Sacramento–San Joaquin basin (40 percent of the land base in California) drained into the bay, mixing with seawater that poured in through the passageway now spanned by the Golden Gate Bridge. Over 10,000 years, these waters gradually submerged the bay boundaries, creating a marshy zone that was twice as large as the open water and river delta combined.

GOPHER
SNAKE

"Settlement" of the bay and delta included diking these waters for salt production, filling them for agriculture, and siphoning off freshwater inputs for domestic water and irrigation. Today, only 5 percent of the original tidal marshes remain. The "conversion" of these marshes is still occurring, though not as wantonly, thanks to the efforts of conservationists and educators who are spreading the *good* news about salt marshes.

Clapper Rail

If the salt marsh had an orchestra, this bird would be its lead instrument. The infamous "voice of the marsh" sounds like old-fashioned clappers, and any loud noise, such as an airplane or your laughter, may trigger a "clapping" throughout the marsh. The rails need this distinctive vocal signature because they can't see each other in the dense jungle of grass blades. Without a way to keep in contact, the vegetation that hides them so well from their predators would suddenly become a liability.

Other adaptations to their habitat are strong, muscled legs and feet that are specially built for walking. Three toes point forward, and one raised toe points backward, acting as a brace. Their bodies are deep but narrow (the inspiration for the phrase "thin as a rail"), enabling them to slip between tightly spaced stalks. The short, rounded wings add very little bulk, but perform admirably when the rail is migrating or flushing from its hiding place.

Rails are also well adapted to change. Although the salt marsh is lavishly appointed with edible plants, animals, and water, its tides make it somewhat unpredictable. Nesting, for instance, takes some forethought. Clapper rails place their nests high above normal tides on a mound of vegetation. Sometimes, despite their planning, a flood tide may sweep into the creeks and rise dangerously close to the eggs. When it does, the clappers go into high gear. They rush around, nearly tipping over backward with the exertion of tugging up grasses. They tuck the grasses under the nest to jack it up, often saving the eggs just in the nick of time. During peak tides, clappers show themselves to be surprisingly good swimmers despite the fact that their feet are not webbed. When water covers their local cupboards, they swim to higher parts of the marsh where food is still accessible.

Look for clapper rails—hiding in the tall cordgrass along tidal creeks or searching for food on the banks. They eat fiddler crabs, crayfish, mollusks, worms, fish, aquatic insects, and other marine animals. Watch while they declaw a fiddler crab—grasping the base of the large claw with their beak, they vigorously shake their head until the claw flies one way and the body another. Rails are usually secretive, but may be forced into view by high tides. At these times, look for them swimming across marsh creeks, crossing marsh roads, or floating on boards. At low tide, they sometimes wander

WILDLIFE LOCATOR CHART—COASTAL SALT MARSH

Illustrations labeled: MARBLED GODWIT, BLACK-CROWNED NIGHT-HERON, WESTERN FENCE LIZARD, SEMIPALMATED PLOVER, SNOWY PLOVER, WILLET, BLACK RAIL

	Feeds from Air	Feeds in Lower Canopy	Feeds on Ground	Feeds in Shallow Water (Wades or Dabbles)	Feeds Underwater
Nests in Tree Canopy	Osprey Black-shouldered Kite		Cattle Egret, Raccoon	Great Blue Heron Black-crowned Night-Heron	
Nests on Ground	Gull-billed Tern Northern Harrier Short-eared Owl	Common Yellowthroat (Also nests in shrubs)	Snowy Plover, Semipalmated Plover, Western Sandpiper, Dunlin, Savannah Sparrow, Song Sparrow, Western Harvest Mouse, Salt-marsh Harvest Mouse	Gadwall Black Rail Clapper Rail American Avocet Willet Long-billed Curlew Marbled Godwit Long-billed Dowitcher	Harbor Seal
Nests Beneath Ground or Debris			Suisun Shrew, Vagrant Shrew, Brush Rabbit, Black-tailed Jackrabbit, California Ground Squirrel, Botta's Pocket Gopher, Deer Mouse, California Vole, Norway Rat, Gray Fox, Long-tailed Weasel, Mink, Striped Skunk, Southern Alligator Lizard, Western Fence Lizard, Gopher Snake		
Nests Above Water			Marsh Wren	American Bittern Least Bittern Black-necked Stilt	Ruddy Duck Muskrat
Nests in Fresh Water			Pacific Treefrog		

out from the marsh edge to bathe in shallows or forage on mud banks. True to their nickname, "marsh hens" bob their head and twitch their tail as they walk. When they fly, they stay low and dangle their legs.

Length: 14–16½ inches.

Look for nests—on the ground in 3- to 4-foot-high cordgrass. The 8- to 10-inch-wide saucer or bowl of dead marsh grasses is set up high on a grass clump, holding eggs about 1 foot above normal high tide. Some nests are domed over with interlocked green blades, rising another foot above the nest. This awning protects the eggs from sunlight and predators.

Look for runways—beaten-down trails in the grass leading to and from the nest.

Look for pellets—small clumps of indigestible material (fish bones, crab shells, etc.) that the rails cough up. Feeding debris and tracks are often nearby.

Look for tracks—chickenlike marks on the muddy shores of creeks, splattered with white droppings the size of a half-dollar.

Listen for—a potpourri of sounds: clacks, grunts, groans, and shrieks. The most well-known call, given just after dawn, shortly before dusk, and more often in the breeding season, is a hoarse, chattering "kek-kek-kek-kek-kek-kek." A surprised group of these birds sound like guinea fowls, giving guttural "rack-k-k-rack-k-k-k-" calls that may go on for several minutes.

Salt-marsh Harvest Mouse

Salt-marsh harvest mice live a rather leisurely life among the pickleweed plants in the midmarsh. The salt content of the water they drink and the plants they eat is high, yet it doesn't seem to bother them. When rising tides flood their haunts, they simply climb up-stalk a bit and wait out the tide, still well hidden in the dense vegetation.

The salt-marsh harvest mouse is a close relative of the western harvest mouse, which can be found in the higher portions of the marsh where upland grasses grow. As a species, the western variety is not nearly so well adapted to a salty diet. Every now and then, however, a few individuals are born with a higher tolerance to salt. Experts believe that a few of these "special" mice might have wandered down to the salt marshes on isolated islands that were once in the San Francisco Bay. Over the next 25,000 years, as these isolated populations adapted to their salty environment, they eventually evolved into a whole different species—the salt-marsh harvest mouse.

Today, it's interesting to compare the progeny with its ancestor and see how the two habitats have shaped them. The "new" variety of harvest mice subsist on green foliage instead of seeds, mainly because there are few seed-bearing plants in the salt marsh. Their intestines are longer than their ancestors', presumably to allow the mice to absorb more water from their food and thus help dilute some of the salt in their body. A third, and very important, difference is their temperament.

When a laboratory-caged western harvest mouse is set free, it leaps wildly from its cage, plunging over the edge of the lab table and scurrying for the wall. It runs pell-mell along the edge until it finds some indentation in which it can hide and quiver. The salt-marsh harvest mouse is decidedly more mellow. It leaves its cage calmly, sniffing the edge of the lab table and plotting its way down. It may bounce to a chair, and then to the floor, where it may pause to take inventory again. Instead of clinging to the cracks, it may prance boldly across the linoleum—in stark contrast to its progenitor.

One likely reason for this difference is habitat. The western harvest mouse lives in the meadows upland of the marsh. In late summer, these meadows dry out and become sparse, exposing the mouse to the eyes of aerial predators. They have good reason to be cautious, and have adapted a nocturnal lifestyle to reduce their risks. Down toward the bay, the salt-marsh mouse is hidden by mats of vegetation year round, and can thus afford to be mellow. This protection has also allowed it to branch out from the strictly nocturnal schedule, and do some of its feeding during the day.

Look for salt-marsh harvest mice—along the ground where pickleweed grows, 6–10 feet above the mean sea level. They avoid the cordgrass gardens because these are flooded too deeply for the mice to be able to climb above the water and still remain out of sight of predators. Thanks to their small size and light weight, they can clamber onto bushes and blades alike. In the winter, they move temporarily to the higher parts of the marsh to escape the highest tides of the year. They venture out of the marsh only in the spring and early summer, when grasslands adjoining the marsh are still lush and green, offering cover. A maximum tide may force them to swim, which they do calmly, of course, bobbing like corks and clinging to floating debris.

Length: Head and body, $2^3/_5$–$3^1/_5$ inches. Tail, $2^1/_5$–$3^2/_5$ inches.

Look for nests—a fist-sized bundle of dried grasses and sedges on the ground or above, with one, two, or three entrances. They change nest sites frequently, especially if the nest has become wet with the tide. Occasionally they are flooded out, but can build another nest in just a few hours.

Listen for—squeaks, squeals, birdlike notes, and chatters, usually only when courting, mating, fighting, or injured.

Harbor Seal

When you see them snoozing on the mud flats or lolling in the pickleweed, you might get the idea that harbor seals are on a lifelong vacation. Actually, they are extremely wary animals, cautiously selecting haul-out sites that are remote enough to discourage land predators, yet close enough to deep water to give them an instant escape route. At the first sign of disturbance, the seals lumber down to the sea, plunging in with a warning slap of their hind flippers.

No matter how sluggish they may look on land, the seals are sheer grace and velocity in water. Natural selection has favored a streamlined, cigar-shaped body that cuts through the water with a minimum of resistance. Their forelimbs, hind limbs, and even their ears have been reduced to cut down on drag. Their underwater vision is enhanced by large, convex eyes that are specially positioned on the top of their head so they can see fish that are swimming above them. Internally, their system is geared to withstand long periods without breathing (up to 23 minutes) and occasional deep-water dives (up to 200 feet). To conserve oxygen when diving, they constrict all peripheral blood vessels, keeping open only those networks serving the major organs: heart, kidney, brain, lungs, and intestines. The seals also have high levels of myoglobin (a substance that binds oxygen) so they don't suffer from oxygen debt in their muscles. To further conserve resources, their heart slows from an average of 85 beats a minute to a low of 15. This allows the seals to sleep on the bottom of the bay if their normal haul-out spots are occupied by tides or intruders. They choose shallow waters for their naps, coming up every 5 minutes or so for a breath of fresh air.

When the coast is clear, the seals clamber onto land for resting, birthing, and caring for their young. They usually congregate in groups of up to 100, having learned that 200 eyes on the lookout are better than 2. Breeding and pupping periods are especially active at the haul-out sites. Later in the summer, courting males and females roll, nuzzle, and cavort in the shallows just off the shore. The male may perform flips and leaps in the air for the female, while she shows her passion by delivering deep, scarring bites to his neck and shoulders.

The female does not actually give birth until the next summer, dropping her pup unceremoniously onto the chilled slab of mud. Mother and young spend their first few moments sniffing each other (important for future identification), and then quickly head for the sea. Seals are born knowing how to swim, but when newborns get tired, they often climb onto the mother's shoulders, hanging on even during dives. After a week, the pup is making its own dives, but is still dependent on its mother for nourishment. Seal milk is 50 percent fat, an incredibly rich concoction compared with the 3–4 percent fat in the cow's milk we drink. The pup nearly doubles its weight in only four weeks on this diet. Even after weaning, the mother continues to look after and accompany the pup for several months. Renowned as devoted mothers, these seals have been known to risk their own lives to save a pup in trouble.

Adults and pups alike were in trouble not long ago, when bounties were offered for each harbor seal killed. The seals were accused of competing with commercial fishing operations, especially in their consumption of salmon. Studies showed that the salmon consumption was actually minimal, and that harbor seals eat noncommercial fish for most of the year. Now, laws to protect marine mammals are beginning to pay off in rising populations. The new "bounty hunter" is more insidious, however. Biologists suspect that pollutants (PCBs) in the water may be contributing to the rising rate of birth defects and miscarriages in these beautiful seals.

Look for harbor seals—hauled out on mud flats, rocks, or sandbars at low tide or in pickleweed beds at high tide. Their napping herds are relatively unstructured, with unrelated seals bedding amiably next to one another. They spend half their time on land, and half in water, searching for fish such as sole, flounder, sculpin, hake, cod, and herring, as well as squid, octopus, clams, and snails. An average dive lasts only 5–6 minutes, so watch for seals coming up for air.

Length: 4–6 feet.

Look for "nursery groups"—between April and September, a group of mothers and very young pups separate from the main colony for the first 2 weeks of the pups' life.

Listen for—the distress calls of young pups. People sometimes think the pups are abandoned when they cry like this. Actually, the mother is usually not far away, and will retrieve the pup shortly.

CALIFORNIA VOLE

SOUTHERN ALLIGATOR LIZARD

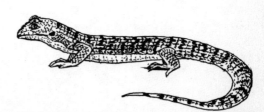

Quillwort

Water Smartweed

CANVASBACK

WESTERN GREBE

GREAT BLUE HERON

BULLFROG

Pondweed

Common Cattail

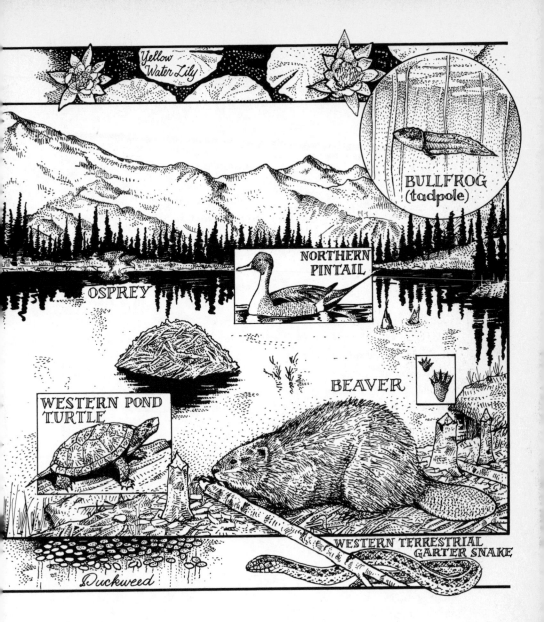

Yellow Water Lily

BULLFROG
(tadpole)

OSPREY

NORTHERN
PINTAIL

BEAVER

WESTERN POND
TURTLE

WESTERN TERRESTRIAL
GARTER SNAKE

Duckweed

Lake and Pond

WHERE TO SEE THIS HABITAT:

Arizona: Glen Canyon National Recreation Area

California: Clear Lake, Delevan, Salton Sea, and Tule Lake national wildlife refuges; Mono Lake (Bureau of Land Management); Plumas, San Bernardino, Sequoia, and Stanislaus national forests; Yosemite National Park

Colorado: Grand Mesa-Uncompahgre, Gunnison, and Roosevelt national forests; Rocky Mountain National Park

Idaho: Bear Lake, Camas, Deer Flat, and Minidoka national wildlife refuges; Targhee National Forest

Kansas: Kirwin National Wildlife Refuge

Montana: Benton Lake, Bowdoin, Ul Bend, Charles M. Russell, and Red Rock Lakes national wildlife refuges; Bitterroot, Flathead, and Kootenai national forests; Glacier National Park

Nebraska: Crescent Lake and Valentine national wildlife refuges

Nevada: Lake Mead National Recreation Area; Railroad Valley Wildlife Management Area; Ruby Lake National Wildlife Refuge

New Mexico: Bitter Lake National Wildlife Refuge

North Dakota: Arrowwood, Audubon, Des Lacs, Lake Alice, Lake Ilo, Long Lake, Lostwood, Tewaukon, and Upper Souris national wildlife refuges

Oklahoma: Salt Plains, Tishomingo, and Washita national wildlife refuges

Oregon: Cold Springs, Malheur, Umatilla, and Upper Klamath national wildlife refuges; Crater Lake National Park; Umpqua National Forest

South Dakota: Lake Andes and Waubay national wildlife refuges; Madison Wildlife Management District

Texas: Buffalo Lake, Hagerman, and Muleshoe national wildlife refuges

Utah: Dixie, Fishlake, and Uinta national forests

Washington: Columbia, Conboy Lake, Toppenish, and Turnbull national wildlife refuges; Colville, Okanogan, and Olympic national forests; Coulee Dam and Ross Lake national recreation areas; North Cascades National Park

Wyoming: Bridger-Teton and Shoshone national forests; Yellowstone National Park

Lake and Pond

BEGINNINGS

To understand the present character of a lake, it helps to know something of its history. Icy-cold "cirque" lakes sit in teacup basins that were scooped out of the side of a peak by alpine glaciers. Lakes farther down the mountain were formed when retreating valley glaciers dumped a ridge of debris across a raging river. Blocks of ice that were buried in the glacial debris melted years later to form small "kettle" lakes. Even flat landscapes such as the northern plains have their glacial souvenirs. From an airplane, you can see a hundred of these "pothole" ponds per square mile, still sparkling in the thumbprints of an ice sheet that melted 10,000 years ago.

At the warmer end of the geologic spectrum are lakes such as Crater Lake in Oregon, which filled the cavity left after a volcano blew its top. Lakes can even form in sand dunes where a windy blowout has carved a bed (e.g., Moses Lake, Washington). Or a lake may be created when the plates of the earth's surface drift together or apart (e.g., Lake Tahoe, California). The great salt lakes of the West are the evaporated remnants of large, sealike lakes that covered much of the northern basin and range country millions of years ago. These lakes are mere slices of their former depth, yet contain the concentrated salts of a much larger body of water.

Even today, you may be able to see a lake in the making. When a river jumps its channel and cuts off a meandering loop, an oxbow lake is born. Or when a beaver family is determined to spread the river beyond its banks, you can see a pond arise in a matter of months. Temporary lakes fill desert basins called playas after heavy rains, then slowly dry up as the sun begins to intensify.

People have surpassed the beavers as the great lake-makers of the West. Dams on the Colorado and the Columbia rivers, for instance, have created huge reservoirs for water, hydroelectric power, and flood control. Ranchers on the plains often dig ponds to "water" their stock. These ponds have become an important alternative to the original plains potholes, many of which have been drained and converted to agricultural fields. In fact, some researchers have suggested that the Central Flyway (a migration corridor) may actually be shifting westward as birds take advantage of these new resting and feeding stopovers.

No matter how they were created, lakes are all headed for the same future. Water entering them brings silt and organic matter from the surrounding slopes. Aquatic plants and animals find their way in and begin to take root, multiply, and die. Their remains add nourishment and encourage the growth of even more organisms. As the bottom builds up with silt and organic matter, plants can take root farther and farther into the center, helping to pump the land dry by giving up their moisture to the air. Slowly, a lake becomes a pond, then a marsh, a wet meadow, a shrub swamp, and perhaps even a forest. This filling in and drying out may take hundreds or even thousands of years. In the case of the 2,000-foot-deep Crater Lake, the future may be millions of years away.

LAKES HAVE LAYERS

Lakes are larger and usually deeper than ponds—deep enough to have a lower layer of water that receives no sunlight. When you tread water, you can often feel this colder layer down by your feet. Life thins out in this vault, where it is too dark for green plants to grow. In the warmer, sunnier layer that you swim in, billions of microscopic plants and animals float suspended around you. They form the basis of the food chain that supports fish, insects, amphibians, birds, and mammals. When this teeming cloud of life dies, the remains filter down through the cold, dark layer, until they reach the muddy ooze of the lake floor. Here life abounds again; a swarming megalopolis of bacteria, bloodworms, midges, flatworms, and other organisms consume the debris and convert it to nutrients such as nitrogen and phosphorous.

Unfortunately, these nutrients don't just rise to the surface waters where they are needed by plants. Nor does oxygen produced by these plants automatically sink down to the ooze layer where it is sorely needed. Since cold water is denser and heavier than warm water, the two layers separate like oil and water. Winds that ripple the surface of the lake circulate the warm layer with itself, but leave the cold layer unruffled.

In regions where winter temperatures plunge, a twice-a-year phenomenon called "overturn" breaks down the barrier and causes the waters to mix and share their resources. In the fall, the sun-warmed upper layer

CHARACTERISTIC PLANTS:

Trees and Shrubs:
blue spruce
bush honeysuckle
narrowleaf cotton-
    wood
peachleaf willow
shrubby cinquefoil
water birch

Herbaceous Plants:
American bistort
American licorice
American lotus
bluebells
brook saxifrage
buck bean
bur reed
buttercups
checkermallow
cinquefoils
Columbian monks-
    hood
common arrowhead
common cattail
common mares-tail
common pipewort
common winterberry
cranberry
duckweeds
elephant heads
featherfoil
fire flags
fleabanes
floating hearts
foxtail barley
fragrant water lily
green false hellebore
hardstem bulrush
heartleaved bittercress
Indian paintbrushes
mannagrass
marsh marigold
meadow arnica
mountain death camas
mountain sorrel

mudwort
narrowleaf bur-reed
Nuttall's sunflower
Parry's primrose
poison-ivy
pondweed
prairie cordgrass
quillwort
rose-crown
scouler's flower
sedges
short-awn foxtail
soft rush
speedwells
spikesedges
summer-cypress
true forget-me-not
tufted loosestrife
watercress
water plantain
water shield
water smartweed
water-starworts
waterweed
water willow
western wheatgrass
wild rice
willow-herbs
yellow iris
yellow pond lily
yellow skunk cabbage
yellow water lily
yellow water buttercup

begins to cool down, until it finally reaches the same temperature as the lower layer. When this happens, the layering breaks down, and the brisk winds can finally stir the water all the way to the bottom. This is what we call fall overturn. The same thing happens in reverse in the spring. The icy upper layer thaws, and the whole lake reaches the magic equilibrium temperature. Winds stir it from top to bottom, mixing plant nutrients from the depths with fresh oxygen from the surface.

SHALLOW, SUNNY, AND GREEN

Ponds, on the other hand, are usually not deep enough to experience this kind of layering. One definition of a pond is that it is shallow enough to support rooted plants all the way across, and thus shallow enough to be warmed all the way to the bottom. You may not be able to see the plants in the center of a pond because they are submerged—their leaves don't float or extend above the surface. As you get closer to the edges of a pond, however, a "bull's-eye" of plants becomes visible. Each ring or zone is inhabited by certain types of plants that are adapted to that particular combination of water depth, substrate, and wave action. Where the conditions change, the next zone of plants begins. The ring closest to the center is composed of plants such as water lilies that sail their leaves atop the surface. The tops of the leaves are coated with a waxy cuticle that repels water, thus keeping the air-breathing pores unclogged. Flotillas of tiny duckweeds, with leaves the size of a matchhead, stipple the water around the wide leaves, dangling their hairy roots beneath them. In the shallows closer to shore, tall, slender emergents thrust their spikes well out of the water. In the mud around the edges, willows and other bushes that can tolerate "wet feet" form a transition zone from water to dry land.

If you walk around the perimeter of a lake, you're bound to find pondlike environments like the one just described. Look in quiet bays or on shores that are protected from the prevailing winds and wave action. The wildlife community in these wet gardens is very similar to what you will find in marshes (see page 105).

WHAT'S IN IT FOR WILDLIFE?

Wetlands in the West are precious. They are without a doubt the most densely populated habitats, attracting not only aquatic species but also land animals that come here for food, water, shade, and protection from enemies. One streamside area in Arizona holds the record for having the densest population of birds per unit area of any place in the United States. Wetlands offer an oasis from the surrounding arid grasses or shrubs, and a break in the expanse of dense conifer forests. Their shoreline is 100 percent "edge," a zone of transition that is renowned for being a magnet for wildlife (see page 23). Wildlife watchers who visit wetlands are rarely disappointed.

While there are similarities among lakes, ponds, and marshes, lakes do offer wildlife something that can't always be found in the other two communities—size and depth. In large lakes, loons have enough room to set up breeding territories, calling to each other with an eerily beautiful music. Lakes are also deep enough to allow them, along with mergansers, grebes, and cormorants, to dive after fish. Other diving birds such as ruddy ducks, ring-necked ducks, redheads, and canvasbacks reach for remote, submerged vegetation. Their special diving adaptations include streamlined bodies, legs that are placed far back for propulsion, and special breathing mechanisms that allow them to tolerate buildups of carbon dioxide. Above them, eagles and ospreys dive like winged rockets from the clouds, emerging from the spray with fighting fish between their talons.

Along the shallower edges of the lake or pond, the profusion of plants lends shade and security to breeding birds, insects, frogs, fish, and salamanders. Eared grebes build dishes of vegetation that actually float atop the water. Rails, bitterns, marsh wrens, coots, and yellow-headed blackbirds build their nests above the water in the thick tufts of emergent plants. The permanent nature of lakes and large ponds appeals to some salamanders that require more than one year to mature. Marshes that might dry up in a season are not nearly as safe a bet.

Food is also plentiful in lakes and ponds. Western water snakes and western painted turtles prowl for slippery prey with just their eyes above the water. Turtles and muskrats dive down to nibble on submerged plants such as pondweeds and waterweeds. Coots (which look like ducks but are actually rails) may dive or linger at the surface, turning lily pads over in search of insect prey. Teals, pintails, and wigeons teach their young to tip-up for food in the plant-choked shallows, and longlegged herons and egrets stand statue-still, waiting for hapless minnows to school within striking distance. These waders often pick up plant seeds in their partially webbed feet, inadvertently helping the pond plants spread to other areas.

The undersides and stems of these plants support an interesting menagerie of protozoans, hydras, snails, and sponges. The slimy, gelatinous layer of algae and tiny animals that coats the stems is called "aufwuchs." Tadpoles scrape this layer off the stems with their rasping mouthparts, while adult frogs climb atop lily pads to bask in the sun. The sun helps them raise their body temperature, digest their food, and may even help control external parasites.

LONG-BILLED CURLEW

LONG-TOED SALAMANDER

AMERICAN COOT

CANVASBACK

EARED GREBE

WESTERN HARVEST MOUSE

WILDLIFE LOCATOR CHART—LAKE AND POND

	Feeds from Air	Feeds on Ground	Feeds in Shallow Water (Wades or Dabbles)	Feeds Underwater (Dives or Dips)
Nests in Tree Canopy	Osprey Bald Eagle		Great Blue Heron	
Nests in Trunk Cavity		Fox Squirrel, Raccoon	Wood Duck	Common Goldeneye Barrow's Goldeneye Bufflehead Hooded Merganser
Nests on Ground	American White Pelican Caspian Tern Common Tern	Common Snipe, California Gull, Northern Waterthrush	Canada Goose Green-winged Teal Mallard Northern Pintail Cinnamon Teal American Wigeon American Avocet Long-billed Curlew	Common Loon Northern Shoveler Ring-necked Duck Wilson's Phalarope
Nests Beneath Ground or Debris	Belted Kingfisher Bank Swallow	Eastern Cottontail, Western Harvest Mouse, Deer Mouse, Hispid Cotton Rat, Mink, Mule Deer, Moose, Pacific Giant Salamander, Western Terrestrial Garter Snake, Common Garter Snake		River Otter Snapping Turtle Western Painted Turtle Western Pond Turtle Checkered Garter Snake Western Ribbon Snake
Nests Above Water			Redhead Black-necked Stilt	Eared Grebe Western Grebe Canvasback American Coot Beaver Muskrat
Nests in Water		Plains Leopard Frog, Spotted Frog, Cascades Frog, Northern Leopard Frog, Long-toed Salamander, Tiger Salamander, Roughskin Newt, California Newt		Bullfrog Mountain Yellow-legged Frog

The shoreline supports yet another community. Wave-scoured gravel or sandy beaches attract spotted sandpipers and killdeer. Quiet, muddy beaches are stippled by the probing bills of long-billed curlews, Wilson's phalaropes, and American avocets. In the dense vegetation on shore, loons and geese will secrete their nests. The insects that are attracted to the blooming profusion of plants on these shores are a good protein supplement in the diet of young chicks.

Because they hold such a precious commodity, lakes and ponds are magnets for species from a cross section of habitats. Landlubbers visit them for food, drinking water, escape cover, and even relief from the heat and insects. Minks and raccoons creep down at night to search for fish, frogs, snakes, and other food. Frogs and salamanders crowd into ponds in the spring for their annual jamboree of mating. At the same time, moose and deer are wading into the water of quiet bays to find sodium-rich aquatic plants. After a winter of eating woody browse, they are literally starved for salt.

Among the most celebrated visitors to western wetlands are the migrant birds that are winging their way to or from their wintering grounds in the southern United States, Mexico, or South America. In spring and fall, you may see enormous rafts of birds on a lake, including scaups, grebes, common goldeneyes, redheads, and buffleheads. At Tule Lake in California, there are sometimes four million birds at one time! Without these feeding and resting stopovers, these birds could not complete the age-old journey to their breeding grounds.

Western Grebe

Breeding time on a grebe lake is like the *Ziegfeld Follies*: beautiful costumes, a cast of thousands, and bursts of spontaneous choreography everywhere you look. The two most beautiful displays are the "weed dance" and the "race," or rushing ceremony. In the weed dance, a male and a female emerge from a dive with weeds dangling from their beaks. As they move toward one another, they begin treading water faster and faster with large, lobed feet, until they actually begin to rise out of the water. Finally, standing atop the water with breasts touching, they intertwine their bills and thrust them skyward as if offering their weeds to the heavens. Gradually they sink down together and resume their casual swimming and loafing. Researchers believe this display reinforces pair bonding between the two birds.

The race can occur at any time of year, and can involve a male and female, two males, or a female and several males. The birds paddle toward each other with fiery red eyes and raucous cries, necks extended and bills pointed at each other. Just before their beaks touch, they turn on a dime, and wind up traveling side by side, mirrored bodies upright and wings partly spread. Their pounding feet roar like rotors, propelling them atop the water as if on tiptoe. Their long, swanlike necks carry their heads high above the water, with bills tilted slightly skyward. After skittering along the surface for 50–100 yards, the racers usually dive under in perfect unison.

Diving is the true forte of the western grebe; in fact, on their breeding grounds, the birds are more likely to use their wings in the water than in the air. Their ankles and toe joints are extremely flexible, enabling them to use their feet as combination paddles-and-rudders. The lobes alongside their toes spread to propel them along at 6½ feet/second, fast enough to catch and spear a fleeing fish. To "short-circuit" their buoyancy and make diving easier, the grebes press the air out of their feathers and their air sacs before they dive. This allows them to disappear instantly and silently from the surface, as veteran grebe watchers will surely attest.

Look for western grebes—diving, swimming, preening, sleeping, or displaying atop the water, often in scattered flocks that number in the hundreds or thousands. Their peak feeding times are from first light to 9 A.M. and from late afternoon until the light begins to wane. Grebes need light to see fish, insects, mollusks, crabs, and other aquatic foods. Don't bother looking on land, as grebes are very much out of their element there. Their legs, placed far back on their body to help them dive, are virtually useless for walking. Flying is also rather limited, most of it occurring during evening migrations. Before they do fly, watch for grebes "taxiing" across a long stretch of water in order to build up the speed needed to lift them into the air.

Length: 22–29 inches.

Look for nests—in May to mid-June, in shallow, vegetated water that is protected from waves, but deep enough to allow the parents to swim underwater when entering or leaving the nest. When building the nest mound, the grebe gathers vegetation from the bottom of the lake and anchors it to the hummocky roots of bulrushes or other plants. The sodden mass may be in as much as 10 feet of water, and may actually float. The 3–4 eggs are placed in a lined depression within the 2-foot-wide mound. These grebes are colonial and may build nests within 2 yards of one another.

Look for grebe chicks—riding on their parent's backs, in a pocket formed by the wing and back feathers. The chicks mount their "gondolas" just after hatching, and spend their first few weeks here. The parents ferry the young out to good fishing grounds, and one parent fishes while the other acts as a floating nest. Occasionally, the gondola will also take a dive with the chicks still attached! The chicks have an unusual patch of skin on their forehead that turns red when they are excited or hungry. This patch may function much like a baby's cry—it alerts the parents to the chick's hunger or discomfort.

Listen for—a rasping, cricketlike "cree-creet" or "creeeet," usually delivered in bouts of 1–5 calls in a row. This advertising call is used to attract potential mates or to help mated pairs keep in touch. Each bird has its own unique call-frequency pattern, which tells other grebes something about its species, its sex, its individual identity, and whether or not it is mated. Other calls include the low clucking call that parents use when delivering food, the ticking call that signals alarm to the chicks, and the intense rackety growl or "kree" uttered during threat displays. The most unusual call is a tea-kettle whistle performed during a head-turning display.

Beaver

According to an American Indian belief, giant beavers fetched the mud with which the earth was built. It's not so outlandish an idea when you consider that beavers, in all their forms, have lived on this continent for a million years—long enough to have modified every watershed in North America. In fact, we owe much of our tillable land to their efforts. Dig down in any farmer's field and you're likely to find silt that long ago accumulated in the stillness of an ancient beaver pond.

When a stream is broken by a series of beaver dams, it spreads over its banks and becomes a necklace of ponds and marshes. The swift water slows enough to support rooted plants and attract insects. In turn, these insects attract aquatic organisms and their predators. The lodges, dams, and canals that beavers construct create new travel lanes or nests for many creatures.

It's not a civic conscience that prompts beavers to do their good works, however. In building dams, they are solving a basic problem of their own; the stream is too shallow and narrow to hide them from the eyes of predators. By spreading the stream into a pond, beavers gain a protective moat for their lodges, as well as a safe travel lane to and from their feeding grounds on the shore.

Beavers cut trees down to get at the succulent leaves, twigs, and bark in the canopy (a novel approach to browsing!). It takes a beaver less than ten minutes to fell a 3-inch-diameter tree, but they've been known to labor for hours over record 60-inchers. Contrary to popular opinion, they don't direct the fall of their trees. Most trees fall toward the water simply because they are lopsided; they have more branches on the side that was near the open water and sun.

By removing the shoreline trees, beavers let in a flood of sunlight that encourages more palatable shrubs and saplings such as aspen, birches, and willows (which are, of course, the beaver's favorites). By removing overstory competitors, the beavers also make way for trees that have been waiting in the understory. By releasing them for growth, beavers actually accelerate the aging process of a forest around the edges of their ponds.

SNAPPING TURTLE

When food supplies around the pond run out, beavers move on, leaving dams that become leakier every year. Eventually the pond drains, and the marsh becomes a meadow, a shrub swamp, then finally a forest with its roots in rich heavier soil. Few other mammals, beside humans and perhaps elephants, can so drastically change their habitat to suit their needs.

Look for beavers—paddling from their lodge every day about the same time (dusk). They work mostly at night, but also during the day in the fall when they are laying in a store of winter food. A family of nine beavers may need as much as a ton of bark to survive the winter! It's easy to tell beavers from muskrats; beavers weigh 45–60 pounds while muskrats weigh only 2–4, and beavers' tails don't show when swimming. Like muskrats, beavers have a complete array of adaptations for water life: a wet suit of waterproof fur, webbed feet to propel them, furry lips that seal watertight behind their chopping teeth, flap valves on their nostrils and ears, transparent eyelids for "goggles," a body that can tolerate high levels of carbon dioxide, and a special air passage that is separate from the larynx so they can breathe while toting branches in the water.

Length: Head and body, 25–30 inches. Tail, 9–10 inches.

Look for lodges—large domes of branches smeared with mud, 5–6 feet above water level, and 12–14 feet wide. They may be built along a bank or in the pond itself. Beavers pile branches together, then swim up under the pile to hollow out a dry center for raising young. The apex of the lodge is loosely constructed to let air in and humid vapor out; in the winter, beaver breath looks like smoke coming from the lodge "chimney." The mud on the outside of the lodge freezes solid to keep predators from clawing their way in. In the summer, look for northern harriers or Canada geese nesting atop the lodge.

Look for dams—2–10 feet high, and up to 2,000 feet long. A pair of beavers can build a 2-foot-high, 12-foot-long dam in two nights, piling brush and tree limbs in the stream and cementing them together with mud, leaves, and rocks. Long poles are dragged over the dam and left on a slant, with their upper end perched on the dam and their lower end anchored in the mud on the downstream side. These buttresses, plastered in place by more debris, help to hold back the weight of the dammed water. Dams are not completely watertight; beavers allow some water to percolate through as a way to ease the pressure. A serious break will bring them running to repair it, however. When beavers build along high-energy streams, they often have to completely rebuild their washed-out dams each year. Many other animals use beaver dams to cross the stream (look for their scats).

Look for canals—winding from the pond up into the forest. Canals carry the beavers to a whole new set of food resources, and allow them to float their logs back to the pond. Hauling these logs overland would be too energy-expensive and risky.

Look for gnaw marks—in a circular pattern around trunks. Stumps are pointed and scarred with broad tooth marks. Some marks may be higher up, indicating that the work was done during winter while the beaver was standing on snow. Branches used to build lodges will often have the bark peeled off.

Look for "mud pies"—mounds of mud up to 1 foot high marked with drops of castoreum, a musk that beavers use to communicate their presence to other animals. There are 50 different volatile substances in castoreum, and every beaver has a unique odor signature. Humans use castoreum in perfumes—also to leave memorable messages! At one time, castoreum was thought to have miraculous healing powers; if taken up the nose it could clear the brain, or if rubbed on the head it could bestow a powerful memory. There may be between 40 and 120 of these scented mounds within the home range of a beaver family.

Look for tracks—splay-toed, 3 inches long, sometimes with only 3 or 4 toes printing. The webbed hindprints are 5 inches wide, twice as wide as the foreprints. Often, the prints will be obliterated by the drag mark of the flat tail.

Listen for—the resounding slap of a beaver's tail on the water, telegraphing danger to the rest of the beaver family. By protecting its relatives, the tail-slapper also protects some of its own genes, even though it risks giving away its own location to predators. If you're close enough, you can easily hear the cries and whimpers of the hungry, begging beaver kits in the lodge. Angry beavers blow through their nostrils.

Bullfrog
Bullfrogs are famous for their legs—those large, meaty, muscular springboards that starred in Mark Twain's "The Celebrated Jumping Frog of

Calaveras County." The frog's jumping ability evolved as a defense against predators such as skunks, raccoons, large birds, snakes, and more recently, the gastronomic purveyors of frog's legs.

When a bullfrog leaps from shore, its forelimbs lift the body up and aim it at a 45-degree angle, which is the most efficient flight path known (our rockets are designed to follow this same trajectory). The thighs and calves propel the frog upward and forward, and the hind feet roll off last, giving a little extra kick. As it travels, it shuts its eyes and withdraws them into its mouth cavity for protection. Landing is the most stressful part of the leap. Frogs have short rigid backbones consisting of only 9 vertebrae instead of the usual 30–100 in the backbone of a newt or salamander. After the forelimbs break the fall, the chest hits the ground, followed by the rest of the underside. Each leap can transport them up to nine times their own length (similar to you jumping 50 feet)!

The final destination is usually the safety of water. Bullfrogs move through the water in much the same way as they leap, but without the vertical component. When they kick their legs back, the water spreads open their webbed feet and gives them something to push against, thus propelling them forward. As they pull their legs back up to their body, their feet fan shut, slicing through the water like feathered oars. Besides humans doing the breaststroke, frogs are the only animals that move this way through the water. When escaping from enemies, the frogs usually head for the bottom, where they can hide among the tangles of aquatic vegetation, breathing for a while through their skin instead of their lungs.

Bullfrogs are perhaps most conspicuous at breeding time when the males move to their favorite croaking spots in the shallows and begin to serenade likely mates with their "jug-o-rum" call. Surprisingly, the frogs produce this far-reaching call with their nostrils and mouth closed tight. While shuttling air back and forth between the mouth and the lungs, they force some of it through slits in the mouth floor. This air inflates internal balloonlike vocal sacs, which resonate to carry the sound up to half a mile away.

Look for bullfrogs—basking onshore or floating in the shallows with just their eyes and nostrils piercing the surface. They are most abundant near a fringe of aquatic vegetation where tadpoles can feed on algae, and adults can hunt insects, lay eggs, and hide from predators. Bullfrogs catch and eat most of their food in the water; in fact, when they catch something on land, they usually jump into the water to eat it. Favorite foods include fish, crayfish, salamanders, young water birds and ducklings, and even their own younger brothers and sisters. During breeding, males float in shallows and females wait near shore until ready to join the males for mating.

Length: 3½–8 inches, our largest western frog.

Look for fighting males—bullfrogs are very territorial during breeding season. If a male intrudes on another male's territory, they will lock fore-limbs in combat, with throats and abdomens touching, and hind legs kicking. The struggle usually ends with one frog being pushed onto its back. You can distinguish males from females by looking for the large, circular ear membrane called the tympanum just behind each eye. In male frogs, this tympanum is much larger than the eye.

Look for eggs—in a filmy disk that may cover up to 15 square feet (3′ × 5′) of surface area on the water and include up to 20,000 eggs contributed by many frogs. You can spot egg masses by looking for foamy air bubbles dotting the jellylike mass. Eggs may be laid from February to June, depending on the onset of the first warm temperatures. Ideal conditions are 80 degree F air temperatures and 70 degree F water temperatures.

Look for tadpoles—up to 6 inches long, with vertically flattened tail, cylindrical body, and no legs. Tadpoles have circular mouthparts lined with rasping teeth that allow them to scrape algae off plant stems and eat decaying vegetation. They are in turn eaten by fish, water birds, other frogs, and water snakes. One of their worst enemies is the giant water bug, which grasps the tadpole with its hooklike forefeet and sucks out its body juices. It takes two or more years for tadpoles to transform into adults. When they hit the shores just after transformation, it may seem like a plague of frogs. For the converging predators, it's more like a feast, during which frog numbers are quickly thinned.

Listen for—a deep, booming "jug-o-rum" in evening and all night during breeding season. To locate the frog that's calling, shine a flashlight in the water where you hear the sound, and have a friend, standing farther down the shore, shine a light where he or she hears the sound. Your frog should be close to where the beams intersect. Females can also call, but are not nearly as loud as males. When accosted, a frog will open its mouth to let out a scream. It also lets out a yelping "yarp" as it leaps into the water.

SPOTTED
FROG

WILSON'S
PHALAROPE

Red-osier Dogwood

Mountain Alder

YUMA MYOTIS

STONEFLY
Adult
Nymph

HARLEQUIN DUCK

AMERICAN DIPPER

OLYMPIC SALAMANDER

Watercress

Bluejoint Reedgrass

Quaking Aspen

Blue Spruce

WILLOW FLYCATCHER

Bog Birch

RACCOON

MINK

TAILED FROG

WATER SHREW

Seep-spring Monkeyflower

Tufted Hairgrass

Mountain Stream

WHERE TO SEE THIS HABITAT:

California: Klamath, Lassen, Plumas, Sequoia, Shasta-Trinity, Six Rivers, and Stanislaus national forests; Yosemite National Park
Colorado: Rio Grande, San Isabel, and White River national forests; Rocky Mountain National Park
Idaho: Clearwater, Idaho Panhandle, Salmon, and Targhee national forests; Grays Lake National Wildlife Refuge
Montana: Gallatin, Kootenai, and Lolo national forests; Glacier National Park
New Mexico: Carson National Forest
Oregon: Rogue River (Bureau of Land Management); Siskiyou, Umpqua, and Wallowa-Whitman national forests
Utah: Uinta National Forest
Washington: Colville and Olympic national forests; North Cascades National Park
Wyoming: Bridger-Teton National Forest; Yellowstone National Park

Mountain Stream

BEGINNINGS

Drops of rain and snow that fall to earth have many possible fates; they may be soaked up by the soil, taken up by plants, intercepted by evaporation, or added to snowpacks and open bodies of water. Eventually, the snows may melt, the groundwater may resurface in a spring, and the lakewater may overflow its banks. Gravity takes over from there, creating a stream that journeys downward, heading inevitably for the deepest folds of the land. As it flows, other streams join it, and they in turn merge into larger rivers flowing wide and slow through the valleys.

On high-mountain hikes, you'll find streams gushing right from the snouts of glaciers. Some of this water, still milky with pulverized rock flour, may have fallen during snowstorms that happened hundreds of years ago! Released now by the sun, the meltwater cuts a channel, tearing rocks and vegetation loose from the banks and grinding pebbles into fine particles that are used like sandpaper to deepen the streambed even further.

Vegetation usually hangs over and shades high-mountain streams while they are still narrow and bounding through the forest. Some alders and willows will colonize areas right along the banks, and in the Rockies, blue spruce and bog willow join the streamside community. Mosses and ferns enjoy the constant cool mist around waterfalls, and the shady banks may be spotted with moisture-loving wildflowers such as seep-spring monkeyflower. The nutrients from leaves, fronds, and needles that fall into the water provide stream organisms with most of their energy.

When the steeply pitching stream drops down into a flatter area—a subalpine meadow, for instance—it often begins to meander. A meander may begin when a stream veers to one side to go around an obstruction such as a boulder. When the water hits the far shore, it "rebounds" back to the other side, following an "S" shape. The full force of the current

CHARACTERISTIC PLANTS:

Trees and Shrubs:
American plum
balsam poplar
beaked hazelnut
Bebb willow
bigleaf maple
black cottonwood
blue spruce
bog birch
bog willow
booth willow
bush honeysuckle
chokecherry
Douglas-fir
Drummond willow
Engelmann spruce
European red elder
Fremont cottonwood
Geyer willow
hawthorns
lodgepole pine
mannagrass
mountain alder
Nebraska sedge
New Mexican locust
Oregon ash
planeleaf willow
ponderosa pine
quaking aspen
red-osier dogwood
ribes (currant)
river birch

Rocky Mountain
  maple
sandbar willow
serviceberry willow
shrubby cinquefoil
smooth barked cot-
  tonwood
subalpine fir
swamp currant
water birch
western azalea
white alder
white fir
wolfs willow
wood's rose
yellow willow

Herbaceous Plants:
arrowleaf groundsel
asters
Baltic rush
beaked sedge
bluegrasses
bluejoint reedgrass
California pitcher
  plant
cinquefoils
elkslip
Fendler's meadowrue
few-flower spikesedge
field horsetail
fowl bluegrass
giant angelica
hardstem bulrush

heartleaved bittercress
marsh cinquefoil
marsh marigold
Merten's rush
mountain bluebell
mudwort
nodding bluegrass
northern bog orchid
Nuttall's sunflower
panicled bulrush
Rocky Mountain rush
scouring-rush
sedges
seep-spring monkey-
  flower
Siskiyou aster
slender wheatgrass
spikesedges
spike trisetum
star Solomon-plume
streambank globemal-
  low
sweetflag
tufted hairgrass
umbrella plant
water sedge
western virgin's-
  bower
white checkermallow
white clover
wild rice
wild strawberry

erodes the outside banks of the "S," while the slower water on the inside curves deposits sand. This erosion and deposition causes the "S" to widen so dramatically that the bends become nearly closed loops. During a high-water episode, the river might cut through the narrow neck of the loop, thus cutting off an "oxbow" of still water. Eventually this pond fills with sediment, allowing marshy plants to take root and creating another valuable wetland for wildlife.

CURRENT AS A FACT OF LIFE

Mountain streams are made up of a series of rapids (fast rocky stretches) followed by pools of deeper, quiet water. As water in the rapids encounters the friction of the rocky bottom, the ensuing turbulence raises particles of sand and silt and keeps them suspended in the water. When this silt-laden water slams against a boulder or log, the rebounding wave is forceful enough to pick up and carry even larger particles. The result is that riffles are usually swept clean of all movables, leaving only the heavier cobbles and gravel. This rocky bed can actually support more kinds of life than a bed of shifting sands, because there are more surfaces for insect larvae, planariums, and algae to attach themselves to.

In one sense, the current in these riffles is a blessing. Like an endless conveyor belt, it delivers bits of food from upstream—leaves and twigs that have fallen into the stream, for instance, or insects that have been dislodged from the rocks. The churning, cresting wavecaps breathe life into the water by mixing in oxygen with every splash while the current continuously flushes away wastes.

On the other hand, this same current can be a challenge, constantly abrading the banks and prying loose what is not anchored in place. River creatures are outfitted in a variety of ways to outfox the force and friction of moving water. Some simply avoid the current—living in eddies behind rocks or burrowing into the streambed. Snails, stonefly nymphs, and flatworms find refuge on the quiet underside of rocks. Paper-thin water pennies are flat enough to fit in the "boundary layer," a quiet zone on the top of the rock where the friction of moving water causes the current to slow down.

Other organisms actually use the current to keep them plastered against the rock or to help them snag a passing meal. The net-building caddisfly larva attaches a funnel-shaped net to the rock, and then periodically creeps out from its crevice to harvest the feast of tiny plants and animals caught in the mesh. Black fly larvae have feathery brushes on their head that comb bits of food from the passing water. They line up on rocks in dense colonies that look like carpets of black moss. With their prolegs clamped tightly to the surface, they let their body stream out with the flow. Should they lose a grip, they simply haul themselves back in with a silken lifeline.

Also growing on the top of rocks are slimy colonies of algae, bacteria, and other tiny creatures, which you might woefully encounter if you try to rock-hop across a stream. Luckily, stream algae reproduce new generations faster than any other kind of algae, quickly replacing the colony you scrape off when you slip. Larger stream plants adapt to frequent tearing by regenerating whole plants from the broken fragments. Submerged plants like watercress and water hypnum are sleek and flexible so they have less drag in the water. Others, like cushiony mosses, are rounded so that water finds the fastest way around them.

WHAT'S IN IT FOR WILDLIFE?

Rivers are one long "edge" habitat—the interface between land and water. True to their edge status, they offer wildlife the bounties of both water and land. Unlike other freshwater habitats that have limited, circular shorelines, the river's edge goes on for miles and miles. Often, it is the only bit of natural vegetation that cuts through the various layers of mountain habitat from glacier to grassland. Elk and other migrating wildlife may use these corridors to safely travel from their high-altitude summer ranges to their lowland winter ranges.

Besides visual cover and protection from predators, wildlife also find thermal relief around rushing rivers. The vegetation that overhangs the banks insulates the air, keeping temperatures cooler in the summer and somewhat warmer in the winter. In addition to cover, these banks provide easy access to drinking water, protected sites for burrows and nests, and a sunny spot for berries and other fruit-producing shrubs to grow. The muddy banks of a river are a great place to look for the tracks of upland animals that visit the river throughout the day. Mule deer and elk, for instance, will come to drink the cool water, and minks and raccoons will come down at night to hunt crayfish or to pick at the carcass trailings of dead fish.

Besides visitors from terrestrial habitats, there are some species that spend almost all their time in or near rivers. The American dipper, for instance, is a uniquely adapted bird that can "fly" to the bottom of a roaring stream, then walk along the rocks, probing for insects. Spotted sandpipers also fish for insects, wading in from the banks with stilted, mechanical strides. Tailed frogs are equally equipped to handle the rush; their "tails" are used to fertilize the female internally, so that the sperm cannot be washed away. The tadpoles keep their place by latching onto rocks with their suctionlike mouth. If you're lucky, you'll spot a tiny water shrew diving to the bottom wrapped in a silvery sheath of air bubbles. Bristles of hair on each paw also trap bubbles of air, allowing the shrew to sprint on top of the water for short distances!

The air above a river comes alive when the wriggling, wormlike insects among the rocks begin to "hatch" or transform into flying adults. Hatching insects float up from the bottom, unfold their new wings, and struggle to break free from the surface or crawl onto rocks and logs. Those that hesitate are whisked down to the pools of hungry trout swirling beneath the rapids. Those that make it into the air are often scooped up by zigzagging bats, flycatchers, swallows, and swifts. Those that stop to rest on the leaves of streamside shrubs may wind up in the beaks of warblers, sparrows, and thrushes.

In addition to insects, the water is alive with small fish, with crustaceans, and occasionally with the hatching eggs of salamanders or frogs. Herons and egrets stand and wait for their dinner to swim by, while belted king-fishers plunge down from above, rattling the air with their famous call. In wider stretches of swift water, you may find mergansers bucking the current, or even a pair of the rare and beautiful harlequin ducks.

Although the stream and its residents seem ruggedly wild, it is a surprisingly fragile place. One of the most insidious threats to clear-running streams is the removal of the streamside vegetation. Once there are no roots to hold the soil, vast plumes of silt may bleed into the water, irritating the gills of fish and amphibians, while blocking the light that algae need. When this silt settles to the bottom, it chokes the rubble community and obliterates the maze of rocky surfaces that makes the streambed so unique. As the smothered community decays, it uses up more and more oxygen. At the same time, the unfiltered sun heats the stream, thus reducing the water's ability to hold dissolved oxygen. This forces out sensitive species such as trout, tailed frogs, and many aquatic insects. Equally alarming results occur when acid deposition, chemicals, or fertilizers make their way into rivers. Because of the speed of the current, containment attempts are rarely fast enough. Eventually, trouble upstream makes its way downstream, affecting all the communities in between.

American Dipper

When you stand on the banks of a roaring mountain torrent, it's hard to believe that anything larger than a water penny could set foot in this river and survive. Just then, you see a starling-sized gray bird emerge from the rapids, perch on a rock, and blink the streamwater from its eyes. Dippers fill a peculiar niche in the upper reaches of wild rivers. Though they are not related to diving birds such as grebes, nor to wading birds such as

WANDERING TATTLER

SPOTTED SANDPIPER

YELLOW WARBLER

MACGILLIVRAY'S WARBLER

MOUNTAIN YELLOW-LEGGED FROG

HOODED MERGANSER

WILDLIFE LOCATOR CHART—MOUNTAIN STREAM

	Feeds from Air	Feeds in Tree Canopy	Feeds on Ground	Feeds Beneath Ground	Feeds in Water
Nests in Tree Canopy	Bald Eagle Copper's Hawk Golden Eagle Great Horned Owl Black-chinned Hummingbird American Redstart	Band-tailed Pigeon Ruby-crowned Kinglet American Robin American Goldfinch			
Nests in Trunk Cavity	American Kestrel Western Flycatcher	Black-capped Chickadee	House Wren, Raccoon		Hooded Merganser
Nests in Shrubs	Willow Flycatcher	Yellow Warbler MacGillivray's Warbler Black-headed Grosbeak			
Nests on Ground			Blue Grouse, Wandering Tattler, Spotted Sandpiper, Mule Deer, Moose		Harlequin Duck American Dipper Water Shrew
Nests Beneath Ground or Debris	Belted Kingfisher Yuma Myotis		Masked Shrew, Nuttalls' Cottontail, Least Chipmunk, Deer Mouse, Montane Vole, Meadow Vole, Water Vole, Western Jumping Mouse, Coyote, Black Bear, Long-tailed Weasel, Mink, Mountain Lion, Bobcat, Blacktail Rattlesnake, Western Terrestrial Garter Snake		River Otter Western Aquatic Garter Snake Blackneck Garter Snake Narrowhead Garter Snake
Nests Above Water					Beaver Muskrat
Nests in Water			Pacific Giant Salamander, Olympic Salamander, Western Toad, Striped Chorus Frog, Cascades Frog, Northern Leopard Frog, Spotted Frog, Wood Frog	Redbelly Newt	Roughskin Newt Tailed Frog Mountain Yellow-legged Frog

sandpipers, they have adopted a fishing style that features both diving and wading. Though dippers are not as highly sophisticated in either activity, there are few competitors that will challenge them in these swift-moving waters.

When dippers enter the stream, a scaly flap keeps water out of their nostrils, and up to 6,300 outer feathers underlain with down keep them warm. Their plumage is well waterproofed with oil from a preening gland that is ten times larger than that of other songbirds in their class. This extra protection allows them to hunt for food even when water is laced with ice.

Dippers usually take shallow dives, and may remain submerged for up to 30 seconds at a time. Their short wings propel them to the bottom, where they stroll along the cobbles, flapping into the current and grasping the slippery surface with their strong claws. Their favorite foods include the larvae of caddisflies, which build tube-shaped houses of sand grains cemented with silk. They also dive for stonefly, mayfly, mosquito, and midge larvae, aquatic worms, and even small fish, clams, and snails. Naturally buoyant, they bob back up to the surface, sometimes exploding straight up out of the water and leveling off with a quaillike buzzing flight.

Look for American dippers—doing their characteristic, full-body dipping (it looks like rapid deep-knee bends) on a rock in the rapids or along the shore. They may dip 40–60 times a minute before diving or hopping to another rock. One interesting (but unproven) hypothesis is that this teetering helps them blend in with the changing light and motion of the lapping waves. You may also see them swooping to their nests, diving from the air, or wading in the shallows along the shore. In flight, they rarely deviate from the contours of the stream, even if a jaunt across land would shorten the distance.

Length: 7–8½ inches.

Look for nests—a 1-foot-wide ball of green and yellow moss on horizontal ledges of cliffs, beams under bridges, the upturned roots of a fallen tree, or even behind a waterfall. Although parents must commute through the waterfall to deliver shipments of food to their young, they are assured that the danger from predators is low. If you find a nest, look for the gaping mouths of dipper nestlings poking out of the arch-shaped side entrance. Don't stay too long, however, because you may be keeping the parents from their hungry brood.

In the winter—you'll still find dippers diving and walking into streams, even when shelves of ice begin to form. If the stream becomes completely iced over, the dippers will seek open water at a lower elevation.

Listen for—a loud, clear, flutelike song, loud enough for you to hear over the roar of the stream. Dippers can be especially vocal in winter when defending their feeding territories.

Water Shrew

It's a big risk for a tiny animal to take, but the water shrew plunges into ice cold water anyway. It keeps its dive brief, just long enough to snare a protein-rich snack, such as a caddisfly or mayfly nymph, planaria, small fish, tadpole, or snail. When it returns to land, it quickly combs the water droplets out of its fur with its hind toes, allowing its body temperature to return to normal.

Even on land, shrews have a hard time keeping warm because their skin area, through which they lose heat, is so large in comparison with the amount of body mass that produces heat. Their metabolism is also maniacally fast, meaning they burn up the food they eat in a very short time. To protect them from losing even more heat, water shrews have thick, velvety hair that traps air bubbles and keeps their fur from becoming completely wet. As they dive, this shimmering, silvery suit of air not only insulates, but also keeps them buoyant.

When underwater, the shrew swims with all four feet as if running. Large, webbed hind feet propel it to the bottom, where it need only shift position slightly to begin trotting along the streambed. As soon as it stops, it bobs quickly back up to the surface. Here, it might opt to take a short sprint on top of the water, balancing on the film of surface tension the way the spidery insects called water striders do. Hairs that form a fringe along the shrew's feet trap bubbles of air beneath them, large enough to support the weight of a running shrew!

Look for water shrews—swimming in or running alongside streams, especially those that have well-vegetated banks with plenty of tree roots, fallen logs, and rocky debris for cover. They are mainly active at night, especially the first several hours after sunset and the first hour before sunrise. You might also see them out during the day, however, quelling their endless appetite.

Length: Head and body, 3½–3⅘ inches. Tail, 2½–3⅕ inches.

Look for nests—balls of vegetation and sticks, as large as 4 inches in diameter, hidden in streamside debris or burrows.

In the winter—shrews remain active, and may be found under overhanging shelves of ice left after the water level recedes.

Listen for—the squeaks of fighting shrews.

Tailed Frog

A frog in a rushing, rocky stream is a horse of an entirely different color. Unlike other frogs, the tailed frog can't serenade its mate in the spring because it has neither voice nor ear membranes. Communication by sound seems to be a moot point anyway, because the roaring torrent monopolizes the air waves. Instead, the male walks along the bottom of the stream in pursuit of a mate. When he finds a female, he clasps her in a traditional frog mating embrace called "amplexus." His forearms are enlarged 2–3 times their normal size at this time of year to help him get a good grip. Instead of simply releasing the sperm in the water and letting it settle over the eggs (the way most frogs do), the tailed frog has had to evolve another adaptation to its rushing stream environment. To prevent its sperm from being washed away, the male fertilizes the female internally with an extension of his body that is erroneously called a "tail." The female must then attach the fertilized eggs to the underside of a rock until they hatch.

The tadpole of the tailed frog seals itself to the rock with a huge sucking disk that surrounds its mouth. It can then bend or close its funnel-shaped nostrils to control the flow of stream water jettisoning through its body. Interestingly, when the nostrils are open, the tadpoles use them to catch small food particles. This supplements their diet of algae that they scrape from rocks with their ring of horny, comblike "teeth."

When an insect floats by, the adult tailed frog doesn't whip out a long sticky tongue like many frogs do; its tongue is short and rather immobile, better adapted for picking off sedentary insects attached to rocks. The frog's lungs are also smaller than those of most frogs, which actually makes them less buoyant, so they can sink to their feeding grounds with ease.

Because the tailed frog has become so specially adapted to cold, rushing, oxygen-rich mountain streams, it is extremely sensitive to change. If, for instance, the streamside vegetation is removed by logging or fire, the sun-drenched stream might become too warm for the frogs. If a large enough area of vegetation is removed, the resulting erosion may cover its hiding rocks with silt and suffocate the insects that it eats. Silty streams soon lose their populations of this fascinating frog.

Look for tailed frogs—by turning over rocks in the stream (please remember to replace them). The frogs may be gray, pink, brown, or black, and usually blend magically into their surroundings. In the spring, look for mating males and females which may stay coupled on the streambed for up to 70 hours. During dry periods, the frogs will stay in the water, but during rains or on cool damp days, they may be found crawling along the banks or even farther from the water.

Length: 1–2 inches.

Look for tadpoles—1½ to 2 inches long, facing upstream, with their mouth attached to rocks (even those in waterfalls!). Tadpoles may also use their mouth to lift themselves onto a spray-drenched rock. Evidently, the algae-grazing may be better here than in the more turbulent spots below.

Look for eggs—in rosarylike chains or clumps of 28–50 colorless eggs (⅓ inch in diameter) attached to the undersurfaces of stones. Eggs are laid from May to September and take a month to hatch.

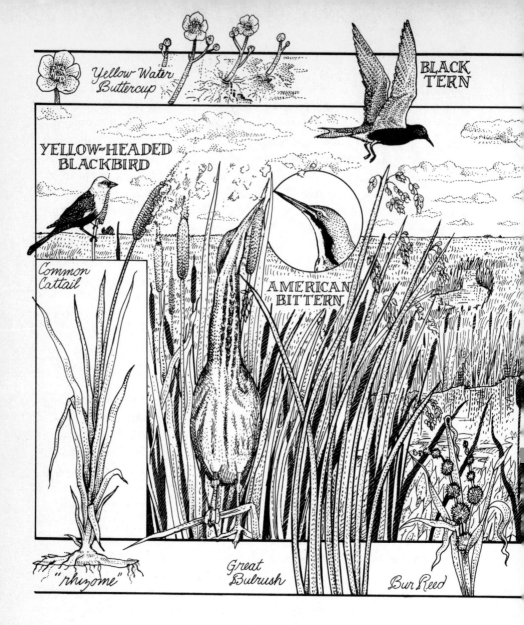

Yellow Water Buttercup

BLACK TERN

YELLOW~HEADED BLACKBIRD

Common Cattail

AMERICAN BITTERN

"rhizome"

Great Bulrush

Bur Reed

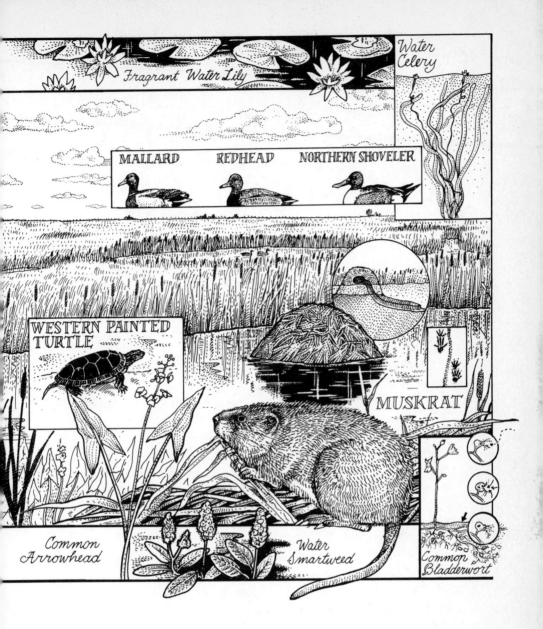

Water Celery

Fragrant Water Lily

MALLARD   REDHEAD   NORTHERN SHOVELER

WESTERN PAINTED TURTLE

MUSKRAT

Common Arrowhead

Water Smartweed

Common Bladderwort

Inland Marsh

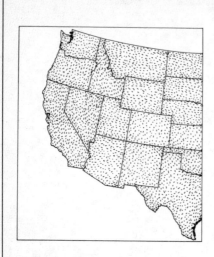

WHERE TO SEE THIS HABITAT:

California: Delevan, Kern, Kesterson, Lower Klamath, Modoc, Sacramento, San Luis, Sutter, and Tule Lake national wildlife refuges
Idaho: Bear Lake, Camas, Grays Lake, and Minidoka national wildlife refuges; Challis National Forest
Kansas: Quivira National Wildlife Refuge
Montana: Charles M. Russell, Medicine Lake, and Red Rock Lakes national wildlife refuges
Nebraska: Crescent Lake and Valentine national wildlife refuges; Rainwater Basin Wildlife Management District
Nevada: Railroad Valley Wildlife Management Area; Ruby Lake National Wildlife Refuge
New Mexico: Bosque del Apache National Wildlife Refuge
North Dakota: Crosby, Devils Lake, Kulm, and Valley City wetland management districts; Des Lacs, J. Clark Salyer, Lake Alice, Lake Ilo, Long Lake, Lostwood, Tewaukon, and Upper Souris national wildlife refuges
Oregon: Klamath Forest, Umatilla, and Upper Klamath national wildlife refuges
South Dakota: Lacreek, Lake Andes, Sand Lake, and Waubay national wildlife refuges; Madison Wildlife Management District
Texas: Hagerman National Wildlife Refuge
Utah: Bear River Migratory Bird Refuge; Fish Springs National Wildlife Refuge
Washington: Toppenish and Turnbull national wildlife refuges

Inland Marsh

BEGINNINGS

A marsh can arise in any basin that holds water long enough for herbaceous, water-loving plants to take root. It can fill in the oxbow of a slow meandering river or be the last watery remnant of an aging lake. The water may be anywhere from "soggy soil" to several feet deep, sparkling in open pools, or hidden beneath a continuous "prairie" of plants. It can be fresh, like most of the marshes in high rainfall areas, or saline, like the tule-bulrush marshes of California and Oregon.

In the shallower portions of the marsh, tall, wandlike plants called emergents grow half in and half out of the water, binding the soft ooze with their mesh of roots and underground stems. Above the water, they bend gracefully with the wind and waves, harboring quiet eddies between their tufts. Grasses, bulrushes, spikesedges, cattails, arrowheads, smartweed, and pickerelweed are some of the more common shallow-grown emergents.

In slightly deeper water, reeds and wild rice take root, and floating-leaved plants such as water lilies sail their flotilla of flat green leaves on the surface. These leaves are connected to tuberous roots by an extra long stem that lets the floating leaves rise as the water levels rise. Buoyant free-floaters such as duckweed have hairy roots that dangle beneath a single floating leaf no larger than a matchhead.

In the deepest, open-water portions of the marsh, rooted submergents such as water celery and bladderwort manage to make food (through photosynthesis) in the murky light that filters down to them. Bubbles of oxygen, which collect on their leaves as they photosynthesize, are sometimes jostled to the surface by nibbling turtles. Bladderworts supplement the food they make by trapping small animals and plants that float by them. Next time you're in a marsh, pull up the branches of a common bladderwort plant, and look for the hundreds of tiny, deflated "bladders" with one-way trap doors. When a minute bit of food brushes against the threshold, the door swings open and the prey is literally vacuumed inside the trap.

Finally, suffusing the water with a St. Patrick's Day green are the millions of tiny suspended plants (the algae). Late in the summer, when fertility in the marsh is at an all-time high, the algae sometimes "bloom" with abandon, creating the typical marshy smell as they decompose. These tiny plants form the basis of the entire marsh food chain, which represents a tremendous volume of organisms. Sometimes, when you are standing at the edge of a marsh with your eyes closed, you can actually hear it hum with life.

The northern plains of North and South Dakota hold some of the nation's most abundant and productive marshes. These "prairie potholes" were created by heavy sheets of ice that melted off the land a mere 10,000 years ago, while civilization was already well under way in the Middle East. The shallow "thumbprints" left by the glacier still fill with spring rains each year. Deeper depressions hold their water longer, but are also subject to highs and lows in the water level.

After several years of low rainfall, a marsh may become so shallow that the pools may dry down completely, making life unbearable for the cattails, bulrushes, and water lilies. As the exposed bottom mud steams and cracks in the sun, the stranded plants and animals will begin to decay. This is good news for the thousands of seeds that have been buried over the years. Nourished by a pulse of nutrients, a crewcut of green quickly covers

---

CHARACTERISTIC PLANTS:

Herbaceous Plants:

American globeflower	giant reed	spotted joe-pye-weed
bluejoint reedgrass	great bulrush	sweetflag
bulrushes	great hedge nettle	tule
bur reed	hardstem bulrush	water celery
common arrowhead	marsh cinquefoil	watercress
common bladderwort	marsh skullcap	water hyacinth
common cattail	narrowleaf bur-reed	water smartweed
common mares-tail	pickerelweed	waterweed
common reed	pondweed	water willow
duckweed	purple meadowrue	yellow iris
elkslip	sedges	yellow pond lily
fragrant water lily	seep-spring monkey-	yellow skunk cabbage
fringed loosestrife	flower	yellow water buttercup
	soft rush	
	spikesedges	

the mud. Side by side, plants from the uplands and the lowlands compete for sun, space, nutrients, and water.

Sedges and grasses will make the strongest comeback at first, enjoying the relatively dry environment. If waters don't return, the marsh may progress to drier stages of wet meadow, shrub swamp, and eventually, if the site is right, a forest. If, however, the skies open and the basin is reflooded, cattails and other water plants will once again have the upper hand. In some prairie potholes, this cycle of drydown and rejuvenation has kept the marsh a marsh for 11,000 years!

THE NINE LIVES OF CATTAILS

The fuzzy brown punk of the cat-o'-nine-tails is the logo of the marsh. This seedhead can be packed with some 250,000 seeds, each equipped with a fluffy parachute that catches in the wind or floats atop the water. Seeds also stick to the fur, feathers, and muddy feet of wildlife, helping to start new cattail colonies wherever they fall off.

A plant as successful as the cattail doesn't depend solely on the whims of animals, waves, or wind to start its next generation, however. Cattails also travel by sending out a horizontal stem (called a rhizome) not far from the parent plant. This stem puts down roots and sends up shoots, creating an entirely new plant. Because it is still connected to the root system of the parent plant, however, the new sprout enjoys a subsidy that independent plants don't have.

Cattails store nutrients in these fleshy rhizomes each autumn, before the upper stalks die. These storage pantries remain alive beneath the ice of a winter marsh, relying on dead, hollow stalks to snorkel air down to them. Their starches fuel early spring growth, sending new stalks skyward at an astonishing rate. Unless, of course, muskrats discover them first.

Muskrats are fond of rhizomes, and will dive deep to dig them up from the bottom. The rafts of floating plants you sometimes see in a marsh are the aftermath of this feeding. Luckily, the indomitable cattail uses even this uprooting to its advantage, floating to a new place and often taking root again.

Muskrats occasionally go through a boom-and-bust cycle in the marsh. Their population may explode after a new flush of cattails appears, and they sometimes wind up eating themselves out of house and home. Under balanced conditions, however, their small-scale harvesting can be a special service, especially to migrating waterfowl. You can watch flocks on any autumn day, wheeling high over a marsh, then funneling down by the hundreds to rest on the muskrat-opened patches of water.

WHAT'S IN IT FOR WILDLIFE?

Even when they are dried and brittle, old cattail stems still provide shelter to many animals that cross the frozen marsh during the winter. Look for ring-necked pheasants and wild turkeys huddling in the windshadow of cattail clumps. Under the ice, muskrats and fish remain alive, and under-the-mud turtles breathe a sort of muddy oxygen.

When the ice begins to thaw, frogs, toads, and salamanders return to the open water of marshes to breed. The thick clusters of plants dampen wave action and create a stable harbor in which to lay their eggs. Insects are also laying their eggs between, under, and on the plants, providing an abundant source of food to quick-tongued frogs. In turn, these amphibians give wading birds, snakes, and land mammals something to hunt for.

Breeding birds also come to the marshes in droves. The air is loud with the courtship calls of yellow-headed blackbirds and others fighting for a patch of marsh in which to nest. The still-standing stalks of last year's plants provide valuable nesting sites for rails, American coots, common moorhens, and waterfowl. The prairie pothole region is a particularly important nursery, producing 50 percent of our ducks in an area that represents only 10 percent of the country's wetlands. Studies have shown that under the best conditions, prairie pothole marshes support 140 ducks per square mile.

The emergent stalks quiet the water and give young ducklings a safe place to develop their muscles for paddling. As a bonus, each plant harbors the larvae of various insects, providing the high-protein diet that ducklings need. As these insects "hatch" they are also scooped from the water surface by black terns and picked off the surrounding vegetation by swamp sparrows and common yellowthroats. Dabbling ducks such as mallards and teals dabble for waterweed and other submerged plants in the shallow end of the marsh. The tubers of arrowhead ("duck potato") are especially popular with migrating waterfowl when they are fueling up for their southern trek.

Farther out, coots turn over the floating leaves of water lilies to find tasty snails for their nestlings to eat. Small frogs that have just developed legs and absorbed their tail also linger near the pads for protection. In the center of the marsh, canvasbacks and redheads dive to find their favorite foods, such as water celery and pondweed, submerged in pools.

The marsh's productivity is legendary. With sun and water in ample supply, plants fill every available space. Thanks to an abundance of decay organisms, the nutrients in fallen plants and animals are quickly recycled back into the community, encouraging even more growth. Compared with the surrounding uplands, a marsh can seem like a lush oasis of life.

Like any habitat, however, the marsh is not a utopia. Those ducks that nest near the edges lose their eggs to minks, foxes, raccoons, crows, magpies, gulls, ground squirrels, bullsnakes, and coyotes. Hawks, snapping turtles, and snakes may take some of the ducklings that do hatch. And the water level can be fickle in a marsh. In the end, the most successful species are those that can exploit the best of the marsh yet can escape to another habitat if the wetland dries up or floods over.

American Bittern

One of the greatest actors in the world is a bird that fools us into thinking it is a plant. The American bittern is not particularly petite, yet it is able to imitate the slender cattails in which it lives with uncanny accuracy. To "become" a stand of cattails, the bird raises its bill skyward and compresses its feathers. Its plumage and even the color of its bill mimic the vertical stripes and shadows of the habitat. The disguise is interrupted only once—by a fiery eye which remains carefully trained on you. When you move, the bittern pivots so its camouflaged breast continues to face you. When a breeze bends the cattails, the bittern bends with them, coming to a standstill when the breeze halts. Even young hatchlings can "bittern," proving that the act is an instinctive one programmed by long years of evolution.

Not even the booming "oong-KA-chunk" call of the bittern can give it away. Even though the booming is loud enough to be heard by females and rival male bitterns up to half a mile away, predators have a hard time tracing its source. Ornithologists refer to this sort of hollow, elusive call as "ventriloquistic." To produce the call, the bittern first gulps air into its esophagus. A specially thickened patch of skin on its throat balloons, then acts like a bellows to force the pocket of trapped air out.

By way of slow, deliberate movements and a great deal of patience, bitterns are also able to remain hidden from their prey. They practice the wade-and-wait method of fishing, keeping their bill level and their eyes directed into the shallows. When a frog, fish, eel, or crustacean happens by, they slowly point their bill toward it, then flash out of their freeze at just the right moment to nab it.

Look for American bitterns—wading in the shallows of the marsh or hiding in the dense vegetation. A bittern keeps its head and body low when running through the cattails. When it stops, it assumes a vertical pose, which it will hold until you are almost on top of it. Suddenly it will flush before you in a roar of wings, sounding an annoyed, nasal "kok-kok-kok" as it labors to get airborne. It flies with dangling legs and sort of floppy wing movements at first, eventually working up to rapid wingbeats.

Length: 23–34 inches.

Look for nests—platforms, a foot or more in diameter, made of dead

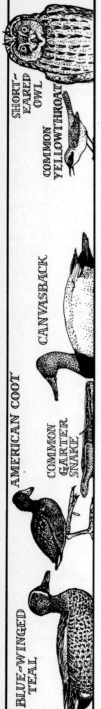

BLUE-WINGED TEAL
AMERICAN COOT
COMMON GARTER SNAKE
CANVASBACK
COMMON YELLOWTHROAT
SHORT-EARED OWL

WILDLIFE LOCATOR CHART—INLAND MARSH

	Feeds from Air	Feeds in Lower Canopy	Feeds on Ground	Feeds in Shallow Water (Wades)	Feeds in Shallow Water (Dabbles)	Feeds Underwater (Dives or Dips)
Nests in Tree Canopy			Raccoon (Nests in Trunk)	Great Blue Heron Snowy Egret Green-backed Heron Black-crowned Night-Heron		
Nests on Ground	Northern Harrier Peregrine Falcon Caspian Tern Short-eared Owl	Common Yellowthroat	White-faced Ibis California Gull Savannah Sparrow Le Conte's Sparrow Song Sparrow	Yellow Rail Virginia Rail Sandhill Crane American Avocet Willet Common Snipe	Canada Goose Green-winged Teal Mallard Northern Pintail Blue-winged Teal Cinnamon Teal Gadwall American Wigeon	American White Pelican Northern Shoveler Ring-necked Duck Wilson's Phalarope
Nests Beneath Ground or Debris			Coyote Mink Red Fox Plains Garter Snake			Nutria Snapping Turtle Western Painted Turtle Northern Water Snake Western Ribbon Snake Common Garter Snake
Nests on Water (Floating nest)	Franklin's Gull Black Tern				Common Moorhen	Pied-billed Grebe Red-necked Grebe Eared Grebe American Coot
Nests Above Water			Marsh Wren Red-winged Blackbird Tricolored Blackbird Yellow-headed Blackbird Brewer's Blackbird	American Bittern Least Bittern	Fulvous Whistling-Duck Trumpeter Swan	Canvasback Redhead Ruddy Duck Muskrat
Nests on Water			Woodhouse's Toad			Bullfrog

cattails, reeds, or sedges built a few inches above the water and surrounded above and on the sides by arching, dense vegetation. Sometimes the nests are directly on the ground, and sometimes they actually float. Up to 5 eggs are laid, from April to July.

Look for runways—one leading into the nest and one leading out. The female fashions these trails by bending stalks down with her weight or clipping them with her bill. Instead of landing or taking off directly from the nest, she sneaks in and out via the runways to keep predators guessing about the nest's whereabouts.

Listen for—a throaty, belching "oong-KA-chunk," repeated several times, usually at dawn or dusk. At the height of breeding season, you may hear it at any time of day or night. Calling bitterns pump their head and neck violently, as if in a coughing fit. Males use the call to build a "fence of sound" around their territory and to attract a mate.

Muskrat

The haystack houses of these water-loving rodents are a familiar site on most marshes. To build them, muskrats pile aquatic plants such as cattails and bulrushes atop a foundation of mud, branches, and other debris. As they cut down plants and dredge up mud around the house, they create a "moat" of open water that protects them from land predators. To form the chamber inside the house, the muskrat gnaws a tunnel up from the foundation almost to the top, chewing out a cavity that sits above the waterline.

When ice caps the marsh, muskrats build yet another structure called a "push-up." They begin by gnawing a 4- to 5-inch hole in the ice, through which they pull or push up vegetation to make a 12- to 18-inch lumpy pile over the hole. A small cavity within this pile gives the muskrats a way station on their under-ice excursions—a place to rest, feed, and breathe. Their winter fare includes roots, stems, and tubers that they find underwater. In a pinch, they can even eat the walls of their own homes.

Look for muskrats—swimming in marshes with no current and plenty of cattails. In the North, the marshes should be at least 3–4 feet deep, so they won't freeze all the way to the bottom in the winter. Here's how to tell a muskrat from a beaver: muskrats are 10 times smaller and sometimes hold their skinny tails out of the water when swimming. Beavers have wide, flat tails that trail underwater. You can usually see muskrats out during the day, feeding on platforms or sunning themselves on their decks, but they may also be active at night, starting at twilight. In spring and fall, muskrats may be on land, even far from the water, looking for new quarters. Drought, high water, or an "eat-out" (when muskrats strip all the cattails from a marsh) may force them from their original marsh.

Length: Head and body, 10–14 inches. Tail, 8–11 inches.

Look for houses—up to 8 feet wide and 5 feet high, randomly arranged in the marsh. A house may be some distance from open water, but usually has water-filled channels that connect it to the pond. Muskrats may also den in burrows in the banks.

Look for push-ups—small piles of vegetation on an ice-covered marsh, used for feeding, resting, and breathing. Push-ups help extend a muskrat's feeding range under the ice.

Look for feeding debris—piles of mussel shells on feeding platforms, or floating rafts of uprooted cattails.

Look for droppings—oval, ½ inch long, deposited in clumps on feeding platforms, rocks, or logs. Small pats of grass, mud, and leaves marked with musk secretions are called scent posts, and help the males and females identify each other.

Look for tracks—in pairs, separated by a stride of 3 inches. The hindprint, 2–3 inches long, is twice as long as the foreprint. Sometimes only 4 of the 5 toes print. Look for the drag mark of the skinny tail.

Listen for—the squeals of young muskrats. Adults are rather quiet, except during mating, when the female can squeal like a bird. As you approach a marsh, you may hear a loud splash as a muskrat plops from the bank, warning its comrades of your presence.

Western Painted Turtle

The painted turtle begins its day by climbing onto its favorite water-soaked log along with as many as fifty of its compatriots, all searching for the life-giving warmth of the sun. Because turtles are ectotherms ("cold-blooded animals"), they must soak up the sun or seek cool water to regulate their body temperature. After a night's sleep on the chilly pond floor, the turtle needs all the solar radiation it can get to rouse it out of its low-temperature stupor. A basking turtle will spread its head and limbs as far as they will go, but close its eyes to avoid harmful ultraviolet rays. Though it may not always keep an eye peeled for danger, the turtle is "listening" for vibrations that travel through the ground or water as sound waves. At the first hint of a canoe paddle splitting the water, all the turtles will slide and plop out of view, becoming incognito except for an occasional set of nostrils piercing the surface.

VIRGINIA
RAIL

MARSH
WREN

Midmorning, the turtles begin nibbling on pondweed stems and algal sprays, flushing frogs, fish, or tadpoles from their hiding places. After a fast chase, the turtle locks the prey in its jaws and tears it into bite-sized pieces with its foreclaws. These "everything eaters" are the scavengers of the marsh community, feeding on the dead as well as the living. To collect particles of food from the surface of the water, the turtle floats along with its head out of the water and its lower jaw dropped so that it's level with the surface. As the turtle retracts its head, water begins to spill into its throat, carrying surface-floating food along with it.

It samples the odors around it by pulsating its throat to draw a steady stream of water in through its nostrils and out through its mouth. Along the way, the chemicals in plant juices and the odors of snails, worms, and other prey are analyzed. Turtles also use chemical messages to find potential mates. After stalking a female for a while, the male will finally pass her and then turn to face her. To put her in the mood for mating, he begins stroking her head and neck with the backs of his elongated foreclaws. If she is receptive, she'll stroke his outstretched forelimbs with her foreclaws. Occasionally, the male will start to swim away, as if trying to lure the female to follow. When she's sufficiently interested, the female sinks to the bottom, where mating can continue for an hour or more, interrupted only by periodic jaunts up to the surface for air.

Look for western painted turtles—in shallow water with a soft bottom, aquatic vegetation, and plenty of basking sites. They rarely venture far from water, except to travel to or from hibernating ponds or when their summer pond dries up. Researchers believe painted turtles use a sun-compass to get their directional bearings, then rely on familiar visual landmarks to find their way back to home ponds. Hatchling turtles just emerging from the nest (on land) have no prior memory of the pond, however. They simply look for the area of brightest illumination—usually the sky over a body of water.

Shell length: 7½–9¾ inches.

Don't disturb nests—dug in late May to early July on sandy or loamy sites, in openings where the sun can warm the soil and help incubate the eggs. In the early evening, the female digs a flask-shaped chamber (less than 3 inches wide) with her hind legs, deposits 4–20 eggs, then covers them with sand and leaves them to hatch on their own. If the eggs are laid late in the summer, the tiny hatchlings may overwinter in the nest rather than risk emerging right at the onset of cold weather.

In the winter—painted turtles burrow as far as 18 inches into the muddy bottom of the pond. Their metabolism slows so that they need very little oxygen and can survive for weeks without surfacing. They "breathe" through membranes in their throat or through thin-walled anal sacs.

Western Azalea

Mountain Bluebell

AMERICAN KESTREL

MONTANE VOLE

LONG-TOED SALAMANDER

CALLIOPE HUMMINGBIRD

Giant Red Paintbrush

WESTERN YELLOWBELLY RACER

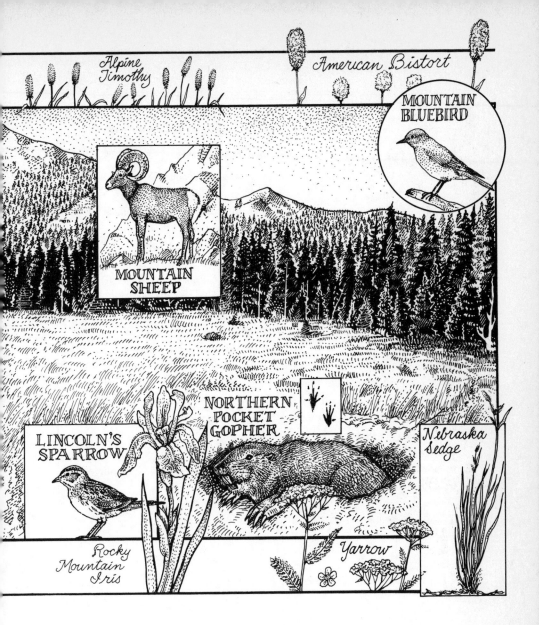

Alpine Timothy

American Bistort

MOUNTAIN BLUEBIRD

MOUNTAIN SHEEP

NORTHERN POCKET GOPHER

Nebraska Sedge

LINCOLN'S SPARROW

Rocky Mountain Iris

Yarrow

Mountain Meadow

WHERE TO SEE THIS HABITAT:

Arizona: Apache-Sitgreaves and Cococino national forests
California: Kings Canyon, Sequoia, and Yosemite national parks; Modoc National Forest
Colorado: Arapaho, Gunnison, Rio Grande, Routt, and White River national forests; Browns Park National Wildlife Refuge; Rocky Mountain National Park
Montana: Benton Lake and Bowdoin national wildlife refuges; Custer and Lewis and Clark national forests; Glacier National Park
Oregon: Deschute, Fremont, Mount Hood, and Wallawa-Whitman national forests; Klamath National Wildlife Refuge
Utah: Fishlake National Forest
Washington: Colville and Okanogan national forests; Conboy Lake National Wildlife Refuge; Mount Ranier, North Cascades, and Olympic national parks
Wyoming: Bridger-Teton and Medicine Bow national forests; Grand Teton and Yellowstone national parks

Mountain Meadow

BEGINNINGS

Natural meadows come in all sizes and shapes, from the dry, sprawling grasslands of the basin country to the wet, springy flower gardens of the subalpine zone. These oases of open space and nutritious forage are located on gentle slopes, broad or rounded ridges, or along streams, rivers, or other water sources. Meadows sometimes arise in the wake of forest destruction—reclothing bare ground after fire, insect attack, logging, or even avalanches. Others begin as lakes, first carved by restless glaciers and later filled in by silt, plants, and animal remains. Still others are on naturally treeless sites—areas that are either too wet, too cold, too dry, or too heavily sodded for vulnerable tree seedlings to get started.

So-called wet meadows—those usually found at subalpine levels—have a water table that is at or close to the surface. Some of these meadows are the offspring of ancient glaciers. Others form on poorly drained sites next to adjacent lakes or streams. The soil is often cold, soggy, and low in oxygen, appealing only to certain moisture-tolerant species such as sedges, rushes, grasses, and willows such as booth, Geyer, and peachleaf. As long as a steady cycle of water flows in and out each year, wet meadows may keep their hold on a site for a long time, resisting the invasion of trees.

"Dry meadows" are usually larger than wet meadows, and can be found on ridgetops, on south-facing slopes, or between open stands of ponderosa pine. In early spring, they are usually saturated with snowmelt and bristling with new growth. Because they are on well-drained soils, however, they dry out quickly, and may be forced into dormancy by mid-summer. This combination of wet springs and dry summers is hard on tiny tree seedlings and ultimately keeps forests from forming on these sites.

Large grassy "parks" that form in the basins between mountains are also underlain by fine-textured soils that drain quickly. Cold air rolls down into the basins from the uplands, creating conditions that are too cold for ponderosa pine. At the same time, these lower elevations don't receive enough moisture to support cold-loving spruces and firs.

Even on sites that could support trees, grasses and sedges have ways of keeping trees at bay. The tough, long-living tufts are each supported by an extensive network of roots that can be 5–10 times larger than the aboveground portion. This stubborn sod usurps much of the growing space, water, and nutrients, making it difficult for a young tree seedling to get its "foot" in the door.

CHARACTERISTIC PLANTS:

Trees and Shrubs:
booth willow
Geyer willow
peachleaf willow
western azalea
wolfs willow

Herbaceous Plants:
alpine bluegrass
alpine milkvetch
alpine timothy
American bistort
arrowleaf groundsel
Baltic rush
beauty cinquefoil
blackhead sedge
bluejoint reedgrass
brookgrass
checkermallow
cliff sedge
cow parsnip
Cusick bluegrass
Dunhead sedge

dwarf plainleaf
ebony sedge
elephant heads
few-flowered spike-
    sedge
field horsetail
forest fleabane
fowl bluegrass
gilias
Greek-valerian
horse cinquefoil
lamb's-tongue
    groundsel
Letterman's needle-
    grass
longleaf squirreltail
louseworts
marsh marigold
marsh skullcap
mat muhly
mountain bluebell
mudwort
muttongrass
Nebraska sedge
nodding bluegrass
one-flower fleabane
ovalhead sedge
paintbrushes

penstemons
Rocky Mountain iris
rosy stonecrop
rushes
saffron groundsel
seep-spring monkey-
    flower
short-awn foxtail
sibbaldia
silver sedge
slender wheatgrass
small bedstraw
smallwing sedge
spikesedges
streambank globemal-
    low
subalpine needlegrass
teacher's sedge
tufted hairgrass
umbel starwort
varileaf cinquefoil
water parsnip
water sedge
wild strawberry
woolly sedge
yarrow

WHAT'S IN IT FOR WILDLIFE?

The blades of sedges and grasses, though individually slim, are densely packed together to form the meadow's "canopy." For jumping mice, meadow voles, and shrews that tunnel under the tangled debris at the base of these stems, this canopy is cover enough. As meadows dry up during the summer, ground squirrels, hoary and yellow-bellied marmots, and badgers head underground to avoid their predators as well as the elements.

Northern pocket gophers are notorious for changing the nature of the meadows that they burrow in. The ridges of bare earth you see in meadows are quickly colonized by pioneering annual plants and fertilized by droppings that the rodents leave in their tunnels. This strip of annuals adds variety to an older meadow dominated by perennials. Burrowing also tends to loosen and aerate the soil while improving its moisture-holding capacity.

At low elevations, shrubby meadows on sun-drenched, south-facing slopes may remain free of snow, serving as an important winter range for mule deer and flocks of tundra birds such as rosy finches. When the animals migrate upslope again in spring, they head for subalpine meadows, where the sun melts the snow off first. Sedges and grasses in these meadows are adapted to cool temperatures and can be actively growing, even under patches of lingering ice. Mule deer, elk, and moose eagerly push the ice aside and continue to forage here throughout the summer.

Many birds also use meadows for feeding, while retiring to nearby forests for cover and nesting. Some of these commuters include rodent-hunters such as sharp-shinned, Cooper's, and red-tailed hawks, northern harriers, goshawks, golden eagles, merlins, and American kestrels. As these daytime hunters return to the forests to roost, they cross paths with great horned owls sailing out for a night's hunt. Swift flyers swoop over meadows

BADGER

VESPER SPARROW · COMMON POORWILL · DARK-EYED JUNCO · ROSY FINCH · ALPINE CHIPMUNK · WHITE-CROWNED SPARROW · GOLDEN EAGLE

WILDLIFE LOCATOR CHART—MOUNTAIN MEADOW

	Feeds from Air	Feeds on Ground	Feeds in Water
Nests in Tree Canopy	Sharp-shinned Hawk, Cooper's Hawk, Northern Goshawk, Red-tailed Hawk, Golden Eagle, Merlin, Great Gray Owl, Black-chinned Hummingbird, Calliope Hummingbird, Allen's Hummingbird	American Robin, Cassin's Finch	
Nests in Trunk Cavity	American Kestrel, Common Barn-Owl, Tree Swallow, Violet-green Swallow	Northern Flicker, Mountain Bluebird	
Nests in Shrubs		Brewer's Sparrow, White-crowned Sparrow	
Nests on Ground	Northern Harrier, Common Nighthawk, Common Poorwill	Blue Grouse, White-tailed Ptarmigan, California Gull, Horned Lark, Water Pipit, Green-tailed Towhee, Vesper Sparrow, Savannah Sparrow, Fox Sparrow, Lincoln's Sparrow, Dark-eyed Junco, Western Meadowlark, Rosy Finch	American Avocet
Nests Beneath Ground or Debris	Northern Rough-winged Swallow, Barn Swallow	Belding's Ground Squirrel, Northern Pocket Gopher, Montane Vole, Pika, Alpine Chipmunk, Hoary Marmot, Yellow-bellied Marmot, Meadow Vole, Western Jumping Mouse, Red Fox, Long-tailed Weasel, Badger, Striped Skunk, Mule Deer, Mountain Sheep, Arboreal Salamander, Ensatina, Rubber Boa, Western Yellowbelly Racer, California Mountain Kingsnake, Gopher Snake	
Nests in Water		Long-toed Salamander, Tiger Salamander, Roughskin Newt, Western Toad, Yosemite Toad, Western Chorus Frog, Cascades Frog, Northern Leopard Frog, Western Spadefoot	Foothill Yellow-legged Frog

to catch insects that are attracted to the flowering herbs and bushes. These hawkers include common poorwills, common nighthawks, tree, violet-green, rough-winged, and barn swallows, and mountain bluebirds, as well as the winged mammals—the bats. Hummingbirds visit meadows for their beautiful, nectar-filled blossoms.

In addition to these visitors from surrounding habitats, the meadow has some breeding residents of its own, including vesper sparrows, savannah sparrows, and, at lower elevations, western meadowlarks. Look for their ground nests and for their eggs, which are often quite narrow at one end. This shape helps stop "rollaway" eggs—they wind up traveling in a circle.

The high density of forest-to-meadow commuters makes the edge of meadows an exciting place for wildlife watching. Keep an eye peeled for foxes, weasels, and coyotes, which will stick to the cover of the edge while watching the field for an easy mammal dinner. Striped skunks also waddle along the border, stopping occasionally to root in the soil for grubs.

If the meadow is adjacent to a stream, the menagerie is even more varied. In large expanses of shady forest or sun-drenched rangelands, these wetland meadows are often the only suitable nesting sites for waterfowl such as mallards. Frogs, salamanders, and turtles are also drawn to these soggy areas, requiring the open water for breeding, feeding, or cover.

Calliope Hummingbird

The calliope hummingbird, weighing only one-tenth of an ounce, is North America's smallest bird. A dragonfly could weigh it down, and a spiderweb could trap it. Nevertheless, it is a powerhouse of adaptation, featuring a flying apparatus that rivals our most sophisticated helicopters, and a brain, heart, and flight muscles that are larger (relative to body size) than any other bird's.

Hummingbird wings beat an incredible 2,000–3,000 times a minute, getting lift and power not only from the downstroke but also from the upstroke. If you could slow down the blur of their wings, you'd see why. Instead of flexing up and down like other birds', the hummingbird's wings rotate at the shoulderblade. Each hovering stroke is a smooth, horizontal figure eight in which the wing flips "palm up" before heading back. This way, the front edge of the wing cuts the air both coming and going, thus keeping the hummer suspended. To zoom forward, they simply tilt the plane of the wing down slightly. To shift into reverse or to lift straight up, they tilt the wing back.

Their internal machinery is equally amazing, beginning with massive flight muscles that take up 25–30 percent of their body weight. Their breastbone is deeply keeled and reinforced with two extra ribs to help them endure the stresses of flight. Meanwhile, their oversized heart is beating up to 1,260 times a minute (when active) and their lungs (at rest) are expanding 250 times a minute. It's an energy output that's 10 times that of a person running 9 miles per hour!

Imagine for a moment how it would feel for you to live the life of a hummingbird. Say you weigh 170 pounds. With a body temperature of 752 degrees F, you would burn 155,000 calories a day and evaporate 100 pounds of perspiration an hour. You'd have to eat 340 pounds of meat every 24 hours or 100 pounds of pure glucose in order to stay alive. If you ran out of water, your skin temperature would soon reach the melting point of lead, and you could eventually ignite!

The fuel that keeps the calliope's engines humming comes from the nectar of 1,000 blossoms a day. The hummer's long, needle-thin bill reaches down into the neck of tubular flowers, and its grooved tongue sucks up the nectar with capillary action. The flower, in turn, has good reason for serving free nectar to the bird. Each time the bird imbibes, its bill becomes dusted with pollen, which in turn fertilizes the next flower the bird visits.

The flowers have coevolved special traits that make them especially attractive to hummingbirds. The flowers are bright red, orange, or yellow, tubular in shape, and reinforced against piercing. At their base is a large reservoir of nectar to reward pollinators with a long "reach." The time of blooming, lack of scent, and size and shape of the flower are designed to discourage other types of nectar lovers, such as bees, that may not be as efficient at delivering the pollen.

Look for calliope hummingbirds— throughout the day, feeding in meadows that are ringed with conifers and splashed with the flowers that calliopes prefer: Indian paintbrushes, gilias, penstemon, red columbine, seep-spring monkeyflower, louseworts, gooseberries, or manzanitas. They tend to forage on the flowers at the lower portions of the plant, whereas most other hummingbirds choose the top flowers. To find the male, look

HORNED
LARK

carefully along the tops of shrubs or small trees where he is sunbathing and preening, no larger than a swollen twig. His iridescent throat is striped with white and purple feathers in a candy-cane effect. Occasionally, he may leave his perch to hawk an insect or home in on some nectar.

Length: 2³⁄₄–3¹⁄₂ inches.

Look for nests—a small, 1¹⁄₂ inch-wide knot on a pine branch, 2–70 feet above the ground, usually situated between two pinecones. The birds cover the outside with pine scales, bark, and lichen until the nest convincingly resembles one of the cones. Nests can also be found in dark aspen thickets near streams. Here, the nests are camouflaged to look like the gray knots of dwarf mistletoe plants that grow on aspen branches. The female always chooses a nest site that is covered from above by foliage. This keeps heat from escaping to the open night sky, and protects the nests from predators and precipitation. By choosing a site on the eastern edge of wooded areas, she also reaps the warming sun as soon as it clears the horizon. This warmth is especially important when females are incubating their eggs, and therefore can't go into the semisleep state of torpor that normally helps hummingbirds save on their internal heating bills. Look for 2- and 3-layer-high nests that have been reused several years in a row.

Look for courtship flights—at the approach of a female hummingbird, the male will launch from his perch and fly straight up for 40–100 feet. At the apex, he'll dive straight down then climb back up, describing a steep "U." These pendulum flights are so accurately executed it looks as if the bird is suspended by a wire.

Listen for—a muffled "bzzt" or "pfft" produced near the bottom of each display swoop. As the male approaches the female, he greets her with a high-pitched "see-ree" sound. While feeding, they utter a soft "tsip" or squeaking noise.

Northern Pocket Gopher

Gophers are designed for digging. Their legs are stubby and muscular, crowned with crescent-shaped claws that scrape and loosen dirt like the blade of a shovel. When these claws get moving, they can plow through 300 yards of sandy soil in a single night. To duplicate this feat, a 150-pound person would have to dig a 17-inch-wide trench 7 miles long! But humans are not nearly so well equipped for the task.

The gophers' large, yellow teeth protrude outside their furry lips so that they can cut roots and remove dirt without swallowing a mouthful. These teeth are constantly growing, kept to a manageable size only by the erosion caused by their gritty diet. If they didn't wear down, these teeth would soon grow one and a half times longer than the gopher! The fur-lined cheeks behind the teeth turn inside out like pants' pockets for easy cleaning. To further keep dirt out of their system, their ears have valves that close, and their eyelids fit so tightly that not even fine-grained sand can make its way in.

In tunnel transit, there's seldom room enough to turn around. This doesn't stop pocket gophers, however; they are just as speedy going backward as they are going forward. Their skin fits loosely, and is covered by short, dense hair that moves back and forth easily. Their touch-sensitive tail curls over them as they back up, acting as a tactile "rearview mirror." Long, sensitive hairs scattered throughout their coat also inform them about their tight-fitting environment. Their extremely narrow hips are an advantage when zipping through tunnels, but a disadvantage when giving birth. Gopher females have evolved a way to circumvent this structural problem, however. Their bodies break down and absorb the central part of their pelvic bones during their first pregnancy so there is an ample gap available by the time they give birth!

Burrows are centers for feeding, resting, traveling, hiding, and giving birth. The horizontal, main tunnel (4–12 inches beneath the surface) has many short branches that the gopher uses as resting spots, as exits to the surface, or as places to store food. Vertical tunnels lead down to the basement level (18–24 inches underground), where the nest chamber is built. Some of the gophers' food (roots and tubers) conveniently dangles down into their home, but for their preferred dish—succulent green leaves and stems—they have to venture up to the surface. Gophers rarely travel far from their holes, however, and as they duck back in, they carefully push soil behind them to form a plug, thus closing the door on flash floods and drop-in predators.

All this burrow building is good for the soil. It lifts sublevel soil up to the surface so that air, water, and solvents can break down minerals and make them available to plants. Surface soil packed down by cattle, logging equipment, or hiking boots is also loosened by the tunneling, allowing nutrients from dead plant remains to percolate down to the lower levels along with oxygen and water. The improved drainage slows spring runoff and allows deep-rooted plants to flourish. Over the course of a year, researchers estimate that one hamster-sized gopher churns up about 1¼ tons of soil!

Animals also benefit from the pocket gopher's endeavors. As many as 22 different species have been found to occupy abandoned gopher tunnels, including tiger salamanders, spadefoot toads, gopher snakes, ground squirrels, meadow voles, and long-tailed weasels. Gophers also benefit from their own roto-tilling; the continual disturbance tends to favor the growth of herbaceous (soft-stemmed) plants, which happen to be their preferred foods.

Look for northern pocket gophers— emerging at dusk, at night, and during the day when it's overcast. They rarely travel more than a few feet, looking for leafy vegetation to stuff in their cheek pockets and carry down to their storage pantries. Gophers need not travel for drinking water; they get the moisture they need from their diet of roots, tubers, and leaves. Males may travel longer distances overland to find the burrows of females, or they may simply break into females' burrows by tunneling beneath the ground. If you want to study gophers, do it from a distance so as to avoid walking atop their burrows. Although they don't have good eyesight, they are acutely aware of vibrations, and will quickly duck under at your first footfall.

Length: Head and body, 5–6½ inches. Tail, 1 ⅝–3 inches.

Look for mounds—fan-shaped sprays of soil, with an upraised surface marked by concentric rings. At the center is a sunken plug of soil, 1–3 inches wide, marking the last time a gopher surfaced. Mounds may be 18–24 inches in diameter and no more than 6 inches high. Since the tunnels are built at a slant rather than straight up, the soil that the gophers push out is fanned away from the hole rather than domed over it. You can figure out which way the tunnel descends by looking at the apron of sand; the tunnel slopes away from the wide side of the apron. In areas where gophers are common, all the soil will be completely turned and reworked every two years.

In the winter—gophers tunnel in the snow to safely get to new foraging areas. In fact, the snow cover allows them to forage in three dimensions; by tunneling up, they can feed in shrubs that are inaccessible to them at other times of year.

Look for soil castings—long ridges of soil crisscrossing the meadow in the spring. During the winter, as gophers tunnel underground, they carry the soil up to the surface and stash it in snow tunnels. These filled storage tunnels look like heavy snakes of soil once the snow melts.

Listen for—huffing and teeth chattering when gophers are fighting, or a squeal of anger when they are annoyed.

Western Yellowbelly Racer

The slender snake coursing through the grass pauses, lifts its upper body and head off the ground, and takes a good look around. Just ahead, a panicked lizard skitters across a runway and disappears. Moving faster than the eye can follow, the snake dashes forward, grabs the lizard with needle-sharp teeth, and pins its struggling body to the ground.

The yellowbelly racer is the Porsche of North American snakes, using its unparalleled speed not only to find food but also to escape its enemies. When trying to get away from you, the racer will often head downslope to pick up even more speed. To keep you guessing, it will begin its retreat with a wild thrashing motion. This focuses your attention on a small patch of ground where the snake used to be. In the meantime, it has switched to a stealthy, silent glide, and before you realize it, the trickster is far from the scene of commotion. Racers will occasionally take to water or climb a small bush to get away, becoming even harder to follow in the the tangle of branches and leafy foliage.

When the snake senses, but is not convinced of, possible danger, it will assume a stately "threat posture." As it parades past the suspicious object, it holds its upper body off the ground and flattens itself laterally so that in profile it looks like a much thicker, larger, and more menacing snake.

Finally, if the racer is cornered, it begins striking and fighting for its life. Though the racer has no poisonous venom, it can leave long scratches as it recoils after a bite. In the process of drawing back, its teeth can actually pull out of its mouth and become embedded in your skin.

In the early morning, the racer may not be up to such a fight. Because they are ectotherms ("cold-blooded"), they need the heat of the sun to help warm their engine up to a good starting temperature. If disturbed when they are still chilly, they may resort to a display that they also use when injured. Instead of striking, the snake merely coils and hides its head under a loop of its body. A thick creamy fluid exudes from its cloaca (an opening on its underside) and spreads over its body as the snake squirms. This musk has a disagreeable odor and presumably discourages all but the hungriest predators. (Getting the musk on your hands will discourage most everyone you know too!)

Look for western yellowbelly racers—hunting in meadows where there is enough vegetation to hide them from prey and predator alike. Don't bother trying to follow an escaping racer with your eyes. Instead, look for the waving grasstops that mark its passage. If you wait a while, you may see the snake circle back to the spot it was flushed from. Also look for basking snakes in sunny spots or atop boulders in the meadow. These snakes prefer higher temperatures than most, and so can usually be found basking more often. Red-tailed hawks circling the meadow above you are also doing some snake-watching; they are the most frequent predators of this snake.

Length: $2\frac{1}{4}$–$4\frac{1}{3}$ feet.

Nests are underground—in old burrows abandoned by pocket gophers, ground squirrels, and other small burrowing animals. The female deposits 7 elongated white eggs and then leaves them to self-incubate and hatch. These burrows are well insulated and have the high humidities that snake eggs require. The flexible shells will gradually absorb moisture during their 51-day incubation, until, at the time of hatching, the eggs are nearly twice as large as they were at laying.

Look for mating racers—two snakes lying side by side with tails intertwined. When courting, the male sidles up alongside the female and ripples its body from head to tail. She may dash away suddenly, but he moves right along with her, struggling to maintain mirrored contact. In between bouts of writhing, he may leave her side to race in a circle around her a few times, always ending up back in courting position. As a signal of acceptance, she finally raises her tail, and they mate. Because of recurved spines in the male's reproductive organ, they are actually locked together during coition. The female sometimes wanders, dragging the male backward behind her. One observer even saw the female climb a shrub with her dangling male companion in tow.

Hibernation dens are underground—in crevices or caves in limestone outcroppings, usually with a sunny southern exposure. The body temperature of hibernating racers can drop below freezing, but they will die if frozen solid.

Listen for—a rustling in dry vegetation, created when an alarmed snake vibrates its tail and thrashes, leaving a sound decoy before it glides to safety.

STRIPED
CHORUS
FROG

STRIPED
RACER

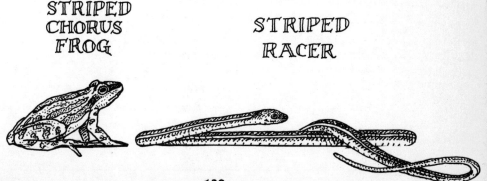

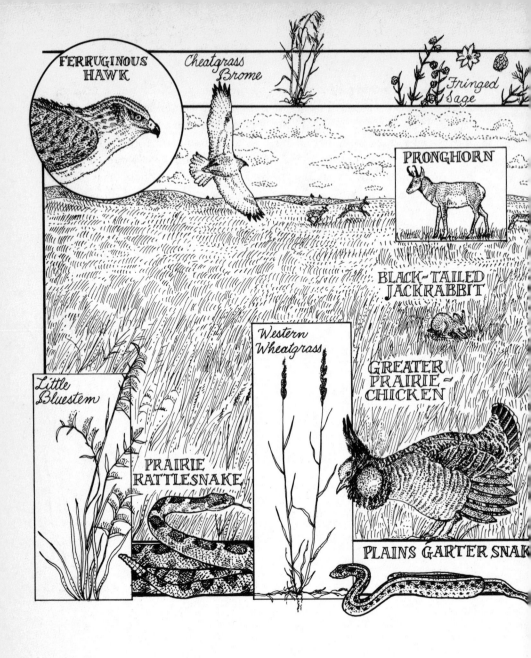

FERRUGINOUS HAWK

Cheatgrass Brome

Fringed Sage

PRONGHORN

BLACK-TAILED JACKRABBIT

Western Wheatgrass

GREATER PRAIRIE-CHICKEN

Little Bluestem

PRAIRIE RATTLESNAKE

PLAINS GARTER SNAKE

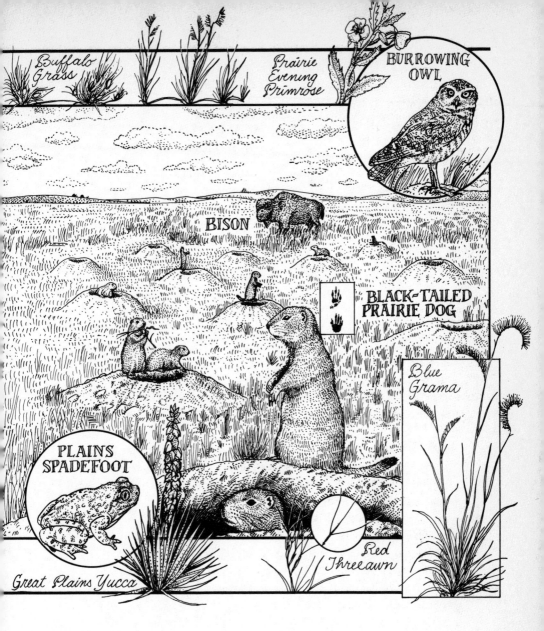

Buffalo Grass

Prairie Evening Primrose

BURROWING OWL

BISON

BLACK-TAILED PRAIRIE DOG

Blue Grama

PLAINS SPADEFOOT

Red Threeawn

Great Plains Yucca

Plains Grassland

WHERE TO SEE THIS HABITAT:

Colorado: Comanche, Kiowa, Oglala, and Pawnee national grasslands
Kansas: Cimmaron National Grassland; Flint Hills, Kirwin, and Quivira national wildlife refuges
Montana: Benton Lake, Bowdoin, Charles M. Russell, Medicine Lake, Red Rock Lakes, and Ul Bend national wildlife refuges; Custer National Forest; National Bison Range
Nebraska: Crescent Lake, Fort Niobrara, and Valentine national wildlife refuges; Nebraska and Samuel R. McKelvie national forests; Oglala National Grassland; Rainwater Basin Wetland Management District
New Mexico: Kiowa National Grassland; Maxwell National Wildlife Refuge
North Dakota: Arrowwood, Audubon, Des Lacs, J. Clark Salyer, Lake Alice, Lake Ilo, Long Lake, Lostwood, Tewaukon, Upper Souris national wildlife refuges; Black Kettle, Cedar River, Little Missouri, and Sheyenne national grasslands; Crosby and Valley City wetland management districts; Theodore Roosevelt National Park
Oklahoma: Black Kettle National Grassland; Salt Plains, Tishomingo, Washita, and Wichita national wildlife refuges
South Dakota: Badlands and Wind Cave national parks; Buffalo Gap, Fort Pierre, and Grand River national grasslands; Lacreek, Lake Andes, and Sand Lake national wildlife refuges
Texas: Caddo, Lyndon B. Johnson, and Rita Blanca national grasslands; Muleshoe National Wildlife Refuge
Wyoming: Thunder Basin National Grassland

Plains Grassland

BEGINNINGS

One hundred million years ago, in what is now the Great Plains, you would have had to climb to the top of a tropical jungle in order to see the horizon. The moist climate that watered this forest gradually changed, in part because the Rockies began rising out of the earth's crust. Warm air masses blowing in from the Pacific dropped their moisture over these new mountains, so by the time the air masses reached the plains, they had precious little rain to offer. The lush, tropical forests suffered in the new climate, and eventually gave way to the more modest, but better-adapted grasses.

The lands within a 200-mile band east of the Rockies are the driest, receiving as little as 10 inches of rain on the average per year. High winds evaporate much of that, creating dry conditions that suit the so-called shortgrasses, such as buffalo grass and blue grama. Farther east, the land begins to emerge from the rain shadow of the Rockies, and precipitation doubles to 20 inches and above. The mixed prairie is found here and, true to its name, contains both short and tall grasses, although it is dominated by midgrasses such as little bluestem, western wheatgrass, prairie junegrass, threadleaf sedge, side-oats grama, threeawns, needlegrasses, and various

PLAINS
POCKET
GOPHER

dry-land sedges. Four hundred miles east of here, the tall grass prairie begins, now existing solely in places saved from the plow.

The Great Plains grasslands, home of the shortgrass and mixed grass prairies, are the subject of this section. The grasses in these areas must endure blistering heat, drying winds, soils that grow dusty by midsummer, occasional years of drought, fires, heavy grazing by livestock, and a long, snowy winter. Luckily, these grasses have had 35 million years to perfect their defenses.

TOUGH AND FLEXIBLE—A SURVIVAL STANDARD

To survive even the driest years, grasses grow gigantic root systems (2 to 3 miles of end-to-end roots for a single plant) festooned with fibrous hairs that track down the slightest trace of water in the root zone. To hold onto the water they capture, bluestems have groups of "hinge cells" on the surface of their blades. These cells contract as they lose water, causing the leaf to roll up like a tube, thus preventing any more moisture from escaping. The midgrasses seem to anticipate drought, growing rapidly in early spring when moisture is available, then shutting down (going semidormant) for the sizzling summer months. When the cool moisture of autumn returns, the grasses come out of retirement to do some last-minute growing.

When it comes time to sow the next generation, special adaptations get the grass seeds off to a good start. Bristles on the seeds called "awns" absorb moisture, twisting and untwisting with changes of humidity. This twisting motion helps screw the barbed seed into the ground, where it is closer to water and protected from the ravages of seedeaters. Even if the seeds fail, however, the tenacious grasses have other, more foolproof ways to regenerate. Sod-forming grasses send out "runners" above or below the ground that take root and become auxiliary plants some distance from the parent plant. Bunchgrasses sprout repeatedly from their base, forming a tuft of as many as 100 stems. Dry conditions favor bunch-type grasses, while moist environments (like your lawn) favor sod growth.

Besides climate, the grasses have had to adapt to the constant pruning by grass-eating animals. Most plants grow from their tips (think of the bright green "candles" of a growing pine), and lose their capacity to grow when this tip is chopped off. Grasses, however, grow from their base, so that when animals snip off the tops, they simply grow out again. This, in a nutshell, is why we have to cut our lawns so often.

You will also find an assortment of forbs (broadleaved herbs) and shrubs in plains grasslands. The forbs grow deep, branched taproots (up to 20 feet in the yucca plant), and therefore don't compete with the shallower roots

CHARACTERISTIC PLANTS:

Trees, Shrubs, and Cacti:
candelabra cactus
eastern redcedar
four-wing saltbush
fringed sage
Great Plains yucca
plains pricklypear
prairie sage
rabbitbrush
Rocky Mountain juniper
sand sagebrush
snakeweed
winter fat

Herbaceous Plants:
asters
big bluestem
blazing star
blowout grass
bluebells
bluebunch wheatgrass
blue grama
bottlebrush squirreltail
buffalo gourd
buffalo grass
cheatgrass brome
common sunflower
curlycup gumweed
dotted blazing-star
false-boneset
foxtail barley
galleta grass
green needlegrass
groundsels
hairy golden aster
hairy grama
heliotrope
Indian-grass
Indian ricegrass
Kentucky bluegrass
large-leaved avens
leadplant
leafy aster
little bluestem
milkvetch
Missouri goldenrod
mountain bladderpod
needle-and-thread
needlegrasses
pincushion cactus
plains muhly
plantains
prairie-clover
prairie coneflower
prairie dropseed
prairie evening primrose
prairie junegrass
redroot amaranth
red threeawn
ring muhly
rose-crown
rough pennyroyal
Russian thistle
sand bluestem
sandhills muhly
sandhills pigweed
scarlet gaura
scarlet globemallow
scurfpeas
secunda bluegrass
sedges
side-oats grama
skullcaps
small soapweed
snow-on-the-mountain
switchgrass
tall dropseed
threadleaf sedge
tumble-grass
virgin's bower
western ragweed
western wheatgrass
wheatgrasses
whitlow-wort
wolftail

Buffalo Grass

of grasses. Prairie shrubs hold onto their water in much the same ways that desert plants do. They are light-colored and coated with moisture-conserving wax or dew-trapping hairs. Cacti also grow among the short-grasses, storing moisture in their succulent pads.

Like the grasses, grassland animals have evolved adaptations to help protect them in this open landscape, where predators can stalk their prey from afar, and alert prey can see their predators well in advance. Prong-horns, for instance, can see as well as we do when we use an 8-power binocular, and can spring away from danger at 60 miles per hour, making them the fastest hoofed animal in the world.

In addition to keen sight and speed, group dynamics also help prairie animals avoid predators. If a pronghorn spots a coyote, it spreads its rump fur in a white flag that signals "danger" to the rest of the herd. In the same way, prairie dogs use a sharp whistle to communicate to one another. Breeding prairie-chickens meet in groups to perform colorful strutting and booming displays, reducing the risk of being singled out by predators.

Because of the wide-open spaces, the songs of prairie birds are usually clearer and louder, carrying farther than those of their forest cousins. Since they don't have perches, many prairie birds have learned to sing on the wing. Be careful when you walk the prairie, because half of all the birds nest on the ground. Their eggs, narrow at one end, are perfectly suited for bare-ground nesting—when they roll, they move in a circle, staying close to home.

Burrowing is another adaptation to prairie living. Prairie animals resort to their underworld to avoid not only predators but also extreme temper-atures and occasional fires. Come winter, animals use these places to sleep or hunker down between food-gathering excursions.

GIVING BACK WHAT YOU TAKE

At one time, before fences, plows, and cattle took their toll, the "bankbook" of the prairie was beautifully balanced. Each spring, the vast network of roots lifted nutrients out of the soil to build green growth up above. Each autumn, the blades would fall back to earth, thus reinvesting the riches they had borrowed. Beneath the ground, the roots remained alive during the winter, seeing a plant through 20, 30, or even 50 growing seasons! When these roots finally decomposed, they left channels that allowed air and water to flow to the bottom layers of soil.

Up above, bison and pronghorn (antelope) reaped the green harvest in different ways, the bison mowing the grasses short, while the pronghorns sought out the forbs. Rather than competing, the prairie's two grazers complemented each other beautifully. Bison practiced a kind of rotation feeding, continually moving to find new sources of tender green growth. This allowed the areas they had just been through to recover from the impact of their visit. In fact, the grasses grew back with renewed vigor thanks to the "pruning" and the added fertilizer (tons of manure and an occasional bison carcass). Rodents also benefited from the new flush of growth, and unwittingly repaired the trampled ground by loosening the soil with their burrowing.

The fires that swept across the flat prairie every 10–15 years were another part of this careful balance. The flames usually moved quickly, crisping the blades with 400-degree heat, but leaving the roots unharmed. In their wake, they left acres of black, smoking soil, exposed to the sun and renewed by the nutrients of the charred grasses. Within weeks, a vigorous rebirth of sprouts painted the earth green. Some of the fires on the plains were deliberately set by Native Americans. They used fire to drive buffalo for easier hunting or to attract the herds with new acres of fresh growth. The impact of these fires, though significant, could not compare with the devastation that would come with the plow, fence, firearms, and cattle brands.

THE HEAVY HAND OF PROGRESS

An estimated 60 million buffalo once roamed the plains, in herds that covered 50 square miles and took days to pass one point. Beginning in 1830, a slaughter of inconceivable proportions brought this population to its knees. At first, the bison were killed for meat and hides, but then the killing became part of a government policy that attempted to force Indians onto reservations. By cutting their major food supply (bison), the United States hoped to make the Indians dependent on government beef, which could be obtained only on reservations. Fifty-five years after the slaughter began, there were only 600 animals left.

Ranchers replaced the nomadic buffalo with cattle, but as they later learned, it was not an equal trade. Unlike the wandering buffalo that gave grasses a chance to recoup, cattle remained in one place. They cropped the native grasses lower and lower until the roots lost vigor, and other grasses, better adapted to the extreme conditions, were able to invade. Some of these, such as Kentucky bluegrass and cheatgrass brome, are exotics that have changed the composition of the original prairie.

Cattle grazing also created a nutrient deficit on the land. Unlike the buffalo that lived, died, and were eventually recycled to the soil, cattle carcasses were shipped out, robbing the prairie of all the nutrients they contained. Their heavy grazing also removed the grass blades that would have normally fallen to the earth. Without this moist, shady mulch, the soil on many sites was baked dry by the sun, leading to a kind of grazing-induced "drought." Even fires were no longer a dependable source of renewal; they had less fuel to burn on, and were usually snuffed out to save homesteads.

Homesteaders who moved onto the land in the late 1800s began to turn the prairie upside down with plows. Without the roots of grasses to hold the soil in place, much of it whipped into the wind, especially during the dustbowl years of the 1930s. By breaking the sod, breaking the fire cycle, and breaking the nutrient flow, we did much to deplete the prairie's resources. Trees and shrubs such as sagebrush and, farther south, mesquite were able to spread. Range managers today attempt to relieve some of these problems by rotating cattle to allow some fields to rest (a technique the bison taught us). Periodic burns are recommended to replicate the natural cleansing of lightning fires. Unfortunately, many of the scars are deep, and will take generations to heal.

WHAT'S IN IT FOR WILDLIFE?

When you consider all the food chains that are tied, directly or indirectly, to grass, you can appreciate the saying "All flesh is grass." The blades themselves offer enough food to support bison that weigh a ton apiece as well as rodents that together weigh even more than the bison. The seeds are relished and stored beneath the ground by a variety of birds, mammals, and insects. Even the dead vegetation feeds the legions of microscopic organisms that together are called "the invisible prairie."

The leaves and twigs of bushes feed mule deer, while cacti, despite their thorns, provide berries for coyote and black-tailed jackrabbits. Beneath the ground, mice, gophers, shrews, and prairie dogs travel intricate tunnels, helping in turn to aerate the soil and ease the flow of water to grass roots. Their tunnel entrances are carefully watched by a whole cadre of predators, including coyotes, badgers, foxes, weasels, and hawks.

Although the opportunities for amphibians are limited on the dry plains, reptiles find easy travel through the grass and plenty of basking sites in addition to food sources such as insects, birds' eggs, and small rodents. Be on the lookout for bullsnakes, racers, prairie rattlesnakes, massasauga, and western box turtles. To find frogs and salamanders, look to watery parts of the plains, where they must congregate each spring to breed.

A prairie dog colony is an ecological hot spot—an absolute must for wildlife watching. The center of the colony is the oldest, and the perennial

LARK SPARROW   CHESTNUT-COLLARED LONGSPUR   PRAIRIE VOLE   WESTERN MEADOWLARK   LARK BUNTING   PRAIRIE FALCON

WILDLIFE LOCATOR CHART—PLAINS GRASSLAND

	Feeds from Air	Feeds on Ground	Feeds in Water
Nests in Tree Canopy	Swainson's Hawk Golden Eagle Ferruginous Hawk Prairie Falcon		
Nests on Ground	Common Nighthawk	Gray Partridge, Lesser Prairie-chicken, Killdeer, Mountain Plover, Long-billed Curlew, Marbled Godwit, Horned Lark, Sprague's Pipit, Clay-colored Sparrow, Lark Bunting, Savannah Sparrow, McCown's Longspur, Chestnut-collared Longspur, Bobolink, Western Meadowlark, Pronghorn, Bison	
Nests Beneath Ground or Debris	Burrowing Owl	Vesper Sparrow, Desert Cottontail, Black-tailed Jackrabbit, Black-tailed Prairie Dog, Plains Pocket Gopher, Hispid Pocket Mouse, Deer Mouse, Prairie Vole, Coyote, Swift Fox, Black-footed Ferret, Badger, California Slender Salamander, Western Box Turtle, Southern Alligator Lizard, Gilbert's Skink, Lesser Earless Lizard, Short-horned Lizard, Eastern Yellowbelly Racer, Prairie Rattlesnake, Ringneck Snake, Night Snake, Common Kingsnake, Milk Snake, Coachwhip, Bullsnake, Longnose Snake, Massasauga, Ground Snake, Plains Blackhead Snake, Plains Garter Snake, Lined Snake	Blackneck Garter Snake Checkered Garter Snake
Nests in Water		Great Plains Toad, Green Toad, Plains Spadefoot, Couch's Spadefoot, Western Spadefoot	Bullfrog

grasses here have been grazed so repeatedly by the prairie dogs that they have given way to annual forbs. Prairie-chickens and sharp-tailed grouse use the open areas as traditional dancing grounds, and the bison come here to wallow in the dust. Meanwhile, the seeds and insects exposed in the thin cover attract western meadowlarks, lark buntings, mourning doves, longspurs, and American magpies. The burrows themselves are home to burrowing owls, ground squirrels, kangaroo rats, black-tailed jackrabbits, tiger salamanders, spadefoot toads, ornate box turtles, and a variety of insects and spiders, including those that spin their webs across unused entrance holes. Look for prairie rattlesnakes emerging from burrows in the spring, while killdeer, mountain plovers, and horned larks prepare to nest on the surface above. The far edges of the colony are more recently colonized, and thus more lightly grazed. This light grazing stimulates the grass to grow more vigorously, attracting other grazers such as pronghorn, deer, bison, and elk.

Another hot spot is the gallery of trees that grow near streams (see Lowland River Forest, page 217). Mule deer retreat to these woody draws to raise their fawns and to find vital winter browse. Migrating birds are also drawn by the availability of cover and water, as are mammals from the surrounding prairie that come here to drink. More birds nest here than anywhere else on the plains, and many amphibians could not breed at all if this ribbon of water didn't run through the grassland. Farther north, glacier-gouged "prairie potholes" are meccas for migrating birds, as well as resident turtles, frogs, water snakes, and salamanders (see Inland Marsh, page 105).

Ferruginous Hawk

Deep in the dew-laced grasses, the ground begins to buckle into a long, black ridge. The hawk, angling low over the plain, draws up short over the spot and hovers for an instant before driving his muscled legs down into the earth. With a few powerful wingbeats, he is airborne again, lifting the still-warm pocket gopher high above the prairie.

Ferruginous hawks are the largest in their class (the buteo hawks), and in their preferred habitat, they are usually the dominant hawk. Jackrabbits and ground squirrels must stay on constant alert for attacks from the ground or from the air. A hawk may stand outside a gopher mound for hours, rising up and pouncing at the slightest flicker of activity. On aerial reconnaissance, they fly 40–60 feet above the ground, in a rocking, side-to-side glide interrupted by occasional wingbeats. They usually dive toward their prey at an angle that helps them intercept the speeding form while remaining in the prey's "blind spot." They sometimes miss on the first strike, giving the rodent time to dash into the shrubs or grasses. Undaunted, the large hawk simply walks in after it, flushing it into another chase. Hawks have also been known to hunt "cooperatively," with one hawk flying high and the other low. As the panicked prey concentrates on getting away from one hawk, the other one swoops down for the kill. Usually the duo is a mated pair with hungry nestlings waiting to be fed.

Before the white settlers arrived, ferruginous hawks were actually common on the prairie. As the "sodbusters" began to remove trees to make room for corn and wheat, the hawks had fewer places to build their nest. Hawks that could find accommodations still didn't have the peace and quiet they require at nesting time. After all the work of building a nest and laying eggs, it takes only one human too close to the nest to convince ferruginous parents to desert the clutch. Even after humans leave an area, signs of human presence continue to affect the birds. Hawks that nest around abandoned homesites, for instance, do not raise as many young as those at completely unspoiled sites.

Look for ferruginous hawks—perched on hunting knolls, low trees, or fence posts, or flying a tilting flight over the grasses. These hawks will also soar in circles like golden eagles do. They are especially attracted to the updrafts inside "thermals," the columns of warm air that rise over sun-baked fields. You can recognize thermals by looking for puffs of fluffy, cumulus clouds that mark the top of the column, where the air begins to cool. Just below the clouds, look for the spiraling hawks with great, 5-foot wingspans.

Length: 22½–25 inches.

Don't disturb nests—in single trees (preferably junipers) or groves along the edge of streams, or in pinyon-juniper forests in remote areas. Tree nests are 3 feet or more in diameter and 1½ feet or more deep. They are reused year after year, growing wider and deeper each time they're repaired, until they are quite conspicuous. These birds may also nest on the ground on hillsides, cutbanks, ridgetops, rocky pinnacles, or the ledge of a cliff. They use sticks up to 1 inch in diameter and line the nest with turf, dried grass, and dried cow or horse dung. For some unknown reason, they'll even garnish the nest with some pronghorn or cow bones. Keep your distance, though; even one disturbance may cause them to desert.

Listen for—harsh alarm cries of "kree-ah" or "kaah, kaah, kaah," sounding like the complaints of a herring gull. They are particularly aggressive when they have young in the nest and have been known to even attack coyotes that range too close.

Black-tailed Prairie Dog

When you walk into a prairie dog town, you trip the alarm on a highly sophisticated security system. One sentinel perched up on its earthern mound begins to bark and urgently flick its tail, sending other dogs back to their mounds. Those dogs immediately around you vanish from the surface, while those somewhat farther away stand atop their mounds and take up the alarm bark. The news spreads through the town like a rippling wave: danger is afoot.

If you sit quietly for long enough, you may see the ghost town on the edges of your forcefield begin to revive. A few dogs will cautiously peek over the rim of their mounds, then slowly climb out to get a better view. If they decide that you are not a threat, they'll throw back their head and let out a joyous, ringing "all-clear" call. Suddenly, like flipping a light switch, the town is back in business: dogs are eating grasses, greeting and grooming each other, mending mounds, and stretching out flat for a midday siesta.

The pupping months of spring are an especially active time. Everywhere you look, exuberant young are exploring their world, and parents are indulging them. The young dogs are allowed to run in and out of other families' burrows, and even over territorial boundaries that adults would never cross. As they get older, however, the pups will be "socialized" and will learn to respect the boundaries that subdivide the town.

A prairie dog town may cover more than 100 acres and have several thousand inhabitants. Within the town, there are several 5- to 10-acre wards that are usually divided by natural boundaries, such as streams and gullies. Each ward contains several social groups, or "coteries," composed of 2–35 dogs (the average is about 8). Animals in the same cotery can use each other's burrows if need be, but those from foreign coteries are considered enemies. When the shadow of a hawk slides over the prairie, however, these territorial boundaries are quickly forgotten. The loud alarm calls are designed to carry across wards until the whole town is alerted.

One menace that prairie dogs have not been able to hide from is the warfare waged by rodent-control programs. In the past, campaigns to "control" prairie dogs on cattle-grazing lands called for eliminating all the prairie dogs from an area (even from a whole state) by poisoning, shooting, etc. Besides stripping the grasslands of one of their most colorful residents, these programs impoverished the many other species that are associated with prairie dog towns. Today, many ranchers are moving away from elimination policies, encouraging instead a balanced prairie dog population, which can actually improve their rangelands.

Look for black-tailed prairie dogs—in areas of shortgrasses, where they can see for long distances in all directions. The residents keep the land "mowed" by clipping vegetation, some of which they eat, and some of which they simply leave on the ground. You are liable to see them standing on their hind legs on the edge of a mound with their front paws dangling on their chest. When wary, they will sink down into their burrow until only their eyes, which sit high on their head, are visible above the rim. Early morning and the hours just before sunset are your best watching times. Midday heat might send them to their burrow for a nap.

Length: Head and body, 11–13 inches. Tail, 3–4 inches.

Look for mounds—cone-shaped piles of dirt, 1–3 feet high and 2–10 feet wide with a 3- to 4-inch-wide entrance hole. This entrance hole leads to a steep, slanting corridor that may plunge 3–10 feet or more into the earth before leveling off for another 10–15 feet. This tunnel may work its way back to a surface escape hole that is well hidden, with no mound to give it away. Blind side tunnels are excavated laterally off the main tunnel and are used as nest chambers, toilets, or refuges when predators or floods invade the main burrow.

Look for feeding signs—pits 1–3 inches deep where prairie dogs have dug up the roots of grasses, usually in the early spring before grasses are green. Also look for clippings of vegetation around the mound. If you find a pile of bones, feathers, or fur, you'll know that carnivorous burrowing owls have moved in.

Look for tracks—1¼ inches long, with 4 toes printing on the foreprint and 5 toes on the hindprint.

Listen for—a wide vocabulary of calls, including the alarm bark, the predator warning cry, the "all-clear" call, snarls, growls, fear screams, and the chattering of teeth. The alarm bark is "tic-uhl, tic-uhl, tic-uhl," with the first syllable a higher pitch than the second. The frequency and intensity are greatest during the first 2 or 3 minutes. After that, the frequency slows to 40 barks/minute, and the call may continue for as long as 1½ hours (usually much shorter). The predator warning cry is more urgent than the alarm bark, and the second syllable is as intense as the first. Prairie dogs don't hesitate when they hear this call; even those at a distance dive immediately into their hole.

BLACK-FOOTED FERRET

Prairie Rattlesnake

There are few sounds more chilling than the dry-bones castanets of a rattlesnake. A fearful response to the rattle seems to be imprinted on human genes, at least in those races that have evolved with these snakes. One theory about the evolution of rattles is that they were intended to warn their predators, and thus avoid an energy-sapping fight. Another theory holds that prairie rattlers used them as warning bells to keep from being stepped on by bison, pronghorn, and other animals. Still another asserts that the rattle developed to lure curious victims into striking distance. Whatever the origin, the use of an auditory defense is ironic because rattlesnakes can't hear the high-frequency sound of their own rattles! Because they have no external ear membranes, their "hearing" is restricted to earth-borne vibrations transmitted via their spinal cord and certain frequencies of airborne vibrations transmitted via their lungs.

Rattlesnakes have other senses, however, that can give them an accurate picture of their environment even in total darkness. Two heat-sensing pits located between the nostrils and the eyes provide an infrared profile of any object that is warmer than its surroundings. By comparing readings received on the right and left sides, the snake can calculate exactly how far away the prey is (even when moving) and judge its strike accordingly.

The snake's legendary forked tongue is also a sensory tool. As the tongue flicks in the air and against the ground, it collects particles of scent, then brings them back into the mouth for detailed analysis. By reading these chemical clues, the snake can easily follow the invisible trail left by a predator, a potential mate, or its retreating quarry.

When its prey is within striking distance, the rattlesnake rears up, catapults its head forward, and opens its mouth a full 180 degrees. The hollow, hypodermiclike fangs are lowered from their sheaths and swung straight out to penetrate deeply and deliver a lethal dose of venom. This venom breaks down the prey's body tissue and blood cells, interferes with blood clotting, and causes the kidneys and lungs to fail. The careful rattler usually keeps its distance while the venom is taking effect, and returns when the prey is subdued enough to safely swallow.

A rattler swallowing a large rat would be like you swallowing a 40-pound suckling pig in one gulp. Its tooth-lined jaws are not fused the way ours are, but are joined with an elastic membrane that stretches to accommodate objects larger than its own head. Each half of the lower jaw as well each of the six bones of the upper jaw and palate can be moved independently up or down, back and forth, or side to side. The snake moves alternating sides of its mouth up the victim, holding on with one side, and then "walking" up with the other, until the victim is completely engulfed. To enable the snake to breathe during this process, its windpipe has an outside extension that is reinforced with cartilage so it won't be crushed. The bones around the brain also have extensions to protect it from the sharp edges of whatever's being swallowed.

Once the prey is past the mouth, the snake puts a kink in its neck to push the "lump" down toward the stomach. The skin along the snake's entire body is pleated and elastic so it can stretch without tearing. It may take as long as an hour to swallow dinner, and even longer to digest it. Because a snake's metabolism is low (only one-tenth a mammal's or bird's), each meal goes a long way. A rattler needs only 6–20 meals a year!

Look for prairie rattlesnakes—between April and October, basking or hunting in the grass. In the hottest part of summer they may restrict their activity to dusk, dawn, and night. They are especially prevalent in areas where their favorite foods—rats, mice, gophers, squirrels, chipmunks, and rabbits—are abundant. The story about rattlesnakes coexisting peacefully with burrowing owls and prairie dogs is partly a tall tale. Though they do live in these burrows, it's free food they are after, not friendship.

Length: 2⅓–5 feet.

Young are born alive—and then quickly disperse from the mother. Young rattlesnakes are eaten by kingsnakes, racers, whipsnakes, coyotes, foxes, bobcats, badgers, hawks, and eagles.

Look for fighting males—locked in a combat dance. The males rear up so that one-third of their length is off the ground and their head is raised at a 45-degree angle. Belly to belly they push each other until one slips or is pushed off by the other. Severe fights progress into side-by-side pushing, neck twining, and wrestling each other to the ground. The snake that exhausts first loses, and must leave the area.

In the winter—they hibernate in underground dens in rocky outcrops, ledges, or burrows beneath the frost line. These communal dens are used year after year, and may be shared by snakes of other species.

Listen for—a dry rustling in the leaves that sounds at first like dry bones clicking together and then rises in intensity and pitch to sound like steam escaping. The rattle trails off to single clicks at the end. A violent, prolonged hissing is also part of the threat display, designed to scare predators away.

WESTERN BOX TURTLE

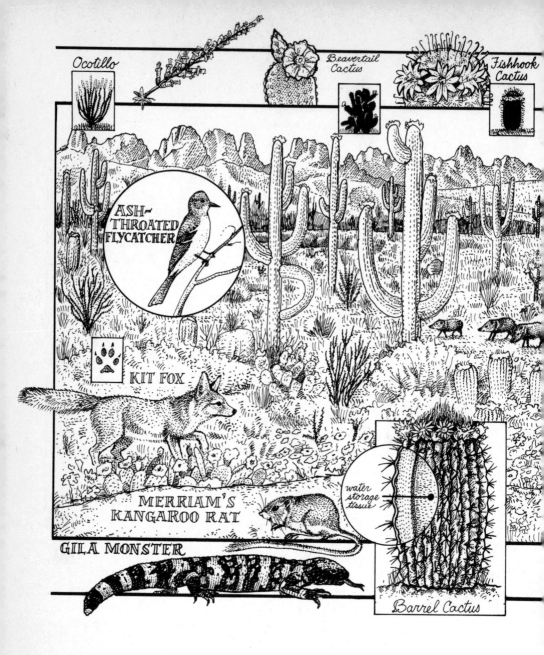

Ocotillo

Beavertail Cactus

Fishhook Cactus

ASH-THROATED FLYCATCHER

KIT FOX

MERRIAM'S KANGAROO RAT

water storage tissue

GILA MONSTER

Barrel Cactus

Foothill "Yellow" Palo Verde

Saguaro

GILA WOODPECKER

COLLARED PECCARY

GREATER ROADRUNNER

REGAL HORNED LIZARD

Desert Marigold

Jumping Cholla

Sonoran
Cactus Desert

WHERE TO SEE THIS HABITAT:

Arizona: Burro Creek (Bureau of Land Management); Cabeza Prieta and Kofa game ranges; Coronado and Tonto national forests; Imperial National Wildlife refuge; Organ Pipe Cactus and Saguaro national monuments
California: Chuckwalla Recreation Land; Joshua Tree National Monument

Sonoran Cactus Desert

ELF OWL

BEGINNINGS

Many people are surprised when they see a desert for the first time. "What are all these plants doing here? Where are the shifting sands?" The four North American deserts do indeed have sand dunes, but over most of their surface, the sands are covered by a patchwork of plant life. In the Great Basin desert of the North (described on page 163), gray-green sagebrush shrubs stretch as far as the eye can see. Farther south, in the Chihuahuan and Mojave deserts, the flora changes to include waving grasslands and tabletop acres of yuccas, creosote, and mesquite. Perhaps the most beautiful of all deserts is the Sonoran cactus desert, famous for its explosion of spring wildflowers and its forests of giant saguaro cacti.

Despite their floristic differences, the deserts of the American West have one important trait in common: low, unpredictable amounts of precipitation. The pattern of global air currents is partly responsible for this aridity. Air currents traveling from the equator to the poles swoop down when they reach the high-pressure system over the southern deserts. The air becomes warmer as it drops, and because it contains very little water vapor the sun is able to penetrate it unhindered, heating the ground surface to high temperatures.

The deserts also lie in a "rain shadow" created by the mountains to the west. When moist air from the Pacific rises over these mountains, it cools off and loses its ability to hold much moisture. After lavishing its store of rain and snow on the western slopes, the wind that arrives in the desert is nearly bone dry.

Of all the deserts, the Sonoran enjoys the most generous rain schedule. Instead of having only one rainy season a year, the Sonoran receives two pulses, one in winter and one in late summer. Even these rains are not always available to the plants and animals, however. Winter rains fall when plants are dormant and many animals are underground or on their winter ranges. Other times, showers are so light that the water is quickly lost to high winds and intense sunshine. Even heavy rains may not fully water the plants. Torrential downpours saturate the upper layer of soil so quickly that the rest is forced to run in sheetlike streams across the surface. Incongruous as it sounds, people have actually drowned in the desert when caught unawares by these walls of rolling floodwaters.

In an environment where rainfall is scant, unpredictable, and often out of reach, plants and animals must fight for every drop they get. This scarcity has shaped the desert ecosystem and created some of the most fascinating adaptations you'll see anywhere.

STAYING GREEN IN THE LAND OF PERPETUAL DROUGHT

Desert plants can be earmarked by the ways in which they handle dry conditions—they are either drought evaders or drought tolerators. "Evaders" are opportunists: they spend their energy reserves all at once when the times are good—namely, in the few short weeks when rains grace the desert. These plants are usually annuals, growing rapidly, flowering, and setting seeds all before drought conditions set in. Some examples of these ephemeral plants include desert chicory, phacelias, bladderpods, and desert marigold.

"Tolerators" try to avoid the harsh consequences of drying out by working overtime, living frugally, and hoarding their savings. To maximize their water "income," these plants put out root systems that are up to six times as large as their aboveground tissue. They tend to monopolize all the water in an area, and occasionally even send out toxins that further discourage competitors. To avoid losing their hard-earned water, tolerators have hairy or waxy, light-reflecting leaves that curl up, drop off, or close their pores when dry winds are blowing and the hot sun is shining.

Cacti are the ultimate tolerators. They have reduced their leaves to spines, and have succulent tissues in which they store large amounts of water. They are also able to store carbon dioxide in the form of organic acids. This allows them to breathe in carbon dioxide during the cool nights, when the threat of losing water vapor is lessened. When the sun comes up again, they can close their pores for most of the day, and use the stored carbon to make sugars.

Perhaps the best-known cactus of all is the giant saguaro, trademark of the Sonoran desert. The roots of the saguaro form a shallow mesh bowl that captures all the moisture within a 90-foot-diameter circle. The cactus stores whatever moisture it can garner in its large, fleshy stem. Its spines slow down air currents right next to the stem, thus helping to shield the pores from moisture-robbing winds. These spines might have also protected the plant against long-ago herbivores such as the giant ground sloth.

The green, photosynthesizing stem of the saguaro, instead of being a smooth cylinder, has vertical pleats like those of a hanging drape. When water is plentiful, the cactus soaks up copious amounts—as much as a ton a day—and the pleats expand to accommodate the full load (up to 8 tons). After several months of drought, the cactus will be deeply pleated again.

Other cacti that store water in their stem include the squat barrel cacti, the oddly branched chollas, and the pad-leaved pricklypear cactus. Some succulents, such as the agaves and yucca, store water in their leaves. Wild cucumber and night-blooming cereus have bulbous roots for storage tanks.

Other drought tolerators have no such storage scheme; they are just plain tough. Their leaves have small, reinforced cells that resist wilting damage, allowing them to actually dry out without dying. The cells maintain a high osmotic pressure that allows them to keep water flowing into the

CHARACTERISTIC PLANTS:

Trees and Shrubs:	Herbaceous Plants:	Cacti:
Anderson lycium	bladderpods	barrel cactus
blue palo verde	buffalo grass	beavertail cactus
brittle bush	desert chicory	buckthorn cholla
cat claw	desert lily	cane cholla
creosote bush	desert marigold	desert Christmas cac-
desert hackberry	filaree	tus
desert ironwood	pale face	fishhook barrel cactus
fairy duster	phacelias	fishhook cactus
foothill "yellow" palo		hedgehog cactus
verde		jumping cholla
jojoba		night-blooming cereus
Mormon tea		ocotillo
smoke tree		organ pipe cactus
velvet mesquite		pincushion cactus
white bur sage		pricklypear cactus
		saguaro
		senita
		yuccas

roots, but resist giving it away to the air (see osmosis discussion on page 67). On a single plant, there may be several kinds of leaves of different hairiness, thickness, and size, some of them specially adapted to drought, and others adapted to rainy times.

Some tolerators support leaves only when moisture is available. Look for the conspicuous ocotillo, a branchless bouquet of thorny, whiplike stems topped with a scarlet flower. After a good rain, these stems put on a whole new set of leaves, only to be dropped when drought returns. The foothill "yellow" palo verde is completely leafless for much of the year but can still manufacture food in its chlorophyll-laced stem and branches. Other plants, such as creosote bush, will drop most leaves, and coat the rest with resins.

STAYING COOL CAN BE THIRSTY WORK

In the process of moving their muscles to find food and water, animals generate heat, which can sometimes build to dangerous levels. Ironically, cooling themselves often means giving up some of the water they have just found. Humans also use a cooling system that involves the loss of water. As the droplets of sweat on our skin change into a gas and evaporate, heat is released, making the surface of our skin feel cooler. Animals may either sweat, pant (which evaporates moisture from the lungs), lick their fur, drool, or even urinate on themselves to capitalize on the cooling action of evaporating water. Of course, the wisest plan is to avoid overheating to begin with.

Animals dodge the heat in a variety of ways. Birds and large mammals that are mobile can fly or walk away to cooler, higher ground or to the oases of waterholes and streams. Those that don't travel much simply use the cooler parts of the habitats they frequent. For example, many birds and some lizards avoid the hot-plate ground surface by perching up in shrubs, while burrowers spend the hottest part of the day underground. Burrows 18 inches under the surface fluctuate only 2 degrees F, regardless of whether the temperature above is soaring or frigid. No wonder 72 percent of all desert animals are burrowers, compared with only 6 percent in forests!

Another way to avoid the heat of the day is to work mainly in the early morning hours or in the cool of the night. Temperatures may plummet by 50 degrees F or more at night, allowing activity without the danger of overheating. Likewise, some seasons are cooler than others. Some birds come here to breed during the spring rains and move on when the mud starts to dry and crack.

Some animals that must be afoot during the hottest months have physical adaptations that help them avoid overheating. Many are pale in color in order to reflect light. Mammals have hair that insulates them from the sun and slows the evaporation from their skin (your clothes do the same thing). Although lizards don't sweat, their scales help keep out some of the heat. Bats and birds such as the lesser nighthawk and common poorwill will go into a daily torpor to beat the heat and conserve energy.

Heat escapes fastest from bare-skinned areas that are ingeniously positioned on animals' bodies. For example, jackrabbits lay in shaded depressions with their large, naked ears flattened over them. As the wind blows across the exposed veins, it cools the hot blood running inside. Birds shuttle their hot blood to bare-skinned legs, and lift their wings to let out some heat.

LIQUID GOLD

Some desert animals can go through their entire lives without drinking a drop of water. Instead, they get their water from seeds, fruits, insects, or animal prey. Burrowing kangaroo rats can sometimes add moisture to their food by storing it in burrows, where the food will absorb moisture from the air. Coyotes often dig in the gravel near dry streambeds to uncover an underground water source. Other animals capitalize on this find as soon as the coyote leaves. Some desert frogs get their water by just sitting on mud—they have an area of thin skin on their lower surface and can absorb 70 percent of their water this way. For most animals, even the early morning dew can be a welcome draft.

The trick to staying alive in this habitat is to hold on to every drop you can find. Birds, as well as some reptiles and mammals, reabsorb the water from their urine and excrete an almost solid waste. Others reingest their feces to get back some of the lost water. Cactus wrens and kangaroo rats have convoluted nasal passages that cool each breath on its way out, thus squeezing out and recouping some of the moisture picked up in the lungs.

WHAT'S IN IT FOR WILDLIFE?

Despite its difficulties, the cactus desert is prime real estate for many creatures. To find the greatest diversity of wildlife, go where the vegetation is thickest and multistoried. Look beneath the shrubs for hiding desert cottontails, black-tailed jackrabbits, and desert tortoises. Look carefully in the branches to find the nests of curve-billed thrashers or the browse marks on twigs nibbled by mule deer in the winter. When the shrubs and small trees are in spring bloom, they attract hordes of insects that in turn attract the ash-throated flycatcher, Say's phoebe, and other insect hawkers. On the stems, look for gila monsters and desert spiny lizards, climbing up in the morning to bask before they begin their hunting.

In burrows between the bushes are round-tailed ground squirrels, cactus mice, desert pocket mice, kangaroo rats, desert iguanas, and western diamondback rattlesnakes, to name a few of the most common. On the surface, you may encounter Sonoran gopher snakes, coachwhips, collared lizards, western whiptails, regal horned lizards, zebratail lizards, side-blotched lizards, and tree lizards. Two species that are uniquely adapted to moving along sandy ground include the fringe-toed lizard and the sidewinder (a rattlesnake). The lizard has fringes on its toes that act like snowshoes to keep it from sinking into the sand. When heat or predators threaten, however, it can just as easily choose to dive and "swim" through the sand. Sidewinders move across the sand by repeatedly throwing a coil of their body sideways, leaving a telltale "J" mark wherever they go. This not only increases their speed but also reduces the amount of actual body contact with the surface.

The saguaro is a major hub of wildlife activity. Spiders, silverfish, moth larvae, and even lizards may live within the pleats. The flowers are pollinated by Mexican long-nosed and Sanborn's long-tongued bats, and the fruits are relished by birds and rodents. Gila woodpeckers and gilded flickers somehow dodge the spines to craft nest holes in the trunk of the saguaro. They fashion their holes in late summer, and during the winter, a thin, woodlike layer forms inside. When the cactus dies, this layer resists decomposition, and these "Saguaro boots" are often found on the desert floor.

As soon as the nests are vacated, western screech-owls, elf owls, flycatchers, and purple martins move in to raise their broods. As the holes age, the third wave of homeowners may include rats, mice, and lizards. Red-tailed hawks place their large stick nests in crotches formed by the great arms of the saguaro, and great horned owls use them once the hawks are gone. White-winged doves will also nest in the branches, making forays out for nectar or fruits.

The ground-hugging pricklypear cactus produces a large, edible fruit called a tuna, and provides a nesting base for desert woodrats. The barrel cactus provides water for these rats, as well as for mice and rabbits that are willing to gnaw past the spines. Humans are not advised to tap cacti for water, however. The saguaro, though it holds 1,000 bathtubs full of water, has a poison in its sap that may kill you.

Other hubs of wildlife activity are springs, seeps, and washes (dry streambeds), where animals find life-giving water, dense vegetation, and

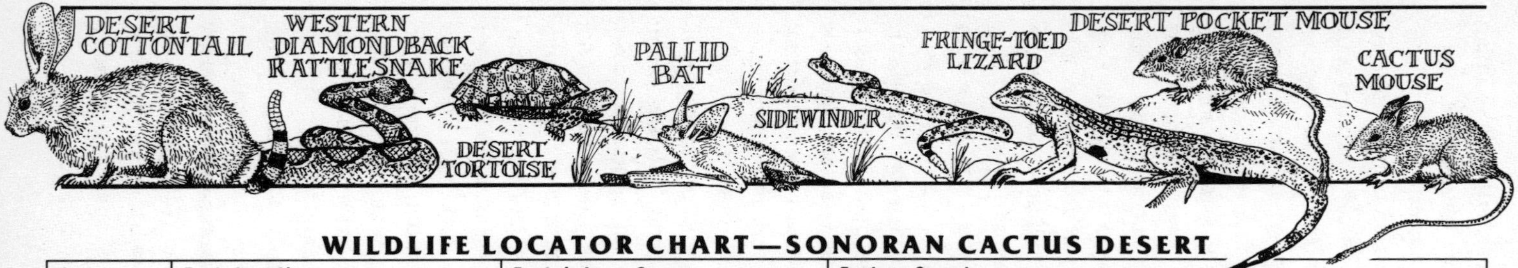

WILDLIFE LOCATOR CHART—SONORAN CACTUS DESERT

	Feeds from Air	Feeds in Lower Canopy	Feeds on Ground
Nests in Tree Canopy	Harris' Hawk Red-tailed Hawk Great Horned Owl		White-winged Dove, Mourning Dove, House Finch
Nests in Trunk Cavity	American Kestrel Northern Flicker Elf Owl Ash-throated Flycatcher Violet-green Swallow Purple Martin	Gila Woodpecker* Ladder-backed Woodpecker* Lucy's Warbler (*Feeds on Trunks)	
Nests in Shrubs or Cacti	Costa's Hummingbird	Verdin Cactus Wren Black-tailed Gnatcatcher	Greater Roadrunner, Bendire's Thrasher, Curve-billed Thrasher, Crissal Thrasher, Le Conte's Thrasher, Pyrrhuloxia, Black-throated Sparrow
Nests on Ground	Turkey Vulture Lesser Nighthawk Common Poorwill Say's Phoebe		Gambel's Quail, Collared Peccary, Mule Deer
Nests Beneath Ground or Debris	Mexican Long-nosed Bat Sanborn's Long-tongued Bat		Pallid Bat, Desert Cottontail, Black-tailed Jackrabbit, Round-tailed Ground Squirrel, Desert Pocket Mouse, Merriam's Kangaroo Rat, Cactus Mouse, Deer Mouse, Desert Woodrat, Coyote, Kit Fox, Jaguar, Bobcat, Desert Tortoise, Zebratail Lizard, Western Whiptail, Collared Lizard, Desert Iguana, Gila Monster, Regal Horned Lizard, Chuckwalla, Desert Spiny Lizard, Fringe-toed Lizard, Brush Lizard, Tree Lizard, Side-blotched Lizard, Western Diamondback Rattlesnake, Sidewinder, Sonoran Mountain Kingsnake, Milk Snake, Texas Blind Snake, Coachwhip, Striped Whipsnake, Sonoran Gopher Snake
Nests in Water			Colorado River Toad, Red-spotted Toad, Canyon Treefrog, Rio Grande Leopard Frog, Great Basin Spadefoot

somewhat cooler temperatures. Washes may appear dry, but usually have runoff water just beneath the surface that can be reached by digging. Water running over a drop-off in the stream may erode a deep tank that holds water for a long time. Birds and larger mammals travel here regularly to drink, and amphibians live here year round, needing the pools for breeding and the moisture to coat their easily parched skins. Best known among the amphibians are red-spotted toad, Rio Grande leopard frog, canyon treefrog, and the huge Colorado river toad (the second largest toad in the United States—also called Sonoran desert toad). Gambel's quail is also seen along washes, as are collared peccaries and the cartoon-famous greater roadrunner.

Wildlife action typically slows during the shimmering heat of midday, except for the occasional turkey vulture hunting in mesmerizing circles for casualties of the heat. The show gets better at dusk, at dawn, and especially at night. Try taking a moonlight hike, and be on the lookout for ubiquitous kangaroo rats looking for seeds, rattlesnakes looking for kangaroo rats, and great horned owls looking for them both. Coyotes, kit foxes, and gray foxes are also afoot at this time, searching for desert pocket mice, cactus mice, and a variety of other rodents.

One note of caution about desert exploration: it *can* become addictive. In the desert, as in few other habitats, you get to see the determining forces of the habitat at work. These forces have produced amazing parallels in form and function, between plants and animals, and between counterparts here and half a world away. Many a naturalist has become smitten by desertphilia, as evidenced by the large and colorful literature about deserts. So forewarned, happy exploring!

Greater Roadrunner

The roadrunner seems to break all the rules of desert-bird design. Unlike other desert-adapted birds that beat the heat by being either small, nocturnal, or able to fly high into the cooler air, the roadrunner is large, active during the day, and flies only rarely. This "ostrich of the desert" depends mostly on its long, pale blue legs for hunting and escape. It can easily gallop along at 15 miles an hour or, in a hurry, can spread its wings and volplane across valleys or down slopes. It negotiates the cactus slalom deftly, pursuing just about any kind of creature that moves, including lizards, scorpions, mice, and rattlesnakes.

Roadrunners have impeccable timing. They raise their broods when prey numbers are at their peak and all desert life is swelling with the moisture of summer rains. They schedule their hunting in the early morning, which is also the time that whiptail lizards, their main "baby food," are out and about. In order for both parents to be away hunting all morning, the nestlings must regulate their own temperature, even when they are a mere 4 and 5 days old. By evolutionary design, roadrunner nestlings are large enough to retain much of their own body heat in the very early hours before the sun reaches them. After this, their black, naked skin acts as a solar panel to absorb heat. Nests are usually built in staghorn cholla, a cactus with spines that deter predators but allow early morning sun directly into the nest. As the sun rises later in the day, the spines provide just a bit of much needed shade. If the nestlings start getting too warm, they flutter their throat, a form of panting that helps cool them by evaporation.

One danger in this kind of panting is that as the moisture from their lungs and throat is lost to the air, salts will begin to build up in their body. No problem for the roadrunner, however; they have special glands in their nose that get rid of this excess salt before it becomes harmful. To help quench the nestling's thirst, the adult regurgitates a clear liquid, and feeds it to the nestling along with its breakfast of lizard.

Adults also have adaptations for regulating their own temperature in the extreme swings of desert days and nights. Instead of burning fuel (food) to keep warm at night, the roadrunner lets its body drop in temperature. It falls into a kind of torpor, which it can afford to do only because it has few predators. In the morning, the groggy roadrunner climbs atop a boulder and spreads its back to the sun. The skin between its shoulder blades is dark black and acts like a solar panel to absorb energy and warm the blood vessels underneath. The bird even spreads its individual feathers to let in more light. This saves 50 percent of the energy the roadrunner would have used if it burned only food to warm itself. Scientists believe there may be yet another benefit of such sunbathing; the heat may cause parasites in the bird's plumage to move restlessly, allowing the bird to easily pick them off.

Look for greater roadrunners—running along the road ahead of slow-moving vehicles or, more commonly, hiding shyly in thickets of mesquite and cactus. They hunt most actively between 7 A.M. and 1 P.M., bringing "lizard after lizard after lizard" back to their nestlings.

Length: 20–24 inches.

Look for nests—a shallow platform of sticks, about 1 foot in diameter, 2–15 feet off the ground, in the dense branches of the cholla cactus or other shrub. They line the nest with whatever they can find blowing around the desert, including snake skins, mesquite pods, feathers, leaves, grasses, and horse and cattle manure. One of the parents spreads itself over the nest to shade the young during their first 3–4 days of life. The parent holds its long tail into the wind so breezes funnel under the tail and over the nestlings! Because the young hatch in a staggered schedule, the roadrunners have an "out" should fickle food supplies in the desert fail: the adult will eat the smaller nestlings, thus removing competition from the older nestlings and giving them a better chance of surviving.

Look for—Maltese-cross tracks in the dust along roads. Each track shows two toes up and two back.

Listen for—an explosive "coo" at nesting season. This sound stimulates the pair to begin their elaborate courtship rituals. Other sounds include a strange whistling "oo-t" that sounds like a breath being drawn in, followed by a loud clatter and crackling noise as the bird snaps its bill.

Collared Peccary

When you finally see your first peccary, you're liable to see your ninth, tenth, or even twentieth at the same time. Most collared peccaries travel in tight-knit, roving bands, and only the very sick or very old are spotted traveling alone. Far more than any other large mammals, the peccaries maintain close physical contact, usually of a nonagressive nature. In the evening they huddle together for warmth under low trees and shrubs. During the day, they feed in loose herds, often stopping for a common gesture called reciprocal rubbing.

In this gesture, two peccaries line up side to side, facing in opposite directions, and rub their heads vigorously over each other's hindquarters. Here, a small nipplelike protrusion on the midline of their back marks the opening of a very important scent gland. Early explorers who noted this gland thought it was a second navel, prompting them to dub the peccary *Dicotyles,* which means "double hollow." The musky secretion, which is a combination of oil and sweat, can actually be ejected by muscles surrounding the glands. Peccaries use this scent to mark the boundaries of their territory by rubbing their glands against rocks, trunks, and other objects.

Researchers who study the piglike animals contend that they live in a world of smells, and that each peccary's scent functions to identify individuals, band the herd together, and delineate the limits of their home range. They also use their sense of smell to find roots, tubers, and bulbs of plants such as morning glory, dock, and gourds under the ground. Their piglike snouts, disk-shaped and naked, lead them to the best underground larders, and help them push aside the soil.

This keen sense of smell makes up for what they lack in sight. So dim is their vision, in fact, that some reports claim that you can walk silently into the midst of collared peccaries, and the animals on either side of you may not see you for a while. As soon as they get a whiff of you, however, they'll begin an unnerving clicking that sounds like castanets. The hackles of coarse hair on their neck will rise a full 6 inches, and they'll suddenly scatter, dissolving into the vegetation nearby.

Peccaries use vegetation not only for protection from predators such as bobcats and jaguars, but also as protection from the baking sun. This ability to find patches of shade and relatively cool spots in a hot landscape is just one of their adaptations to desert living. They are also able to adjust their activity schedule to work around the hot temperatures. In the winter, when it is cool, they spend most of their time in open areas and are active for longer periods during midday. In the thick of summer, they stay in heavy vegetation during early morning and evening hours and conduct most of their business in the cool of the night. They also coordinate their breeding season to coincide with the times of best food availability, namely July and August, after the summer rains.

Another adaptation to desert living is their ability to survive for up to six days without drinking any water. When dehydrated, peccaries are able to reduce the amount of water that evaporates from their body by 68 percent. They are also able to reabsorb the water from their urine before they release it, thus cutting down on this water loss by 93 percent. When free water is scarce, they can get all the moisture they need from pricklypear cactus pads. Although their feces are full of spines, these cacti evidently pass through the peccaries' digestive system without harming them.

Look for collared peccaries—early in the morning or late in the evening, in herds of 6–20 animals, rooting in the ground for tubers and bulbs, or feeding on cacti (especially pricklypear), ephemerals, forbs, acorns, and fruits. Another good place to find them is along the edges of water holes. During the hottest part of the summer, they bed down during the day in thickets and are active mostly at night. In the winter, you'll find them out and about during midday.

Length: 34¼–40 inches.

Look for nests—shallow, unlined depressions in the ground under trees and shrubs.

Look for feeding pits—shallow, saucer-shaped excavations where the

WHITE-WINGED DOVE

herd has dug for underground tubers, roots, rhizomes, and bulbs. Also look for bite marks on cactus plants.

Look for droppings—large and segmented, often full of spines. When feeding on succulent vegetation, scats are soft like cow pies.

Look for tracks—in overlapping pairs separated by a stride of 6–10 inches. Oblong, cloven prints are 1–1½ inches long.

Smell for—a light, skunky odor where herds have been feeding.

Listen for—a barking alarm "cough" given at the first sign of danger, or a squeal when frightened or injuried.

Regal Horned Lizard

The Mexicans called them "sacred toads" because they seemed to weep tears of blood. Today we know that these squat, spiny reptiles are lizards, not toads, and that the shooting "tears of blood" are actually a defense mechanism. When threatened, the horned lizard constricts its major veins, causing sinuses in the head to fill with dammed blood. This swelling is normally employed to help lizards loosen their facial skin so they can shed it easily. In this case, a second pair of muscles is tightened, forcing the blood pressure to go still higher around their eye sockets. Blood sinuses located here eventually rupture under the pressure, and a horsehair stream of blood comes spraying out of a pore in the lower eyelid. These lizards can shoot from both eyes at once, one at a time, or even backward, hitting a target as far as 4 feet away!

Though not nearly as dramatic, regal horned lizards have other defense mechanisms that you (as a potential enemy) might witness. To avoid being seen, they embed their sloping snout in the sand like the blade of a plow, then tilt side to side, using their spines to shovel out a depression. Casting sand up over their back as they dig, the lizards eventually bury themselves until only their nostrils and eyes show. If you dig one out and pick it up, it is liable to go rigid, deflating its lungs and extending its feet in a masterful imitation of death. On the ground, this move would flatten its body against the sand, where its coloring would help it disappear.

When cornered by a predator, these lizards puff up with air, or elevate their collar of spines, presumably to make themselves harder to swallow. Snakes find out the hard way that regal horned lizards can be a dangerous meal—the spines are sharp enough to pierce the esophagus and kill a snake. Don't tell the roadrunner, though; it regularly dines on horned lizards with no ill effects.

To shake off the chill of a desert night, the lizards spend the early morning basking on a rock or sandy area, flattening their body and tilting it up to receive the most direct dose of sun rays. Their body color changes depending on both temperature and light conditions. Whenever the temperature is low or the light is bright, their skin automatically darkens, presumably to absorb more sun. They turn pale as temperatures rise or lights become dim. When the air reaches a dangerously hot 100 degrees F, they stay pale regardless of how bright the light is.

Look for regal horned lizards—basking on rocks or running swiftly to the shelter of a shrub or cactus. They have four prominent spines at the back of their neck, and three at each temple, forming a medieval-looking crown of armor around their head. The spines of a lizard-in-hiding may be all you see poking out from a patch of disturbed soil. In early morning and just before sunset, they hunt for ants and other insects with a sit-and-wait strategy that conserves energy. When they see prey, they stalk slowly—a step or two at a time—using their long, sticky tongue to close the final gap. At night, they burrow beneath the soil to stay safe from predators and dropping temperatures. Come winter, they will hibernate in the burrows of other animals.

Length: 3½–6½ inches.

Eggs are underground—in sandy or gravelly areas with good drainage and exposure to the sun's warming rays. In July or August, the female digs a slanted tunnel, leading 6–8 inches beneath the surface, with a small chamber for eggs at one end. She lays 7–33 (average 21) eggs, rolling each one into the sandy chamber with her hindquarters. With pelvic twists, she covers all the eggs with sand, then scratches at the entrance to hide the evidence of the tunnel. The eggs will incubate on their own with the help of the sun's warmth.

Listen for—a popping sound as the spray of blood pours forth from the eye. Some lizards hiss as part of their ferocious act, or rattle their tail in the dry vegetation.

COSTA'S HUMMINGBIRD

CACTUS WREN

CURVE-BILLED THRASHER

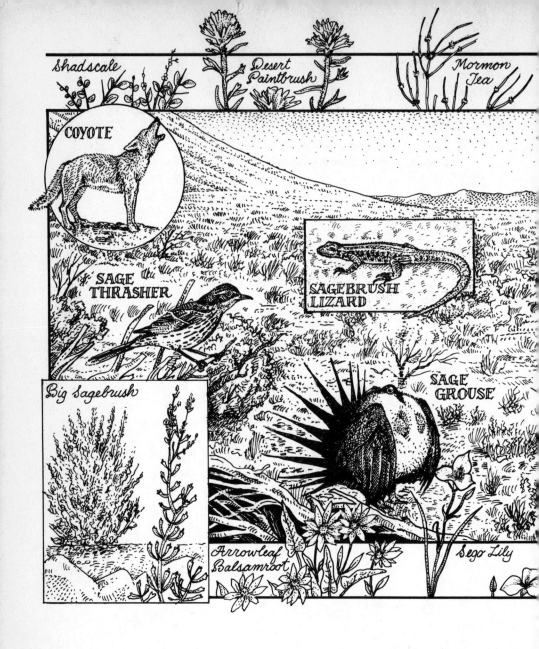

Shadscale

Desert Paintbrush

Mormon Tea

COYOTE

SAGE THRASHER

SAGEBRUSH LIZARD

SAGE GROUSE

Big Sagebrush

Arrowleaf Balsamroot

Sego Lily

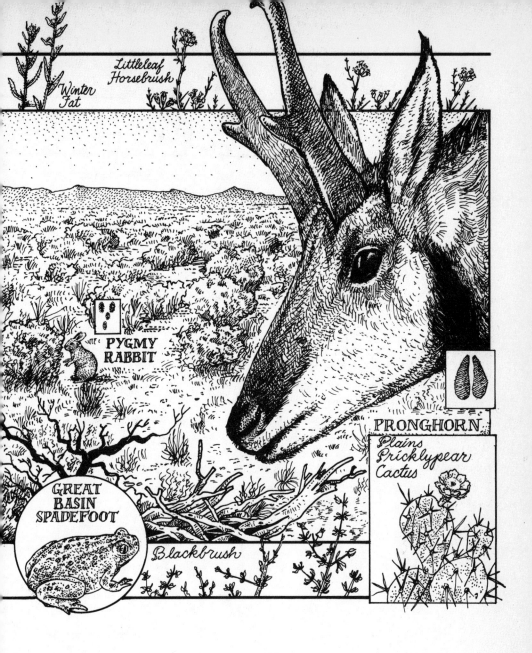

Winter Fat

Littleleaf Horsebrush

PYGMY RABBIT

PRONGHORN

GREAT BASIN SPADEFOOT

Blackbrush

Plains Pricklypear Cactus

Sagebrush Desert

WHERE TO SEE THIS HABITAT:

California: Clear Lake National Wildlife Refuge; Modoc National Forest

Colorado: Dinosaur National Monument

Idaho: Camas and Minidoka national wildlife refuges; Caribou, Sawtooth, and Targhee national forests; Curlew National Grassland

Nevada: Black Rock Desert (Bureau of Land Management); Charles Sheldon Antelope Range; Great Basin National Park; Humboldt and Toiyabe national forests; Ruby Lake and Stillwater national wildlife refuges; Sheldon National Antelope Refuge

Oregon: Crooked River National Grassland; Hart Mountain National Antelope Range; Malheur and Ochoo national forests; Malheur National Wildlife Refuge; Ouyhee River Canyon (Bureau of Land Management)

Utah: Ashley and Dixie national forests; Bear River and Fish Springs national wildlife refuges; Bryce Canyon and Zion national parks; Glen Canyon National Recreation Area

Sagebrush Desert

BEGINNINGS

In some parts of the intermountain West, you can travel for days and see nothing but dusty, gray-green shrubs interspersed with forbs (broadleaf herbs) and grasses. For some people, it's the definition of monotony; but for those who understand sagebrush ecology and the controversy that surrounds this land, it can be a fascinating landscape.

If you look at a topographic map of the basin and range country, you can see the long, fairly parallel strings of mountain ranges interrupted by broad basins and valleys. This up-and-down landscape is actually a desert, despite the fact that temperatures fall below freezing in the cold winters. The Sierras and other high mountains to the west shut this "enclosed desert" off from moist Pacific winds. Even when precipitation does fall, it is not always available to the plants. Much of it falls in winter and leaches straight through the soil, untapped by the dormant roots. In summer, moisture is robbed from the soil by high, persistent winds.

Sagebrush and its associates have learned to find scarce water and hold onto it. The roots of big sagebrush cover an area up to 90 feet in diameter, or three times its crown diameter. Within this circle, no other plants can get established because the water is being usurped. To make the most of any weather, sagebrush sports two different types of leaves: one suited for moist periods and one better adapted to dry periods. These leaves provide important forage for a number of wildlife species, while the low, compact crown provides essential cover. Crush the leaf to find out how this shrub, which is actually a variey of wormwood, got its name. Although it is not a sage, it has a sweetish, sagelike odor.

Growing along with big sagebrush are other species of sagebrush, as well as rubber rabbitbrush, gooseberry, antelope bitterbrush, chokecherry, snowberry, Mormon teas, winter fat, spiny hopsage, and littleleaf horsebrush (which is toxic to cattle). The grasses in the desert vary depending on where you are, but include bottlebrush squirreltail, alkali sacaton, Indian ricegrass, needlegrasses, galleta, bluegrasses, wheatgrasses, and wildrye. The colorful, flowering forbs include locoweeds, sego lilies, Indian paintbrushes, phloxes, lupines, globemallows, and a variety of members of the sunflower family. The only major cactus is the low, spreading pricklypear cactus.

In valley bottoms, sagebrush often yields to shadscale and other shrubs such as true greasewood. Shadscale is a salt-tolerant species, and is prevalent in areas where lakes (even ancient glacial lakes) have dried up and left salt deposits, or where marine shales are outcropping. In areas that are too salty

CHARACTERISTIC PLANTS:

Trees, Shrubs, and Vines:
antelope bitterbrush
big sagebrush
blackbrush
cherries
curlleaf cercocarpus
four-wing saltbush
gooseberries
greasewood
green ephedra
green rabbitbrush
iodine bush
littleleaf horsebrush
low sagebrush
Mormon tea
Nuttall saltbush
phacelias
plains pricklypear
rubber rabbitbrush
shadscale
snowberries
spiny hopsage

western serviceberry
whitethorn acacia
winter fat
Wood's rose

Herbaceous Plants:
alkali sacaton
arrowleaf balsamroot
beaked hawksbeard
blanket-flower
blue grama
bottlebrush squirrel-
 tail
buckwheats
cheatgrass brome
desert dandelion
desert paintbrush
foxtail barley
galleta grass
giant wildrye
goldenrod
Gunnison's mariposa
hairy golden aster
hood phlox

Idaho fescue
Indian paintbrushes
Indian ricegrass
larkspur
locoweeds
longleaf phlox
lupines
meadow death camas
milkvetch
mule's ears
muttongrass
needle-and-thread
needlegrasses
Nevada bluegrass
prairie junegrass
red threeawn
scarlet gilia
scarlet globemallow
secunda bluegrass
sego lily
silvery lupine
slender wheatgrass
thickspike wheatgrass
western wheatgrass
yarrow

even for these shrubs, you'll find iodine bush, spike grass, rushes, alkali sacaton, and pickleweed.

In its native state, this mixture of shrubs, forbs, and grasses was home to a variety of wildlife species that used sagebrush for food and cover, or grazed on the greening grasses and forbs. Beginning in the late 1800s, a new cadre of grazers—sheep and cattle—began to work in this land. Their grazing and trampling touched off a controversy that is still very much alive, and unresolved, today.

HOW MUCH SAGEBRUSH IS TOO MUCH?

Cattle don't particularly like the taste of sagebrush. When they graze an area, they pick at the grasses first, then the forbs, but they usually ignore the shrubs. If too many cattle are allowed to graze in one area long enough, they may weaken the native grasses and open the ground to invasion. The uneaten sagebrush starts to spread and become dense, while exotic annuals such as cheatgrass brome start to edge out native perennial grasses and forbs. When the shrubs get thick, sheep have a harder time squeezing through, and cattle have to hunt harder to find a diminishing amount of quality forage.

In the eyes of ranchers, this sort of range is "depleted" because it can no longer produce a maximum number of well-fed cattle and sheep. In many cases, the runaway sagebrush is seen as the culprit. With financial assistance from the government, private landowners and federal land managers try to "rehabilitate" the range by burning, cutting, or poisoning sagebrush, then reseeding with wheatgrasses from the Soviet Union.

A number of concerns about "range rehabilitation" have been voiced. One is the problem of erosion. The thick stands of sagebrush hold the soil well, and when they are removed, wind and water are free to work their magic. Ideally, the seeded grass, if given a chance to develop, will hold the soil down just as well. Unfortunately, that depends on the better judgment of ranchers, who, in their eagerness to recoup the cost of control, could conceivably graze their cattle too heavily the first year, leaving the soil exposed to the elements.

Another concern is the effect of herbicides on animals and, ultimately, on humans. Studies assure us that these herbicides break down rapidly, but they assume that the detoxifying organisms are working in an environment that has warm temperatures, moisture, and organic matter in the soil. Only one of these conditions (high temperatures) is characteristic of the sagebrush region during the late spring spraying season.

The loudest warning bells are being sounded by wildlife professionals who are concerned about the loss of habitat for native fauna that depend on sagebrush. A few of the species closely tied to this shrub are sage grouse, sage thrasher, sage sparrow, pygmy rabbit, mule deer, pronghorn, and sagebrush lizard. There are many others, such as Brewer's sparrow, that are tied to the shrub-form for nesting.

The greatest controversy today concerns projects that completely remove sagebrush and replace all the native forbs with wheatgrasses. Without the shrubs for cover and food, most of the sagebrush-associated species will have to move elsewhere, *if* there are suitable habitats available. Even if some shrubs return, the loss of forbs makes the habitat unattractive to grazers such as pronghorns and mule deer, which depend on these forbs during the summer months.

Today, new approaches to range rehabilitation are being tested. The idea is to create a mosaic of shrubs for feeding and cover, mixed with open areas for performing displays (see Sage Grouse, page 170). First, the very shrubby, overgrazed stands are thinned to a more natural condition where 20–40 percent of the canopy is sagebrush. Where bare areas must be replanted, the recommended seed mix includes seeds of forbs as well as grasses. These minor modifications should help improve the range for livestock, while at the same time giving wildlife a boost.

WHAT'S IN IT FOR WILDLIFE?

Wildlife use different facets of the sagebrush ecosystem at different times of the year, depending on their needs. Sage grouse eat nothing but the leaves of sagebrush from October through April, then switch to the understory forbs and grasses when nesting and rearing broods. Pronghorns, dependent on sagebrush for most the year, also switch to forbs in the summer. Mule deer are particularly dependent on the cover of sagebrush when rearing their fawns, hiding from enemies, or escaping the bitter winter winds. They nibble the shrubs that shelter them in winter, switching to grasses in the spring and forbs in the summer.

Natural selection has "trained" these animals to seek out the most nutritious foods available in any season. Because green plants are most nutritious when they are sprouting or budding, wildlife favor young plants or the youngest parts of plants. Ideally, they look for places that offer an ever-ripening menu of these young foods. The greater selection of different forbs and grasses (a sign of a healthy range), the better the chances that one of them will be peaking at any given time. Long after the last of these peaking plants has dried up and blown away, sagebrush leaves still hold

WILDLIFE LOCATOR CHART—SAGEBRUSH DESERT

GREEN-TAILED TOWHEE

BREWER'S SPARROW

BLACK-THROATED SPARROW

SAGEBRUSH VOLE

LAZULI BUNTING

GRAY FLYCATCHER

	Feeds from Air	Feeds in Tree Canopy	Feeds on Trunk	Feeds on Ground
Nests in Tree Canopy	Harris' Hawk, Swainson's Hawk, Red-tailed Hawk, Ferruginous Hawk, Golden Eagle, Long-eared Owl, Great Horned Owl, Vermilion Flycatcher	Pinyon Jay, Blue-gray Gnatcatcher		Mourning Dove, Chihuahuan Raven, House Finch
Nests in Trunk Cavity	American Kestrel		Ladder-backed Woodpecker	Mountain Bluebird
Nests in Shrubs or Cacti	Gray Flycatcher, Loggerhead Shrike	Black-tailed Gnatcatcher, Lazuli Bunting		Greater Roadrunner, Sage Thrasher, Bendire's Thrasher, Brewer's Sparrow, Sage Sparrow, Black-chinned Sparrow, Black-throated Sparrow
Nests on Ground	Northern Harrier, Prairie Falcon, Common Poorwill, Say's Phoebe	Clay-colored Sparrow		Sage Grouse, Gambel's Quail, Horned Lark, Common Raven, Green-tailed Towhee, Vesper Sparrow, Lark Sparrow, Western Meadowlark, Mule Deer, Pronghorn
Nests Beneath Ground or Debris	Burrowing Owl			Merriam's Shrew, Desert Shrew, Pygmy Rabbit, Desert Cottontail, Black-tailed Jackrabbit, Least Chipmunk, Townsend's Ground Squirrel, Great Basin Pocket Mouse, Desert Pocket Mouse, Dark Kangaroo Mouse, Deer Mouse, Sagebrush Vole, Coyote, Western Whiptail, Desert Grassland Whiptail, Gila Monster, Sagebrush Lizard, Glossy Snake, Western Rattlesnake, Night Snake, Common Kingsnake, Great Basin Gopher Snake, Longnose Snake, Massasauga
Nests in Water				Tiger Salamander, Western Spadefoot, Great Basin Spadefoot

their allure; they're a good source of protein, and are available even in the winter when snow covers most other foods.

The thermal cover provided by sagebrush shrubs is as important as their food value. When an animal overheats in the sun, it may lose precious water supplies through sweating, panting, etc. By cooling down in the shade of the sagebrush, the animal need not use as much water to lower its body temperature. Animals must also spend energy to replace lost heat when temperatures are low. By blocking the wind, snow, or rain, the shrubs allow the animal to save this energy and use it for more productive processes such as growing, storing reserves, reproducing, and taking care of its young.

A variety of songbirds such as sage sparrow and Brewer's sparrow build their nests in the sagebrush shrubs. Pygmy rabbits use the thick clumps of sagebrush almost exclusively for food and cover. Least chipmunks are also highly dependent on sagebrush, and may be the most abundant mammals in this habitat. The best opportunities for wildlife viewing will be in stands that are diverse—low shrubs next to clumps of tall shrubs, open areas next to stands of pinyon-juniper or curlleaf cercocarpus, and, of course, those that have streamside areas nearby.

Sage Grouse

The sagebrush community is both bed and board to the sage grouse. The shrubs block the wind, the snow, and the extreme sun, while screening the birds from the eyes of roving predators. Because this shelter is evergreen and edible at all times of the year, dinner is never more than a neck's stretch away.

Throughout the year, sage grouse move from stand to stand to find the right density of sagebrush to meet their needs. In the spring, they build nests in areas that have a 20–40 percent canopy cover. Once the brood hatches, the family moves to more open stands to look for succulent forbs such as desert dandelion and yarrow. When these forbs mature and dry, the broods move upslope, where the forbs are still green.

In late August, even these upland forbs begin to dry out, forcing the hens and their broods downslope once again to dense sagebrush stands. Here, the winter snows are not nearly as deep, and the grouse can reach the leaves of the taller sagebrush plants sticking out of the snow. Unlike most birds that barely eke out a living in the winter, the well-fed sage grouse is usually in good condition in the spring, ready to face three months of energetic courtship and nesting activities.

In the still of dawn, you can barely make out the silhouettes of the males parading in the sparsely vegetated opening. This is an ancestral "lek"—a courtship ground where generations of grouse have collected by the hundreds to strut, display, defend their territories, and pass on their genes. "Lekking" in large groups may have evolved as a response to the openness of prairie habitats. Since predators are liable to see any bird that steps out on the flatland, it makes sense for each bird to surround itself with other birds, thus reducing the individual's chances of being the one eaten.

The males arrive first in order to claim territories and defend them against intruders. They face off shoulder to shoulder along their boundaries, striking each other with their wings. The fights are ritualized rather than bloodthirsty; few cocks are actually harmed in these battles. The master cock is he who secures the prime territory, the one that includes an area called the "mating center." This is where the females mill around, watch the males strut, and eventually consent to mate. If the mating center is completely within the master cock's territory, only he has the privilege of mating with the females there. There are times, however, when he is overwhelmed by females. While he is occupied, the males that have managed to secure a territory next to the mating center may have a chance to move in and mate.

During the day, the males congregate for loafing and feeding in stands of sagebrush with 20–50 percent canopy closure. Unfortunately, this is also the density at which "range rehabilitation" measures are recommended (see page 167). In the past, treatments that removed all sagebrush and associated forbs rendered millions of acres useless for the magnificent sage grouse. Hopefully, the days of unrestrained sagebrush "control" are over, and the interests of wildlife will be factored in before the spray planes fly.

Look for sage grouse—on the ground, nesting, breeding, courting, feeding, and loafing in sagebrush stands of various densities, depending on the time of year. Sage grouse reach their greatest densities in areas that contain a water source within a mile or two. They feed on leaves of sagebrush, especially in the winter, and on the soft parts (leaves, blossoms, pods, and buds) of herbaceous plants whenever they're available. They are active during the day, and roost in a circle at night.

Length: 26–30 inches.

Look for nests—in a slight depression on the ground beneath or between sagebrush shrubs. Grouse line the scrape with grasses and sage leaves. The male takes no part in nest building, incubating, or raising the young.

Look for courting grouse—in low, sparse sagebrush or in an area denuded of vegetation. The strutting grounds are usually less than 10 acres in size and are often located near a water source. The males perform in early morning, evening, and sometimes all night in the moonlight, as a way to both advertise their territories and entice females. The grouse holds himself upright with the long, pointed tail feathers erect and fanned. His white neck feathers are raised, the yellow comb over each eye is expanded, and the pale yellow chest sac is partially filled with air. As he struts, the grouse swishes his wings, fills and empties his chest sacs with a resonant pop, and makes cooing sounds. All of this seems to impress the females tremendously, and one male is able to mate with several in succession.

Listen for—quacking as the female arrives at the lekking ground. During the male's display, listen for the "swish-swish-coo-oo poink" sounds. Fighting males cry out harshly.

Pronghorn

According to tribal legend, the Blackfoot Indian god molded the pronghorn antelope out of soil from the mountains. When he turned his creation loose in the rocky alpine country, it quickly tripped and hurt itself. He then carried the pronghorn down to the open plains and watched with great pleasure as the animal sprinted away effortlessly, obviously at home in this sprawling habitat.

Other Indian tribes thought the pronghorn had supernatural powers, perhaps because of its phenomenal spotting-scope vision and its ability to leap 20 feet and run up to 60 miles per hour. Although it can sustain its maximum speed for only half a mile or so, it can easily cruise at 30–40 miles an hour for up to 7 miles at a stretch. Keep an eye on your side mirror when driving in pronghorn country; you may find a herd gaining on you, racing neck and neck with your car, then suddenly crossing over in front of you as if to signal victory.

Their keen eyesight and legendary speed are both adaptations that help them avoid predators such as coyotes and human hunters. Their herding instinct is also a protective measure, ensuring that at any time, several sharp eyes and ears are on the lookout. Their wide-set eyes have a broad sweep of vision, and can detect movement at a distance of 4 miles. When one pronghorn senses danger, it will signal alarm to all others by flaring the white hairs on its rump patch. The other pronghorns also flare in response, thus spreading the message throughout the herd. As they run away, they form a long, elliptical shape, keeping the youngest members stashed safely in the protected middle of the group.

In the winter, their herds greatly increase in size, totaling as many as 100 or more animals. They feed mainly on the evergreen leaves of big sagebrush. When snows accumulate and cover these plants, the herd goes wandering in search of areas with a shallower snowpack. It's at this time of year that they meet a most formidable enemy: the range fence. Although pronghorns are capable of leaping over even the highest fence, they are reluctant to do so. In the summer, they'll gladly wiggle under a fence or between the horizontal strands of wire (even with the resultant scratches), but only a rare individual will actually leap over. When deep snow blocks their wiggling route, a herd will be brought to a standstill, miles away from adequate food supplies. Many ranchers who are aware of this fact are beginning to build fences that can fold down in parts to accommodate these drifting herds.

In the spring these large herds break up into groups of 10–15, the does staying with their yearlings, and the males traveling together in bachelor groups. In May and June, the does seek isolation in order to "drop" one or two fawns. This is a literal term, because, like sheep and goats, the pronghorns stand while giving birth. The drop to earth is thought to stimulate breathing in the newborns. The female hides each newborn in a separate bed, then grazes some distance away so as not to advertise their presence to predators. When she visits every few hours to nurse, she eats the fawns' feces and urine, presumably so that predators won't be drawn by the odors.

In the meantime, the bachelor males are engaged in ritualized contests in which they establish their rank. They push one another head to head, using the forked prongs of their antlers to catch and deflect their opponent's horns. In the fall, the bachelor groups will disperse, and the dominant male from each group will begin to herd up his harem of does and mark his territory with scent from his cheek gland, urine, and feces. He patrols the borders of his territory tirelessly, working to keep his does in, while keeping the eager bachelor males out. When a male tries to intrude, he is met by the staring, snorting threat display of the owner. If he doesn't back down, a fight may ensue, leading occasionally to the death of one bull. Usually, thanks to the prearranged hierarchy system, the lesser bull bows out before the confrontation gets dangerous.

Look for pronghorns—in open sagebrush country that has less than 30 percent shrub cover and plenty of understory herbaceous plants. Pronghorns feed on shrubs throughout the year, but depend completely on sagebrush in the winter (up to 5½ pounds/day). In the warm months, they prefer forbs (i.e., succulent herbs, not grasses). Before white people settled this region, an estimated 40–60 million pronghorn roamed freely. By 1900, hunting pressure and a spate of severe weather had shaved their numbers down to 17,000. Today, restocking and management have brought them up to 400,000. You may have to get out of your car and hike to see large numbers, however; pronghorn use the undulating landscape ingeniously, and an indentation may swallow a whole herd.

Size: Head and body length, up to 4½ feet. Shoulder height, 3 feet.

Look for babysitting groups—one doe followed by an entourage of fawns, including many that don't belong to her. This rotating day-care system seems to work quite well, allowing all the mothers in the herd to get some "time away from the kids" so they can concentrate on foraging.

Look for tracks—shaped like split hearts, about 3 inches long. The front hooves, which absorb the shock of the leap, are larger than the back.

Look for scat—small oval, elongated, bell, or acorn-shaped droppings. In the summer, when pronghorns are feeding on succulent forbs, their droppings are soft and stuck together.

Listen for—a snort or "laugh" that has been described as a "descending, sneezelike cough." Males warn intruders with this snort.

Great Basin Spadefoot

The desert would seem to be no place for a thin-skinned toad that needs a constant supply of moisture in order to keep breathing and raise a brood. Yet the spadefoot toad is a classic sagebrush resident, ingeniously adapted to escape the heat and make the most of the brief and fickle moisture. It takes refuge from the sun by digging itself beneath the ground to a level where the soil keeps its skin moist and cool. It shovels itself in, back-end first, by rotating its "spade," a crescent-shaped projection on the side of its hind foot. When night falls, it reverses the process, and spends the darkest hours hopping on the sagebrush flats, collecting insects with its long, sticky tongue.

A furious, drenching cloudburst is a green-light to the spadefoot toads. They come to the surface by the hundreds after a good rain, searching for shallow basins or dried-up creekbeds that now hold, however briefly, a shimmer of water. The first male to reach a puddle begins a loud, rasping snore that assembles the troops from hundreds of yards around. Other males descend in droves, and before long, they too are swimming back and forth with their heads buoyed high on their ballooning vocal sacs.

Finding a female in the dark, crowded pool is a matter of trial and error. A swimming male will clasp eagerly to any swimming form, be it male or female. If his "mate" snores at him, he knows to let go, grabbing frog after frog until he finds a nonsnoring female with 300–500 eggs he can fertilize.

The countdown starts at the moment of fertilization, when the egg cells begin dividing and multiplying at a mind-boggling rate. Forty-eight hours later, the tiny ovals are already squiggling tadpoles, changing so fast you can almost watch them grow. Their tadpole stage is a sprint to maturity, lasting only two weeks instead of the more leisurely 4- to 6-week schedule of most frogs. Spadefoot tadpoles have every reason to rush, however, because their temporary pools are lowered a little by the sun each day.

Finding enough to eat in this shrinking pool is a problem that the tadpoles tackle together. In a behavior that is unusual for amphibians, the tadpoles form feeding groups, swimming along the bottom like a school of fish. Their waving tails create a current that stirs up mud, leaves, and nutrients that they can eat. They also don't hesitate to devour their own brothers and sisters that die or falter. This may seem cruel, but actually makes good biological sense in a habitat where resources dwindle daily. The weaker tadpoles die so the hardy few can live long enough to become adults and pass on their genes.

Sometimes, the pool dries up before the tadpoles have a chance to transform into landlubbers. In this case, their remains are added to the bottom mud, and are then eaten by next year's young. Interestingly, these tadpole-fed tadpoles transform into adults faster than most other tadpoles. It's as if they get a "message" that this is a shallow pool and not likely to last for the full schedule of maturity.

In the final days of drawdown, spadefoot tadpoles attempt to delay the inevitable drying. Working in groups, they use their tail to scoop out a hole in the mud, thus concentrating the last bit of water into a pool. This way, the surface area of water exposed to evaporation is minimized, buying the tadpoles a little more time. In the desert, even an hour can make a difference in whether or not they are able to transform.

Look for Great Basin spadefoots—hunting for insects at night or heading for breeding pools after a rain. Dry periods and winters are spent in underground burrows, often enveloped in a cocoonlike layer of dead skin that keeps them moist. Some observers claim that you can get a spadefoot to surface by stomping on the ground above its burrow. The skin of spadefoot toads is relatively smooth and covered with glands that excrete a peppery-tasting, musty-smelling substance that may protect them from predators that have discriminating palates.

Length: 1½–2 inches.

Look for eggs—from April to July, in small (less than 1 inch wide) masses of 10–42 eggs, attached to stalks of vegetation in the quiet water of temporary pools or in irrigation ditches, slow streams, or reservoirs. The adults deposit several of these masses in separate locations; all told, a single female may lay up to 500 eggs. The top of the mass is dark olive, and the bottom is creamy or silvery white. Two jelly envelopes protect each egg.

Listen for—a series of low-pitched, throaty, rapid "wa-wa-wa's."

SAGEBRUSH LIZARD

California Black Oak

California White Oak

Blue Oak

ACORN WOODPECKER

BOBCAT

Toyon

GILBERT'S SKINK

DEER MOUSE

Creeping Wintergreen

Red Raspberry

Engelmann Oak

Canyon Live Oak

Interior Live Oak

California Live Oak

WESTERN GRAY SQUIRREL

BAND-TAILED PIGEON

ARBOREAL SALAMANDER

STRIPED SKUNK

California Buckthorn

Digger Pine

Oak Woodland

WHERE TO SEE THIS HABITAT:

California: Angeles, Los Padres, Mendocino, and Shasta-Trinity national forests

Oak Woodland

BEGINNINGS

The oaks of California, with their broad, green leaves and bushels of meaty acorns, are a welcome twist in a landscape stereotyped by grasses, chaparral, and cone-bearing conifers. The "typical" oak woodland is hard to describe. Some are parklike and open, with a sea of grasses waving beneath scattered trees. Others are dense, with understories that include needleleaf trees such as Digger pine, and shrubs such as chamise and manzanita. Most occur in valleys and foothills, sandwiched just above dry grasslands and below moister mountain forests. Of the 15 different oaks that rule the groves, some are leaf-droppers, like their eastern relatives, and others keep their broad leaves throughout the year. Both strategies are an attempt to deal with the chronic problems of low moisture and temperature stress.

Trees that drop their leaves manage to avoid times of poor growing conditions (e.g., cold winters) by going into a sort of dormancy until conditions improve. They must balance the energy they save, however, with the cost of putting on a whole new set of leaves each year. Such deciduous oaks include the Oregon white, blue, California black, and California white.

The evergreen oaks (e.g., canyon live oak, interior live oak, California live oak, and Engelmann oak) have a different approach to resource scarcity. By retaining their leaves throughout the year, they can take advantage of fluctuating conditions. When moisture becomes available, the leaves are in place and ready to produce food for the tree, even during warm spells in the winter. When conditions are very dry, they can close the tiny gas-exchanging pores on their leaves. A thick, leathery cuticle helps to hold in what little moisture the ground offers. After two years, the leaves fall off, but not all at once. Their cycles are staggered, so that some leaves are always left on the tree. By holding onto each leaf for two years, these trees can hold onto their nutrients that much longer.

For millions of years, both types of oaks have survived and improved despite the myriad organisms that eat their twigs, leaves, and buds, and collect nearly all their acorns each year. When humans entered the picture, however, this well-adapted ecosystem was suddenly faced with stress of an unprecedented kind.

MINING THE WOODLANDS

Oak woodlands have been the "forest next door" for many human populations. When the Native Americans settled in the rich Californian valleys, they set small fires to clear the ground before acorn gathering and to help drive game animals so they would be easier to hunt. From what we can tell today, however, their impact was not detrimental.

The largest impact on the oak woodlands has been the result of overgrazing by livestock. Starting in 1769, the Spanish missionaries brought their faith and their animals to the valley oak forests. The stress of too many mouths on too little land weakened the perennial bunchgrasses beneath the oaks and paved the way for aggressive plants such as wild oats, cheatgrass brome, mouse barley, and fescues whose seeds had "hitchhiked" in with shipments from Europe. Those oak seedlings that were not eaten

---

CHARACTERISTIC PLANTS:

Trees, Shrubs, and Vines:
blue elder
blue oak
buckbrush
California black oak
California buckeye
California buckthorn
California juniper
California-laurel
California live oak
California redbud
California white oak
canyon live oak

chamise
Coulter pine
creeping wintergreen
Digger pine
Engelmann oak
hollyleaf buckthorn
interior live oak
lemonade sumac
mariposa manzanita
Oregon white oak
Pacific madrone
Parry manzanita
red raspberry
southern California
    walnut

sugar sumac
toyon
whiteleaf manzanita

Herbaceous Plants:
bracken fern
bromegrasses
California wild grape
California yerba-santa
fescues
needlegrass
oatgrasses
silvery lupine

---

directly by cattle now had to compete for moisture with the new exotic plants. Meanwhile, the Spaniards were systematically killing coyotes, grizzly bears, and mountain lions to protect their livestock. With these natural predators gone, the populations of deer and rodents soared. Armies of these animals ate acorns, nibbled seedling roots, and put even more pressure on the young oaks.

The removal of oaks was not always seen as a loss, however. In fact, the U.S. government used to advise and even pay landowners to remove the "weed" oaks and convert the woodlands to cattle-grazing lands. Oaks were also removed to make room for crops. The early settlers, knowing that the presence of valley oaks was a sign of the richest soil, cleared extensive tracts of these native oaks. Tracts were also harvested for fuelwood and timber, especially during the mining era.

Riparian areas were particularly hard hit. It seems our streamside galleries are but faint shadows of their former junglelike majesty. Historical accounts show that there were once 775,000 acres of forests lining rivers in the Sacramento Valley, forming a band 300 yards wide along each side. Today, we have only 12,000 acres of these cool, parklike river forests left.

Since 1945, many more woodlands have been bulldozed to make room for sprawling suburbs. Ironically, cities named for their oaks, such as Thousand Oaks, Encino, and Sherman Oaks, are now left with only token examples of their natural heritage. The individual survivors (now real estate assets) must fight the ravages of asphalt, overwatering, grade changes, and pruning.

Even the woodlands that remain on the fringes of "civilization" have been altered. For the past 50 years we've routinely suppressed fires, even those that would have helped the woodland by clearing out the accumulated dead wood under the trees. By thwarting these "housekeeping" fires, we have allowed a large fuel load to build up, and encouraged the invasion of highly flammable pines and chaparral species such as manzanita and chamise. With these firebrands in the understory, a runaway fire would now most likely be hot enough to kill the mature oaks. Although they might well return someday, their interim loss would drastically affect the wildlife that depend on them.

WHAT'S IN IT FOR WILDLIFE?

The oak woodland's greatest calling card is its annual crop of acorns. Not every oak species bears a bumper crop each year, but because there are so many different types of oak, one or more is likely to be in "cycle" in a given year. Much of the community revolves around this nugget of high-caloric energy. In one relatively easy-to-gather package, an acorn gives an animal a large dose of energy. To get the same amount of nutrition from a diet of smaller seeds, an animal would have to spend a lot more time and energy collecting. The cost/benefit ratios are so good, in fact, that acorn-eaters have the luxury of being able to gather more acorns than they need at the moment. Dusky-footed woodrats cache them in their large stick homes; gray squirrels and Steller's and scrub jays bury them in the soil; chipmunks haul them underground; and acorn woodpeckers carve out holes for them in large storage trees called granaries. By storing acorns for later use, these animals can extend the harvest even when the trees and forest floor are empty.

Mule deer eat more than 300 acorns a day in the fall, storing them in a blanket of fat that will sustain them through the winter. Acorns are also important to band-tailed pigeons, plain titmice, Lewis' woodpeckers, wild turkeys, tree squirrels, bears, and quail. Even wood ducks from nearby wetlands will waddle overland to harvest the acorn crop.

Wood ducks aren't the only interlopers from other habitats. The guest list includes species from grasslands, chaparral, and needleleaf forests that adjoin and intermix with the woodlands. Anna's hummingbirds, orange-crowned warblers, brown towhees, and California quail are attracted to the chaparral shrubs that sometimes grow under the oaks. Shrubland rodents such as voles and pocket gophers come to feed on oak leaves, grass seeds, and berries and, in turn, attract predators such as hawks, owls, and weasels.

Come winter, many of the visitors are from out of state. Winters are normally mild and snow-free (except in the northernmost parts of the range), allowing wintering ruby-crowned kinglets and yellow-rumped warblers to find insects in the green foliage. Rufous-sided towhees, golden-crowned sparrows, white-crowned sparrows, and dark-eyed juncos also winter here, using the year-round foliage not only for foraging but also as a shield from the eyes of their predators. Mule deer wander downslope to find green grasses and succulent oak seedlings, while their predators, the mountain lions, descend in close pursuit.

Oaks also produce specialty items you might not think of. For instance, acorn woodpeckers drill "wells" in the trees in late winter, lapping the sugary sap that trickles out. Lawrence's goldfinch seeks out insects that cause "galls"—the round balls that you often see on oak twigs. Western bluebirds and phainopeplas make a special trip to feed on the berries of dwarf mistletoe, a tiny parasitic plant that infects and weakens oak trees.

Oaks offer wildlife a choice of nesting, feeding, hiding, and hunting sites in each of their different growth forms. Some species of oaks have light, open canopies that let sun in, while others are dense all the way to the ground. The bark of one species may be deeply fissured and full of

WILDLIFE LOCATOR CHART—OAK WOODLAND

	Feeds from Air	Feeds in Upper Canopy	Feeds in Lower Canopy	Feeds on Ground
Nests in Tree Canopy	Black-shouldered Kite Swainson's Hawk Red-tailed Hawk Golden Eagle Great Horned Owl Black-chinned Hummingbird Anna's Hummingbird Cassin's Kingbird Western Kingbird Loggerhead Shrike	Blue-gray Gnatcatcher Hepatic Tanager Western Tanager	Band-tailed Pigeon Bushtit Hutton's Vireo Phainopepla Black-throated Gray Warbler	Scrub Jay, Yellow-billed Magpie, Lesser Goldfinch, Lawrence's Goldfinch
Nests in Trunk Cavity	Western Screech-Owl Northern Pygmy-Owl Lewis' Woodpecker Dusky-capped Flycatcher Ash-throated Flycatcher Western Bluebird	Acorn Woodpecker	Nuttall's Woodpecker* White-breasted Nuthatch* Plain Titmouse House Wren (*Feeds on Trunk)	Wood Duck, Bewick's Wren, Western Gray Squirrel
Nests in Shrubs		Black-headed Grosbeak		Northern Mockingbird, Brown Towhee
Nests on Ground	Common Poorwill		Orange-crowned Warbler Virginia's Warbler	Wild Turkey, Montezuma Quail, California Quail, Lark Sparrow, Dusky-footed Woodrat, Mule Deer
Nests Beneath Ground or Debris	Western Pipistrelle Pallid Bat			Virginia Opossum, Merriam's Chipmunk, California Ground Squirrel, Botta's Pocket Gopher, California Pocket Mouse, Heermann's Kangaroo Rat, Brush Mouse, Deer Mouse, Gray Fox, Black Bear, Ringtail, Striped Skunk, Mountain Lion, Bobcat, Arboreal Salamander, Western Toad, Western Spadefoot, Gilbert's Skink, Western Rattlesnake, Gopher Snake

NUTTALL'S WOODPECKER

LEWIS' WOODPECKER

PLAIN TITMOUSE

HUTTON'S VIREO

WESTERN SPADEFOOT

BLACK-THROATED GRAY WARBLER

BLUE-GRAY GNATCATCHER

SCRUB JAY

insects, while another is markedly smooth and good for sap-drilling. A rich-rooted oak may tower, while oaks on poor sites hunker down like shrubs. This horizontal and vertical variety creates a wealth of different zones that animals can exploit without competing with one another.

When oaks are scattered in a grassy plain, the area is referred to as a savanna. Savannas offer the amenities of both grassland and forest—grasses for rodents to nibble and hide in, and perching trees from which predators may watch them. Other species gravitate to savannas to nest in the branches and feed on insects rising from the grasses. Look above to find soaring red-tailed hawks, Swainson's hawks, and golden eagles looking for scampering rodents such as California ground squirrels, white-footed mice, Merriam's chipmunks, and California pocket mice. Other savanna birds include loggerhead shrikes, Brewer's blackbirds, and yellow-billed magpies.

Closely spaced oaks provide thermal and escape cover for at least 55 California mammals, including gray fox, bobcat, and black bear. The tightly spaced canopies provide a continuous highway for arboreal roadsters such as fox and western gray squirrels. Dead oaks remain useful for many years, harboring cavity nesters such as raccoons and daytime roosters such as pallid bats. Once fallen, these oaks make good cover for deer mice and striped skunks, as well as moist haunts for reptiles and amphibians.

Acorn Woodpecker

Normally, acorn woodpeckers have all their bases covered. While the acorn crop is booming, they work as a flock to collect far more acorns than they can eat, storing the extras in communal warehouses, usually in dead trees. Each acorn is tapped point-first into a specially drilled hole in the trunk. For 2 months afterward, a few "custodial" woodpeckers remain at the trees, carefully tending the acorns. As the acorns dry and shrink, they must be moved to smaller, better-fitting holes. Nearly all will be moved at least once before they find permanent homes. This pantry will feed the woodpeckers throughout the winter and even through the middle of the next summer. By "thinking" ahead this way, the woodpeckers save themselves the hazards of migrating to a southern climate to find food.

Every now and then, however, even the conscientious acorn woodpecker makes a mistake. Sometimes, you'll find pebbles in the holes instead of acorns. Or you'll find empty holes in the walls of buildings where woodpeckers have hammered in acorn after acorn, only to have them slip through and pile up on the floor inside. The woodpeckers also use the desiccation cracks of telephone poles as a larder. When rains moisten the pole, the wood sometimes swells, breaking the acorns like a nutcracker. In dry weather, the cracks might open up, dropping the acorns all at once. Luckily, these instances are the exception, not the rule.

Look for acorn woodpeckers—in flocks of 3–12 birds, using their bill to twist acorns from twigs, or occasionally picking them from the ground. Their head is strikingly colored with a harlequin pattern of black and white, and their rump is a bright white. Look for them clinging to trunks, where they may be excavating nests or storing and retrieving acorns. You may also see a group of woodpeckers flying from the tops of trees to capture moths and flies in the air, the way flycatchers do.

Length: 8–9½ inches.

Look for nest holes—1³/₅ inches in diameter and 12–60 feet up in the trunk of a dead tree. All the birds in a flock work to excavate the nest, which may take up to 3 months to complete. Incubating and raising the brood are also community affairs. The parents incubate for the first few days, and then share the job with 10 or more other birds. The helpers replace each other every 2–5 minutes, and, at the most, no bird has more than a 17-minute duty. Once the young hatch, they are fed 24–28 times an hour by the loyal flock. Woodpeckers may nest 2–3 times a year.

Look for storage trees—peppered with acorns; up to 50,000 have been found in a single tree! Their favorite oaks, in order of preference, seem to be black oak, valley oak, coast live oak, and blue oak. They prefer groves that have many different kinds of oak—as backup in case one of the species fails to produce in a given year. Other stored foods include almonds, pecans, walnuts, cherries, and insects. Alternate storage spots include old nest holes, cavities in trees, utility poles, and furrows in bark. Woodpeckers will also drill holes randomly on a trunk to drink sap.

Look for acorn shells—and insect remains on the ground beneath traditional feeding "anvils." Anvils are branches or stubs with a viselike crevice that holds the food in place while the woodpecker pecks it into pieces.

Listen for—a talkative "jacob, jacob" (also sounds like "crackup-crackup") given when two birds meet. The "aak-a-ak-a-ak" call is exchanged when tending birds replace each other at the nest. Calls are also used to defend the 10- to 15-acre territory that includes nest, roost, and acorn-laden oak groves. Many animals are interested in pirating the carefully collected crop, including Lewis' woodpeckers, Nuttall's woodpeckers, scrub jays, squirrels, and chipmunks. Their nest holes are also coveted and often usurped by starlings and bluebirds. Acorn woodpeckers rarely drum.

Striped Skunk

It's no wonder you frequently see (or smell) them strewn along the highway. Skunks aren't accustomed to rushing out of harm's way; in fact, when it comes to conflicts, the running shoe is usually on the other foot (or on all four of them). Most animals have learned to yield when they see the black and white of a skunk. These colors are worn by a special fraternity of animals that use a chemical spray to defend themselves. Animals react to these colors the way we react to the familiar shape and hue of a stop sign.

Skunk musk (a creamy yellow substance that glows in the dark) is produced in special glands on either side of the anus, and is sprayed through tiny nipples that protrude when the skunk lifts its tail. Their spray can't kill you, but it will leave your eyes tearing and your stomach turning.

Skunks will avoid spraying whenever they can. Like the fighting reflex in most animals, spraying is a last resort with drawbacks of its own for the skunk. Musk is physiologically expensive to produce, so skunks are hesitant to waste it. They must also be careful not to spray themselves because they are not immune to their own poison!

Before they fire, skunks issue plenty of warnings; they stamp their feet, shuffle backward, chatter, plume their tails dramatically, or even walk on their forepaws in a handstand. If the intruder still doesn't take the hint, the skunk raises its tail and curves its body into a "U" with the head and rear facing the enemy. Using special muscles, they are able to shoot up, down, or to the side, from one barrel or two. Up to 10 feet they are highly accurate, and can usually hit a large target as far away as 16 feet.

Look for striped skunks—waddling along woodland borders at dusk, and feeding on insects such as grasshoppers, beetles, and crickets in open areas at night. They also dig into beehives, squashing the enraged bees with their paws. By day they doze in fencerows, hollow trees, rock crevices, or abandoned burrows.

Length: Head and body, 13–18 inches. Tail, 7–10 inches.

Look for nests—in burrows 6–20 feet long (occasionally up to 50 feet) with several chambers. Dens may have as many as 5 entrances, each 8 inches in diameter. The skunk lines the nest chamber with a bushel of leaves, gathering them under its body and shuffling them along. Just before giving birth, the female may temporarily remove all the nesting material, perhaps to guard the young from being strangled in the grasses and leaves. Another threat to her offspring is their father; if the nest is left unattended, he may eat them.

Look for feeding signs—the ground may be pitted where the skunk was digging and rooting. When it eats eggs (such as those of turtles), it bites off one end and licks out the contents, leaving a mass of shells.

Look for tracks—5-toed, 1¼–2 inches long, and tapering toward the back. The prints are in a "shuffling" formation, with a stride of 4–6 inches.

Listen for—the hissing and teeth-clicking of an angry skunk.

Arboreal Salamander

Arboreal salamanders are built to climb. Their gear includes stout legs, a round, tapered tail that can wrap around twigs, and toes that are broadened at the tip for traction. These toes are lined with blood sinuses, allowing the salamander to use them for breathing—almost like gills. The rest of their skin is also permeable, and they can absorb oxygen directly into their bloodstream as long as a thin coat of water surrounds them. This same film is also their main source of drinking water, which is absorbed rather than sipped. Even common smells reach these lungless salamanders in a watery form; a groove from their lips to their nostrils delivers a steady stream of waterborne aromas that tell them about their surroundings.

A lack of normal lungs has not robbed this salamander of an auditory repertoire, however. When surprised in its hiding spot, the arboreal salamander makes a mouselike squeak by contracting its throat to force air out through its jaws and nostrils. If this warning is not heeded, the salamander will stand up on its tiptoes, lower its head, and wave its lifted tail at the enemy. This is the salamander's way of cutting its losses. If the predator strikes at the moving bait, the tail breaks off easily from the rest of the body. A foul-smelling liquid oozes from its surface, usually curbing the predator's appetite and allowing the torso to get away unscathed. A new tail—essential for climbing and balance—will grow back shortly.

Look for arboreal salamanders—under logs, stumps, stones, bark, boards, or on the ground surface after the first fall or winter rains. As long as conditions remain moist, they will be active throughout winter and ready to breed again in early spring. When the ground starts to dry up in early summer, the salamanders retreat to moist chambers in rotten logs, in hollow trees, or under the ground. As many as 35 salamanders have been found in communal retreats. Along the coast they are associated with coast live oaks, and in the Sierra Nevada they are found in forests of interior and black oaks and Digger and ponderosa pines. They can darken the color of their skin automatically, which helps them absorb more warmth from the sun.

Length: 4¼–7¼ inches.

Eggs are enclosed—in rotting logs, tree cavities (especially oaks), or underground burrows. The female attaches the grapelike masses of 12–19 eggs to the roof of the cavity with slender, jellylike stalks. She tends the eggs for 3–4 months, moistening them with fluids from her skin and bladder. Without her care, the eggs would soon mold and spoil.

Listen for—a mouselike squeak when the salamander is alarmed.

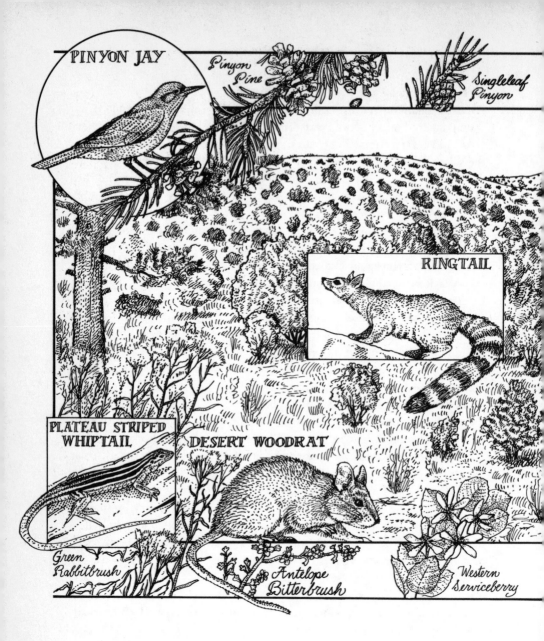

PINYON JAY

Pinyon
Pine

Singleleaf
Pinyon

RINGTAIL

PLATEAU STRIPED
WHIPTAIL

DESERT WOODRAT

Green
Rabbitbrush

Antelope
Bitterbrush

Western
Serviceberry

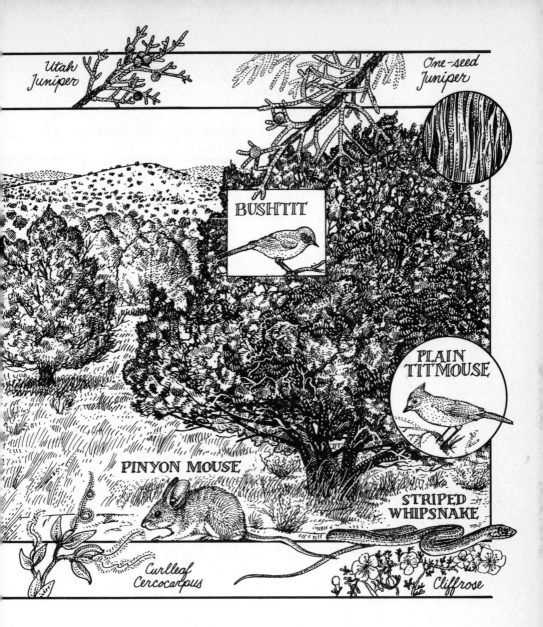

Utah Juniper

One-seed Juniper

BUSHTIT

PLAIN TITMOUSE

PINYON MOUSE

STRIPED WHIPSNAKE

Curlleaf Cercocarpus

Cliffrose

Pinyon-Juniper Woodland

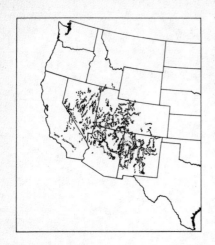

WHERE TO SEE THIS HABITAT:

Arizona: Apache-Sitgreaves, Coconino, Coronado, Kaibab, Prescott, and Tonto national forests; Canyon de Chelly National Monument; Grand Canyon National Park
California: Clear Lake National Wildlife Refuge; Eastern Mojave Recreation Land
Nevada: Desert National Wildlife Refuge; Humboldt and Toiyabe national forests; Sheldon National Antelope Refuge
New Mexico: Bosque, Cibola, Gila, Lincoln, and Santa Fe national forests; Del Apache, Las Vegas, and Sevilleta national wildlife refuges
Oregon: Carson, Deschutes and Ochoco national forests; Crooked River National Grassland
Utah: Arches, Bryce Canyon, Canyonlands, and Zion national parks; Ashley, Dixie, Fishlake, and Manti-La Sal national forests

Pinyon-Juniper Woodland

BEGINNINGS

There's something very appealing about the pygmy woodlands of the Great Basin and the Colorado Plateau. Native cultures were headquartered here for centuries before the Europeans arrived, finding the mix of small trees, grasses, forbs, and shrubs to be a lucrative hunting and foraging ground. In Africa, a similar woodland and savanna setting was home to the very earliest tribes of humans. In modern days, we still plant trees and shrubs around our homes to try to create the kind of shade-and-sun mixture found naturally in the pinyon-juniper woodland.

Pinyon pines and junipers are usually less than 30 and no more than 50 feet tall, with short, twisted trunks and wide, spreading crowns. You can find them growing in the zone just above grasslands and sagebrush and just below ponderosa pines. In the lower reaches of this zone, where the competition for moisture can be fierce, the trees are widely spaced, and their crowns rarely touch. Their compact form, scalelike leaves (juniper), and low numbers of needles per bundle (pinyon) are designed to cut down on the amount of surface area whipped by moisture-robbing winds. As you climb to the upper fringes of the pinyon-juniper zone (or wherever moisture becomes more abundant), you'll find the trees growing closer together, with less of an understory beneath them.

Despite a challenging environment, these trees have actually begun to expand their range over parts of the West, invading meadows and seeding into the grassy spaces between the trees. According to one theory, cattle may have encouraged the invasion by grazing away the grass competitors and freeing up new sources of soil moisture. Others attribute the change to a climatic cycle or to the suppression of fires that used to periodically kill the seedlings in meadows. Whatever the reason, the success of such an invasion depends first and foremost on a way to get seeds into new areas.

Here in the pinyon-juniper woodland, the trees, birds, and mammals have coevolved, creating some of the most fascinating plant-animal relationships in the West.

HOW TO ENTICE A PINYON JAY

In an arid climate, where the upper layers of soil dry out quickly (even after a rain), moist germination sites are hard to come by. One response is to grow a seed that is large enough and packed with enough "fuel" to help the tiny rootlet get down to water as quickly as possible. Pinyons do indeed have a large seed, but their adaptations don't stop there. Rather than merely dropping these heavy seeds beneath the parent plant where they will be forced to compete for moisture, the pinyon pine has evolved "enticer" traits to get animals and birds to carry the nuts away.

First of all, a pinyon nut is a feast worth searching for. Each nut contains 60 percent fat and packs away a whopping number of calories per ounce. Secondly, because the cones are tilted up and the cone scales are short and spineless, the seeds are easy for the birds to find and extract. Their wingless, streamlined shape fits comfortably in a bird's throat pouch, enabling the bird to conveniently transport the seeds to caching sites where seeds are buried for the coming winter.

Pinyon nuts are so easy to love, in fact, that their fans eat most of the seed crop in a normal year, leaving little for tree reproduction. Luckily, the pinyon pines have evolved a strategy to make sure that some of their seeds will be spared. Every few years, the trees in a given locale will produce a bumper crop of cones, swamping the birds and mammals with more than they can eat. Some of these seeds sprout where they land, and others come up in clumps from caches that were never retrieved.

Junipers have similar cycles of bumper crops. One such crop in Arizona yielded 20,000 berries per cubic meter of foliage! To attract as many consumers as possible, the junipers advertise their berries with a bright blue or red color, and then retain them on the tree throughout the winter. A single juniper berry rewards its harvester with 315 calories worth of energy. In return, the animal's digestive juices help dissolve the seeds' protective coat so that they are ready to germinate as soon as they're "planted" (complete with built-in manure). Berries that simply fall and rot beneath their parents are not nearly as likely to sprout.

Animal distributors of pinyon nuts and juniper berries have in turn developed physical and behavioral adaptations that make them better seed transporters. Clark's nutcrackers have a special pouch in front of and below their tongue in which they can carry up to 90 seeds at a time. In 100 days,

CHARACTERISTIC PLANTS:

Trees, Shrubs, and Vines:

alligator juniper
antelope bitterbrush
apache plume
banana yucca
big sagebrush
blackbrush
California juniper
candelabra cactus
canyon live oak
ceanothuses
cercocarpuses (mountain mahogany)
chamise
cliffrose
creambush oceanspray
curlleaf cercocarpus
Emory oak
European red elder
four-wing saltbush
Gambel oak
gray oak
Jeffrey pine
Mohave yucca
Mormon tea
one-seed juniper
Parry nolina
pinyon pine
ponderosa pine
redshank
Rocky Mountain juniper
Rocky Mountain maple
rubber rabbitbrush
shadscale
shrub live oak
singleleaf pinyon
skunkbrush
snakeweed
snowberries
snowbrush ceanothus
Utah juniper
wax currant
western juniper
western serviceberry

Herbaceous Plants:

arrowleaf balsamroot
bluebunch wheatgrass
blue grama
bottlebrush squirreltail
buckwheats
cheatgrass brome
curlycup gumweed
desert needlegrass
fleabanes
galleta grass
hairy golden aster
Idaho fescue
Indian ricegrass
muttongrass
needle-and-thread
New Mexican feathergrass
pinnate tansymustard
prairie sunflower
pricklypear cactus
red threeawn
Russian thistle
scarlet globemallow
secunda bluegrass
side-oats grama
spike fescue
western wheatgrass
wild four-o'clock
yarrow

Western Serviceberry

one bird can cache as many as 33,000 seeds. Pinyon jays have an expandable esophagus that can hold 56 seeds, allowing an entire flock of these birds (50–500) to cache an estimated 4.5 million seeds in a good year.

When flocking birds such as American robins and bluebirds leave the woodlands to search for water, they may fly over a variety of habitats, excreting their cargo of digested berries along the way. These species have an important role in restocking juniper woodlands that have been destroyed and converted to grazing lands. Mammals that help distribute pinyon seeds in caches or droppings include Abert's squirrel, pinyon mice, woodrats, rock squirrels, chipmunks, and black bears.

WHAT'S IN IT FOR WILDLIFE?

Because pinyon-juniper woodlands are within "commuting" distance of a wide variety of habitats, it's not unusual to find pinyon-juniper animals running alongside those of sagebrush shrublands, grasslands, chaparral, needleleaf forests, or even deserts. This mosaic of types presents mobile wildlife with excellent food and cover options. Within the woodland itself, the tree, shrub, and herb layers provide enough vertical diversity to allow species to nest and feed in various layers without competing for the same sites.

Subtle differences between junipers and pinyon pines also present wildlife with options. Pinyon pines, for instance, may be preferred by birds that eat foliage insects because they have more surface area per tree for the birds to work on. Pinyon pine is also the tree of choice for snag nesters and trunk feeders because its branches break off easily, giving insects and fungi an easy way to enter and kill the tree. Once it's dead, a pinyon snag may remain standing for up to ten years, developing a soft interior that woodpeckers prefer. Juniper snags, on the other hand, remain hard and difficult to excavate. Junipers are often favored, however, by birds that build branch nests, such as black-throated gray warblers and black-chinned hummingbirds. Many other species use the stringy bark of juniper to line their nests.

The openings in woodlands are as important to wildlife as the scattered trees. Early spring grasses green up first in these openings, providing vital nutrition for winter-weary deer, rabbits, and other herbivores. Insects, grass seeds, and mushrooms attract burrowing rodents and ground-feeding birds. Hawks and owls that would normally need to travel to find a meadow can often hunt right from the same tree they nest and roost in. Also, don't forget to glance up above the tree canopies to find birds of prey circling for their dinners. At any moment, a rodent's bold dash to an entrance hole might be interrupted by the talons of a Swainson's, red-tailed, or ferruginous hawk, a golden eagle, or a prairie falcon.

As invading trees begin to close up the woodland overstory, the undergrowth starts to dwindle. Still, these dense woodlands are used by larger animals such as mule deer and elk for thermal and hiding cover. Even when crowded, these trees continue to produce the woodland's most popular attractions: energy-rich pinyon nuts and juniper berries.

Trees full of fruits attract noisy flocks of juncos, bluebirds, robins, sparrows, and jays in the winter months, many of which have migrated from northern forests. In warmer parts of the pinyon-juniper range, the winters are mild enough to support insects that flycatchers, warblers, wrens, and gnatcatchers relish. Mountain species such as Clark's nutcrackers, Steller's jays, and rosy finches may make a vertical migration down the mountain when snows cover their food sources.

Mammals also commute to the low-elevation pinyon-juniper woodlands as winter closes in. Black bears and Abert's squirrels come down in the fall to stock up on nuts and berries. Elk and mule deer find shelter as well as emergency browse. Hot on their trail are mountain lions and coyotes, hoping to snare a malnourished yearling or an old, slow member of the herd. Occasionally, they scare a wintering black-tailed jackrabbit from beneath a shrub, then quickly run it down.

In addition to the seasonal guests, there are many permanent residents that are closely associated with the pinyon-juniper habitat. The core group of birds includes pinyon jay, plain titmouse, bushtit, Bewick's wren, and black-throated gray warbler. Also common in these woodlands are Virginia's warblers, blue-gray gnatcatchers, ash-throated flycatchers, scrub jays, and gray vireos.

Mammals both large and small also find year-round food and lodging in the woodlands. Pronghorn graze at the edges where the woodland gives way to open areas. Mountain sheep may appear in high, rimrock areas that have plenty of escape cover but also happen to support pinyons and junipers. Mammal predators such as bobcats, foxes, long-tailed weasels, badgers, and ringtails are attracted by the booming rodent population.

The two most characteristic small rodents are desert woodrats and pinyon mice. Woodrat nests, piled around the stump of a tree or in a rock crevice, hold up to ten bushels of twigs, leaves, and debris—including bones, cactus, deer hide, human trash and treasure, and a cache of pinyon nuts and juniper berries. Pinyon mice build their nests in the hollow trunks of junipers, which they may climb to find berries. Also look for the tracks of brush mice in the dust, disappearing when they reach the base of a tree they've used for a getaway route. The scaled bark at the base of the tree may be the work of porcupines hungry for the sweet inner layer just below.

Holes in the ground may lead to the underground lairs of pocket gophers, California ground squirrels, rock squirrels, golden-mantled ground squirrels, kangaroo rats, and Colorado and least chipmunks.

Warm temperatures, abundant rock crevices and other hiding places make the woodlands especially attractive to reptiles. The striped whipsnake speeds along the ground with its head held high in search of rodents. Colorado checkered whiptails creep close to the ground, easily disarming a cantankerous scorpion. The western spadefoot (a toad) remains dormant deep in the ground during the driest parts of the summer, emerging when enough collected water is available for breeding and laying eggs. Other amphibians are similarly restricted to watery areas.

Pinyon Jay

There may be as many as 500 dark-blue pinyon jays combing all corners of the woodland at once. Nearly half of the birds will be walking or hopping along the ground, probing with their bill for pine seeds or insects. Others will be hammering into downed logs, poking into trunks, or flaking away bark to expose food. Still others will be hanging chickadee-fashion from cones, or tearing into tender new growth at the tips of the branches.

The flock drifts through the woods as it feeds, covering 1 mile an hour, or as many as 13 miles in a day. All the birds may decide to move at once, or they may travel in shifts, one group flying over another in leapfrog fashion. Each jaunt to a new site is usually about a quarter of a mile.

Longer flights of 1–2 miles are initiated by a few individuals that fly up to the branches and begin a sharp, loud "krawking." This seems to be contagious, and soon most of the flock is up in the branches calling. Within a few minutes, they take to the air in a long, black stream that rolls and swirls as it flies. The members in the front of the flock then peel off and return to the point in the forest where they started. After rousing some remaining jays in the trees, they will fly off after them. Meanwhile, the new front members of the flock start to peel off and turn back, while the middle group assumes the lead. The flock circulates this way a few times until the whole flock moves forward, eventually reaching a feeding or watering site 1–2 miles away.

Birds that flock this close together have had to override their innate tendency to be aggressive toward one another. Watch a flock for a while, especially on small, rich food sites where they may literally be landing on top of one another. You'll see some brief aggressive encounters, but not nearly what you would expect from a less social species. For the pinyon jay, the dividends of social behavior are more than worth the occasional inconvenience of cramped living.

Flock feeding is a systematic way to exploit a limited, unpredictable,

BLACK-THROATED GRAY WARBLER

WESTERN SCREECH-OWL

BLACK-CHINNED HUMMINGBIRD

GRAY VIREO

VIRGINIA'S WARBLER

TREE LIZARD

ASH-THROATED FLYCATCHER

SWAINSON'S HAWK

WILDLIFE LOCATOR CHART—PINYON-JUNIPER WOODLAND

	Feeds from Air	Feeds in Upper Canopy	Feeds in Lower Canopy	Feeds on Ground
Nests in Tree Canopy	Cooper's Hawk Swainson's Hawk Red-tailed Hawk Ferruginous Hawk Golden Eagle Great Horned Owl Black-chinned Hummingbird American Redstart	Pinyon Jay Clark's Nutcracker Blue-gray Gnatcatcher	Band-tailed Pigeon Bushtit Black-throated Gray Warbler Scott's Oriole American Goldfinch	Bald Eagle, Mourning Dove, Steller's Jay, Scrub Jay, American Robin, Chipping Sparrow, House Finch, Abert's Squirrel
Nests in Trunk Cavity	American Kestrel Western Screech-Owl Ash-throated Flycatcher		Ladder-backed Woodpecker (Feeds on Trunk) Black-capped Chickadee Plain Titmouse	Common Raven, Bewick's Wren, Mountain Bluebird, Pinyon Mouse
Nests on Shrubs	Gray Flycatcher Loggerhead Shrike	Black-headed Grosbeak	Gray Vireo Black-throated Sparrow	Northern Mockingbird Brown Towhee White-crowned Sparrow
Nests on Ground	Prairie Falcon Common Poorwill Townsend's Solitaire		Virginia's Warbler	Scaled Quail, Gambel's Quail, Rosy Finch, Mule Deer, Pronghorn, Mountain Sheep
Nests Beneath Ground or Debris				Nuttall's Cottontail, Black-tailed Jackrabbit, Cliff Chipmunk, Colorado Chipmunk, Rock Squirrel, California Ground Squirrel, Rock Pocket Mouse, Brush Mouse, Rock Mouse, Bushy-tailed Woodrat, Desert Woodrat, Mexican Woodrat, Coyote, Gray Fox, Black Bear, Ringtail, Long-tailed Weasel, Mountain Lion, Bobcat, Colorado Checkered Whiptail, Desert Grassland Whiptail, Plateau Striped Whiptail, Collared Lizard, Many-lined Skink, Short-horned Lizard, Sagebrush Lizard, Eastern Fence Lizard, Side-blotched Lizard, Tree Lizard, Great Basin Rattlesnake, Striped Racer

and seasonal food supply such as pinyon pine seeds. Because it has so many members, a flock can spread out and find good feeding sites that might be too widely scattered for a single jay to find on its own. Also, the 4–12 sentinels posted high in the trees take care of surveillance so the rest of the flock can concentrate on feeding. When a predator approaches, the sentinels issue a loud, rhythmic "krawk-krawk-krawk," which sends all the jays scurrying for the upper branches. This system of food finding and predator warning works so well that other species often join the jay flocks to take advantage of it. Some common jay associates include starlings, downy woodpeckers, hairy woodpeckers, northern flickers, and Clark's nutcrackers.

Look for pinyon jays—foraging, flying, and roosting in pinyon-juniper or ponderosa pine forests. All members of the flock assemble for the main foraging feast of the year—the pinyon pine seed ripening in August. The jays pick all the seeds from a cone, and instead of eating them on the spot, they stuff several in their throat and carry them to communal caching sites. Using their feet and bills to scratch away the litter, they bury their throatful of seeds near the trunk of a tree, usually on the south side. Come winter, this placement will make it easier for the jays to dig up their treasures. Snows are likely to be lightest here, not only because of the umbrella of tree boughs, but because the sun melts the south side of a tree first. When cone crops fail, flocks may be forced to travel hundreds of miles away from traditional home ranges.

Length: 9–11¾ inches.

Look for nests—bulky platforms of twigs with a smaller cup in the center built of plant fibers, rootlets, paper, wool, and hair. The nests are placed on the warmer, south side of the tree, in branches of pinyons, junipers, and scrub oaks, usually 3–20 feet up (higher in ponderosa pines). A hundred birds may nest in a colony, but each tree holds only one nest.

Look for courting birds—pairing up and separating from the flock for part of the day toward the end of winter. They establish and strengthen pair bonds through a series of rituals, including a silent food transfer, a noisy begging for food, a presentation of nest-building materials, and shopping for a courtship site. The pair returns to the main flock for feeding, for roosting, or when the danger or movement call is issued. After the young leave the nest, the flock breaks up into smaller groups of fledglings and their parents. Throughout the breeding season, the year-old, nonbreeding jays (which are gray instead of blue) form their own flock.

Look for feeding debris—torn-apart cones beneath pines. Seed-burying sites are usually close to traditional nesting grounds.

Listen for—the rhythmic "krawk-krawk-krawk" of a sentinel announcing a predator's presence. After repeating the call two or three times, the sentinel flies to within 10–15 feet of the intruder and continues to call while hopping from branch to branch. Eventually, up to 15 jays may leave the flock to gang up on the predator. These "mobbing" birds may harass a stubborn great horned owl for 45 minutes before it finally agrees to move. Feeding flocks are most noisy early in the morning when members are calling to one another. Courting and nest-building jays also keep in close voice contact. Their vocal repertoire includes cawing, mewing, chattering, and jaylike cries. Also characteristic is their high-pitched "caaaa," often quavering at the end like a laugh.

Desert Woodrat

The story is told of campers who emptied their pockets before crawling into their tent, only to find their coins and car keys missing the next morning. In their place were shreds of juniper bark, a piece of pricklypear cactus, and a pinecone. Luckily, the campers knew something about the habits of the famous "pack rats" of the Southwest. They were able to find their stolen loot amid a jumbled pile of bones and sticks wedged into a rocky crevice a short distance away.

Woodrats are compulsive collectors. But they don't actually "trade" items as we imagine; rather, they simply drop what they are carrying when they find something that looks more appealing. Everything they collect becomes part of their nest, which may be a large pyramid at the base of a cactus, shrub, or tree, or a stuffed-tight opening in a rocky ledge. This odd fortress serves as a protection against predators, foul weather, and the hot sun. An abandoned nest is usually rediscovered by another pack rat, and is thus kept in use for generations.

In the arid Southwest, nests are slow to break down, even after thousands of years! These ancient nests are invaluable to biologists who study the sticks, the stuffing, and the fecal matter to find out what kind of life was around when the nest was built. The American Indians also knew the value of woodrat nests. Each year, tribe members filled their baskets with rich pine nuts that the rats had assiduously collected.

Once you know where a woodrat's home is, you might watch it (at a binocular's distance) for signs of nesting activity. The young rats spend most of their first few weeks securely attached to their mother's teats. In fact, their incisors are flared out at top and bottom to form a perfect six-sided grip. This comes in handy when the female is forced to flee the nest. Instead of leaving her young at the mercy of snake, hawk, or owl, she escapes with them still firmly attached. She might even climb a tree or scramble up a rockface, faithfully toting her genetic investments along with her.

Look for desert woodrats—at night, scurrying about on the limbs of shrubs, over rock surfaces, and along well-worn trails. They are punctual and predictable, so you have a good chance of seeing them if you wait by one of their favorite trails. During these forays, they feed on succulent herbs, cactus joints, stems, twigs, tender bark, seeds, or berries. They may bring some of the food back to their nest and dry it out on the horizontal rack of sticks and bones that forms the floor of their home. They also collect human artifacts on these excursions—including everything from socks to shotgun shells. Shiny objects seem to be most appealing.

Length: Head and body, 5⁴/₅–7 inches. Tail, 4¹/₃–6 ²/₅ inches.

Look for nests—conspicuous collections of sticks, bones, cactus joints, and other debris wedged into a cliff crevice, a ledge on a rocky outcrop, or breaks in a pile of fallen boulders. This "stuffing" serves to discourage digging predators, such as coyotes. Inside there is an 8-inch-wide cup of softer material that is used as a nursery. From 1 to 6 young may be born, but usually only 4 have a good chance of surviving because the mother has only 4 nipples. Nests may also be built up around the abandoned nests of ground squirrels or kangaroo rats.

Look for runways—well-worn ruts radiating from the nest out into the grasses and shrubs. They are narrower than rabbit trails and usually marked by the tracks of last night's excursions.

Listen as—they drum their hind feet on the ground or vibrate their tail in the dry vegetation—two ways in which they announce themselves.

Plateau Striped Whiptail

The researchers who first collected this lizard for study thought perhaps they'd made a mistake. Although they had collected them randomly, every one of their samples was female! They collected again and again, but each time the samples turned out all-female. The real test came when these captive females began to reproduce *without access to male lizards* and their offspring were also all females. After three or four generations, the results were conclusive; plateau striped whiptails are a unisexual species that reproduces via parthenogenesis, commonly known as virgin birth.

Hundreds of studies later, the phenomenon is not quite as puzzling as it once was. Twenty-four different species of reptiles have been found to be all-female or to have portions of their population that are all-female. In the case of the plateau striped whiptail, researchers speculate that the all-female species came about after two "normal" species of lizards (i.e., having both males and females) mated with one another.

Nearly every one of their offspring was probably sterile, however, by virtue of the fact that the parents were from two separate species (just as mules, the offspring of horses and donkeys, are sterile). Eventually, one female hybrid was born with the capacity for virgin birth. Instead of having eggs that had only one set of chromosomes waiting for a male "donation," she produced eggs with a full complement of chromosomes—her own. She was thus able to pass her adaptations on to a carbon-copy offspring, who in turn passed them on again.

Because the hybrid female came from two species of slightly different habitats, she and her offspring were endowed with the adaptations to both. For this reason, the hybrids did well in transitional or marginal habitats. Today, for instance, plateau striped whiptails are most prevalent at the margins of pinyon-juniper forests, where junipers blend into grasslands.

The advantage of virgin birth is that the genetic "recipe" of adaptations to this environment is preserved and replicated in each member of the population. The other advantage is that it takes only one female to start a whole new population. This way, if a female finds a preferred habitat, she can colonize it without waiting for a male to come along. Also, because each member of the population can produce young, the rate of reproduction is at least twice that of male-female populations.

What these populations lack, however, is a rapid mechanism for adjusting to sudden changes. Male-female pairing, in which genes from two individuals are combined, has a better chance of producing a genetic breakthrough—an adaptation that would allow the offspring to survive in new conditions. While this kind of breakthrough is possible in all-female populations, it would take much longer to occur. For the time being, however, the all-female strategy seems to be working quite well for the whiptails of the pinyon-juniper woodland.

Look for plateau striped whiptails—in early morning, pausing between their frenzied hunting forays to bask in patches of sunlight. This high-strung lifestyle gives them a slightly higher metabolic rate and body temperature than that of other lizards, making it important for them to cool down in the shade occasionally. Whiptails often dig for their dinners, flipping over sticks and tearing into termite castles with their forefeet. They also dig their own burrows to hibernate, often choosing a site beneath a rock so that rain can't cave in the roof.

Length: 8-10¾ inches.

Eggs are underground—buried in soft soil or in termite castles.

Look for "mating" whiptails—assuming postures that are identical to those used in male-female mating. One female slides her tail beneath the other's and bends her body into a donut shape. This may help to synchronize ovulation and egg laying, as well as influence how often eggs are laid and how many clutches are laid in a season. In captivity, females caged together always laid more clutches than those housed alone.

Quaking Aspen

Mountain Alder

WARBLING VIREO

MOOSE

LONG-TAILED WEASEL

TIGER SALAMANDER

Common Snowberry

Kinnikinnik

Chokecherry

Lodgepole Pine

Wood's Rose

NORTHERN GOSHAWK

YELLOW-BELLIED SAPSUCKER

RUFFED GROUSE

Silvery Lupine

SHORT-HORNED LIZARD

Showy Fleabane

Blue Columbine

Aspen Forest

WHERE TO SEE THIS HABITAT:

Arizona: Kaibab National Forest
California: Inyo and Tahoe national forests
Colorado: Arapaho, Grand Mesa-Uncompahgre, Gunnison, Pike, Routt, San Juan, and White River national forests; Rocky Mountain National Park
Idaho: Caribou National Forest
Montana: Glacier National Park; Lewis and Clark National Forest
Nevada: Humboldt and Toiyabe national forests; Sheldon National Antelope Refuge
New Mexico: Cibola National Forest
North Dakota: Lostwood National Wildlife Refuge
Utah: Cache, Fishlake, Manti-La Sal, and Uinta national forests
Wyoming: Medicine Bow National Forest

Aspen Forest

BEGINNINGS

Aspens are often called phoenix trees, because, like the mythical bird, they seem to rise up from the ashes of destruction. Shortly after a forest falls to fire, logging, insect attack, or avalanche, the bare ground grows green again with aspen sprouts—as many as 100,000 per acre. This rebirth is possible because the aspen roots belowground remain alive, and are genetically programmed to take advantage of openings in the forest. When a tree dies, growing points on the roots come to life, producing replacement suckers (clones) that head straight for the sun. Each new sucker is nourished by the already established root network, and thus has an edge over other tree seedlings that must rely on their own spindly rootlets.

Besides healing the scars of forest devastation, aspens also invade rocky, wet, or poor-soil sites that are unsuitable for most other trees' seedlings. Although they are primarily associated with mid-elevations (below lodgepole forests), aspens may be found anywhere from lowland river corridors to cold subalpine meadow borders. This wide range of growing sites puts them in contact with an assorted crew of associates, including willows, alders, black and narrowleaf cottonwoods, lodgepole pine, Jeffrey pine, ponderosa pine, red fir, white fir, subalpine fir, Douglas-fir, and Engelmann spruce. Because of this wide range and mixed company, their understories differ from place to place. Some ubiquitous shrubs to look for are snowberries, western serviceberry, chokecherry, and kinnikinnik.

PASSING THE BATON

Although aspens may lead the pack in the beginning of the growing race, they are usually outdistanced by longer-lived, shade-tolerant needleleaf trees. You can often see these "climax" trees—e.g., Douglas-fir, Engelmann spruce, or subalpine fir—growing in the understory and creating a two-tiered forest. Aspens actually help their successors by shading the ground and fertilizing it with a mulch of rapidly decaying leaves. Ironically, the aspen's own sun-loving seedlings are at a disadvantage in this shady, litter-laden forest.

In some areas, however, needleleaf trees are the ones at a disadvantage. The aspen forest may be too far from a needleleaf seed source, or the soil may be too dry, wet, or frost-prone for needleleaf seedlings to take root. In these cases, the aspen suckers have an uncontested shot at the openings created when one or two larger aspens fall. In these stable communities, aspen may reign for as long as 1,000 years, suckering again and again. Each stem that arises from the parent root network is a genetic duplicate of its parent and of the other suckered trees around it. Large clones of single-sex aspen may cover as many as 100 acres (though they are usually much smaller), and could actually be considered one organism.

The bright, shivering leaves of quaking aspen are a welcome counterpoint to the solemn greens of the western pines, spruces, and firs. In the fall, their brilliant yellow-to-orange fireworks flicker like candles on the slopes. This variety is appreciated not only by humans but by wildlife as well.

WHAT'S IN IT FOR WILDLIFE?

After a hike through a hot, drowsy meadow, the darkness of an aspen forest beckons. Step inside, and you'll notice that the air is cooler, the ground moister, the vegetation more layered, and the insects thicker than they were in the meadow. Now you know why you are likely to see and hear more wildlife here than in surrounding habitats. Unlike conifer canopies that are closed and shaded throughout the year, aspen canopies let in more sun (especially when bare in spring and fall) and encourage lush undergrowth. This, in turn, provides not only food but also valuable cover.

Grasses, forbs, and shrubs of various heights camouflage the ground and low shrub nests of birds such as hermit thrush, Townsend's solitaire, dark-eyed junco, white-crowned and Lincoln's sparrows, veery, ovenbird, common nighthawk, and MacGillivray's and orange-crowned warblers. The upper canopy provides camouflaged nesting sites for western wood-pewees, American robins, warbling vireos, yellow-rumped warblers, western tanagers, Cassin's finches, and least and dusky flycatchers. Since these birds like to forage in the open, their nests are often found at the edge of aspen habitat, especially where it opens into a meadow or wetland area.

Female elk seek the seclusion of aspen forests to give birth to their calves. Blue and ruffed grouse also retire to the aspens when nesting and when displaying in the fall. White-tailed and mule deer often disappear into a shimmering, leafy thicket, especially during hunting season. When mixed with needleleaf trees, the aspens are an even more effective screen.

CHARACTERISTIC PLANTS:

Trees and Shrubs:
alders
antelope bitterbrush
Bebb willow
black cottonwood
Canada buffaloberry
chokecherry
common juniper
creeping Oregon
   grape
curlleaf cercocarpus
Douglas-fir
Engelmann spruce
highbush cranberry
kinnikinnik
limber honeysuckle
lodgepole pine
Mexican pinyon
mooseberry
mountain-lover
narrowleaf cotton-
   wood
paper birch

ponderosa pine
quaking aspen
red-osier dogwood
Rocky Mountain
   maple
roses
scarlet elder
snowberries
subalpine fir
western serviceberry
white fir
willows
Wood's rose

Herbaceous Plants:
American licorice
American vetch
blue columbine
bluegrasses
blue wildrye
bracken fern

bromegrasses
common arrowhead
cow parsnip
Fendler's meadowrue
Gray's lousewort
Gunnison's mariposa
orange sneezeweed
prairie junegrass
purple onion-grass
Richardson's
   geranium
sedges
showy fleabane
silvery lupine
slender wheatgrass
sweetscented bedstraw
Thurber fescue
whitestem gooseberry
wild strawberry
yarrow

Besides good cover, aspen forests offer wildlife a plethora of foods from treetop to grass root. Elk stop here to fuel up during their spring and fall migrations up and down the mountain, leaving browsing signs as high as their heads will reach. White-tailed and mule deer eat the tender leaves and sprouts in summer, then gorge themselves on fallen leaves in the fall. In winter, lower-elevation aspens become important emergency food for elk, mule deer, and snowshoe hare. Even the snow-tunneling mice and voles get into the browsing act; look for their brown gnawing scars on the lower trunks of aspens. Ruffed grouse, which depend on aspen buds and catkins in the spring, move to larger trees in the winter, feeding mainly on the male floral buds. These larger trees may also contain a porcupine, swaying in the breeze as it nibbles the sweet inner bark of the aspen. Black bears may climb the same trees (leaving claw marks on the smooth trunk) to reach buds, catkins, or birds' nests full of eggs. In the fall, they may strip berries from bushes beneath the aspen.

The ground layer of succulent greenery under aspen boughs provides a great variety of side dishes, attracting grazers such as elk, western jumping mice, snowshoe hares, and northern pocket gophers. Seedeaters such as deer mice, western jumping mice, least chipmunks, red squirrels, and southern red-backed voles are especially common where aspens are mixed with needleleaf trees. These rodents provide northern goshawks, great horned owls, long-tailed weasels, and other predators with plenty of action.

Insects also find plenty to eat in the grassy layer beneath parklike stands of aspen. They in turn attract blue and ruffed grouse females and their protein-hungry chicks, as well as airborne insect hunters such as hoary bats, swifts, tree swallows, and purple martins. Short-horned lizards gravitate to these open spots in the morning, collecting the sun they need to start their "engines." In the shadier spots, tiger salamanders and western toads lay low, soaking in the moisture under the leaves and fallen logs. Also abundant, but secretive, are the insect-eating dusky and masked shrews.

Even the underground is a popular place in an aspen forest. The deep snowpacks typical of this habitat protect the soil from freezing, and allow burrowing to continue all winter. When the snow melts, look for the telltale soil castings of the northern pocket gopher (see Northern Pocket Gopher, page 125).

Aspens are short-lived species, maturing in only 30 years and falling prey to competition, insects, and diseases in as little as 50 years. In mature and overmature aspen stands, 6–20 percent of the standing trees are dead. These softening snags are easy for woodpeckers to excavate, and are usually full of juicy insects busy breaking down the wood. Even trees that are hard on the outside may be soft inside with heartrot. These "hard snags" make good denning trees for cavity nesters such as sapsuckers, woodpeckers, northern flickers, chickadees, nuthatches, bluebirds, house wrens, owls, flycatchers, swallows, and flying squirrels. Of these, only the woodpeckers, sapsuckers, flickers, chickadees, and nuthatches are capable of excavating their own holes; the rest must scramble to occupy the abandoned nests of these important "pathfinder" species. Sapsuckers and downy and hairy woodpeckers seem to prefer aspens over other trees for nest sites.

When the old aspen stands are suddenly removed by fire or harvesting, young, fast-growing aspens sprout up in "dog-hair" thickets. For several years, the most nutritious parts of the tree are within easy reach of moose, elk, and mule deer. Shrub-nesters such as flycatchers, sparrows, warblers, and cuckoos suddenly have their pick of well-protected sites. These smaller trees are also important to beavers, which seem to prefer 2-inch-diameter stems for their dam and lodge construction.

Yellow-bellied Sapsucker*

In a world overrun with leaf-eating, nut-cracking, twig-chomping, bark-chewing organisms, the sap-lapping sapsucker has found a unique and relatively untapped food source in the aspen forest. Sap is the lifeblood of the tree, carrying sugars from the leaves to the rest of the tree. To tap this lifeblood, the sapsucker drills tiny wells in the bark, analogous to the buckets we humans attach to sugar maple trees. Sap continues to run into these wells for several days, allowing the sapsucker to come back for seconds.

Unlike the industrial-strength "jackhammers" of wood-boring wood-peckers, the bill of the sapsucker is more delicately structured. The tongue, instead of being long and covered with spines, is short and fringed with hairs that lap up the sap from the wells. Sapsuckers also help themselves to the sugary, delicate cambium layer just beneath the tree's bark. The cells in this layer are long and tubular; together they make up the "veins" of the tree's circulatory system. If the sapsucker bores a ring of holes around the tree, there is a chance that these veins could be girdled, thus cutting off food supplies to the roots. Luckily, most groupings of sapsucker holes appear on only one side of the tree.

Besides sipping sap and scraping cambium, sapsuckers also scour the surface of the bark for crawling insects or dart out to snatch winged forms. For most of their protein, however, they simply visit their "flypaper"—the sticky oozing of sap that attracts and traps wasps, hornets, flies, ants, butterflies, moths, and other insects. These wells quickly become an ecological hot spot, providing food and drink for red squirrels, flying squirrels, warblers, and hummingbirds.

Sapsuckers communicate with a complex language of calls and physical

*Much of this information also applies to red-naped and red-breasted sapsuckers.

WHITE-BREASTED NUTHATCH • BLUE GROUSE • DOWNY WOODPECKER • VIOLET-GREEN SWALLOW • TREE SWALLOW • LEAST CHIPMUNK • HAIRY WOODPECKER

WILDLIFE LOCATOR CHART—ASPEN FOREST

	Feeds from Air	Feeds in Tree Canopy	Feeds on Trunk	Feeds on Ground
Nests in Tree Canopy	Cooper's Hawk Northern Goshawk Great Horned Owl Olive-sided Flycatcher Least Flycatcher Western Wood-Pewee Hoary Bat	Yellow-billed Cuckoo American Robin Solitary Vireo Warbling Vireo Red-eyed Vireo Yellow-rumped Warbler Western Tanager		Mourning Dove
Nests in Trunk Cavity	Flammulated Owl Northern Pygmy-Owl Northern Saw-whet Owl Western Flycatcher Tree Swallow Violet-green Swallow	Black-capped Chickadee Mountain Chickadee House Wren	Red-breasted Sapsucker Yellow-bellied Sapsucker Red-naped Sapsucker Downy Woodpecker Hairy Woodpecker White-breasted Nuthatch	Northern Flicker, Western Bluebird, Mountain Bluebird
Nests in Shrubs	Dusky Flycatcher	Yellow Warbler MacGillivray's Warbler White-crowned Sparrow		Swainson's Thrush
Nests on Ground	Turkey Vulture Common Nighthawk Townsend's Solitaire	Orange-crowned Warbler Wilson's Warbler Song Sparrow		Blue Grouse, Ruffed Grouse, Hermit Thrush, Veery, Ovenbird, Lincoln's Sparrow, Dark-eyed Junco, Snowshoe Hare, Dusky-footed Woodrat, Elk, Mule Deer, White-tailed Deer, Moose
Nests Beneath Ground or Debris	Long-legged Myotis			Masked Shrew, Dusky Shrew, Nuttall's Cottontail, Mountain Beaver, Least Chipmunk, Golden-mantled Ground Squirrel, Northern Pocket Gopher, Deer Mouse, Southern Red-backed Vole, Montane Vole, Western Jumping Mouse, Porcupine, Black Bear, Ermine, Long-tailed Weasel, Striped Skunk, Short-horned Lizard, Smooth Green Snake
Nests in Water				Tiger Salamander, Western Toad, Wood Frog

gestures. At breeding time, watch for the males advertising their territory with drumming and a distinctive courtship flight designed to show off their black markings. Females may also engage in signal drumming and synchronized head-bobbing displays. These gestures bond the pair and reinforce their attachment to the nest site. Other displays include bill raising (in which the bill is turned away from the mate as if to say "no threat") and head swinging. Naturalist Arnold Bent once commented that the head-swinging display reminded him of a maestro conducting an orchestra. Other displays include crest raising, bill directing, bowing, throat fluffing, wing flicking, and wing drooping.

Look for yellow-bellied sapsuckers—clinging to the bark and branches, tapping softly as they make their small perforations in the living bark. Their holes have been found on at least 275 different species of trees, shrubs, and vines. The sapsuckers begin to leave their breeding grounds in August, moving to the southern United States, Central America, and the West Indies for the winter. There are three species of closely related sapsuckers occurring in the West: red-naped (Rocky Mountains and Great Basin); red-breasted (northwest coast and Sierra Nevada); and yellow-bellied (Great Plains).

Length: 8–9 inches.

Look for nest holes—8 to 40 feet off the ground in live aspens, poplars, and other trees with decaying hearts, or in dead trees or branches. The entrance is 1¼–1½ inches in diameter, often facing south or east. Nearby, there may be a few half-finished nesting attempts. To locate an active nest, listen for loud, wheezy cries of the begging nestlings. Sapsucker young are much louder than other woodpecker young. Every 15 minutes, one of the parents flies in with a new beakful of squirming ants, while the relieved bird exits to go hunting. As they change places, watch for the head-bobbing and calling display. If you hear chiseling inside the cavity, it may be the parent chipping away at the walls of the abode, creating shavings to cover the nestlings' wastes.

Look for feeding wells—most evident on the trunks of smooth-barked trees. The excavations are a quarter-inch in diameter, and are square, round, or elongated. Holes are often drilled in a series of closely spaced, horizontal bands, which can also look like columns. When these scars heal over, they sometimes leave crisscross marks in the bark, or they merge into large, compound scars.

Listen for—a "mew" or "whee-ur." Their call note is "chee-aa" or "c-waan." At the nesting hole, family members communicate with a "yew-ick, yew-ick" or a low "tuck." Many other calls are used to express different moods, including cries that sound like those of a hawk or jay. You can tell a sapsucker by the nasal, mewling, catlike quality of its calls.

Long-tailed Weasel

When a weasel stalks a cottontail rabbit, it's like a house cat going after an animal the size of a white-tailed deer. The weasel is a skinny rodent, only 1½ inches in diameter, with short legs, a long tail, and a phenomenally ferocious demeanor. The weasel jumps on the rabbit's back before it has time to so much as tense a muscle. It wraps its tubular body around the victim, riding for dear life as the rabbit thrashes through the undergrowth, rolling over and over on the ground. Eventually, the weasel makes its way to the back of the rabbit's neck, where it delivers a precise surgical bite through the neck vertebrae, killing the rabbit instantly. It's this kind of performance that led one Idaho biologist to comment, "If a weasel was as big as a cougar, no one would dare venture outside."

For weasels, this aggressive, predatory nature is a survival tool, especially in cold weather. Their serpentine body shape, though it allows them to follow prey down tiny burrows, can be a hindrance when it comes to retaining heat. Considering their body mass, weasels have a lot of skin area through which heat can escape. Unlike animals that can roll themselves into a sphere for warmth, the weasel can only manage to curl up on its side in a flattened disk. It also has short fur, again good for tunneling but bad for insulating. A weasel therefore needs up to twice as much energy as other mammals its size. For a female with young, this translates into a food requirement of two-thirds her own weight each day—comparable to a 125-pound woman eating 83 pounds of food a day! Also because of their svelte shape, their stomach can hold only an ounce of meat at a time. They are compelled, therefore, to hunt frequently and to store what they cannot finish.

This need for constant fuel has led to an actual size difference between males and females. Males are much larger, and thus exploit larger prey than females do. Going after different prey presumably allows the weasels to live in the same habitat without putting competitive stress on one another.

Both males and females are equipped with the physical tools to track down prey and the spunk to take on animals 30 times their size. They have enormous stamina, and their senses of smell, hearing, and eyesight

WOOD
FROG

WESTERN
TOAD

are remarkably keen, making them among the continent's most efficient predators.

Look for long-tailed weasels—bounding along the ground with arched back, like an inchworm in high gear. They move their head from side to side, sniffing every nook and cranny for possible prey. They usually walk 3½ zigzagging miles a night, though they don't venture more than a few hundred yards total from the den. Preoccupied with the search, they may be oblivious, even to their own prey doubling back beside them. During the day they nap, often in the burrows of mice, muskrats, or ground squirrels that they devoured the night before.

Length: Males—head and body, 9–10½ inches; tail 4–6 inches. Females—head and body, 8–9 inches; tail, 3–5 inches.

Look for dens—in shallow burrows (commandeered from prey species), in rock piles, under roots of trees or stumps, or in hollow logs. The nest is often lined with fur, feathers, bones, and other "trophies" of the hunt. Caches of as many as 100 mice and rats have been found in or near dens. Whenever weasels foul their nest, they cover it with grasses, resulting in a layered nest floor.

In the winter—in northern regions, weasels replace their brown coat with a white one. The tip of their tail remains black, helping to confuse predators. The predator keys in on the black against the white snow and swoops down on it, usually missing the main body, and giving the weasel a chance to escape. Look for drag marks in the snow, or holes where the weasel has plunged into the snow.

Look for pellets—of regurgitated fur.

Look for droppings—dark brown or black, long, slender, segmented, and tapered at one end, left on rocks, logs, or stumps. Look carefully for embedded bone chips and hair.

Look for tracks—with 4 toes printing, in strides that vary from 12 inches to 20 inches when running. The hindprints, ¾ inch wide and 1 inch long, are twice as long as the foreprints.

Smell for—a skunky odor discharged at the slightest provocation or to mark territory. Females scent to let males know they want to mate.

Listen for—a characteristic, rapid "took-took-took." They also let out a raucous screech to startle their prey and their predators. When in pain, they squeal; when annoyed, they stamp their feet. Hunting weasels hiss, and females whistle a high-pitched reedy note when pursued by males.

Short-horned Lizard

Most of the strange and spiny horned lizards are found in deserts, where they have adapted ways to beat the heat, the sun, and their ever-circling predators (see Regal Horned Lizard, page 160). The northern variety of short-horned lizard has all these qualities plus the ability to tolerate cool body temperatures (down to 37 degrees F) and higher elevations.

Unlike birds and mammals that must metabolize food in order to stay warm, lizards are "ectotherms," meaning they take on the temperature of the outside environment. They are therefore keen to the thermal differences between night and day, dawn and noon, sun and shade, or soil and subsoil. To keep their body close to a comfortable 95 degrees, they have learned to exploit these differences.

When they awake, for instance, they emerge from underground beds to bask in the sun. At first, they expose just their head in an effort to get their sluggish brain working so they can recognize danger and get away from it. The head heats up especially quickly, because the major veins that drain blood from the brain are positioned right next to the arteries that send blood up. As sun-warmed blood leaves the brain, it transfers some of its heat to the cooler blood entering, thus helping to concentrate the warmth in the head area. When it's time for the rest of the body to catch up, the lizard constricts muscles in its head so that draining blood must escape through smaller veins elsewhere in the head. Because these are not next to the cool arterial blood, the warmth proceeds directly to the body without being lost. Before long, the body is as warm and alert as the brain, and the lizard can start its day aboveground.

The lizard will usually continue to bask, finding a sunny spot on the floor of an open aspen stand. The flat shape of the lizard's back presents a wide saucer to collect rays. To spread the surface even farther, the lizard separates its ribs and pulls them forward. By jacking up one or the other sets of legs, it tilts the plane of its back so it lays nearly perpendicular to the rays from the rising sun. Finally, to protect the inner organs from a harmful dose of ultraviolet rays, its body cavity is lined with a blocking layer of black pigment.

How does the lizard know when to come in from the sun? Researchers believe that a small translucent spot on the top of the head, midway between the eyes, plays a part in regulating their basking. This "third eye," called the pineal gland, has a transparent outer covering, a retina, and even a lens for concentrating light, yet it isn't actually an eye. Researchers are still working to explain its mysterious role.

Once the lizard is warm enough, it can start hunting, mating, or hiding from predators. Every now and then it must stop in the sun to boost its temperature, or flatten out in the shade to transfer excess heat to the cool ground. If the midday temperature becomes too hot, the lizard shimmies its way underground by moving its spine-encrusted head and body back and forth. Later in the afternoon, the lizard emerges for the second time that day, seeking shade instead of sun. Eventually, as the air cools, the lizard starts to bask again, turning its back fully into the setting sun before it climbs underground to sleep.

Look for short-horned lizards—frozen in place so as not to be seen by you or by airborne predators such as hawks, falcons, or loggerhead shrikes. Their flat, flush stance eliminates a ground shadow and their coloring "paints" them into the background. The spines along their sides help break up the smooth outline so it's not recognizable from the air. Before a lizard spots you, you may see it basking in its "push-up" posture to get the full impact of the sun. They also run for short distances, then take up the freeze stance again. Once cornered, they may try to convince you that they are not an easy morsel to swallow. They'll swell up with air, lower their head, and raise their spines (which can dig into your hands if you are holding them). Many snakes find out too late that these spines are sharp enough to pierce a slender throat.

Length: $2\frac{1}{2}$–$5\frac{7}{8}$ inches.

Young are born alive—after a 3-month incubation inside the lizard's body. When the 5–36 wriggling young first emerge, they are cylindrical in shape. With their first, lung-filling breath, however, they slowly widen into their characteristic saucer shape.

TREE
SWALLOW

NORTHERN
POCKET
GOPHER

SOUTHERN
RED-BACKED
VOLE

TIGER
SALAMANDER

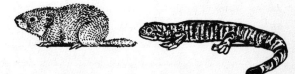

NORTHERN ORIOLE

Plains Cottonwood

Black Cottonwood

BELTED KINGFISHER

RIVER OTTER

"oxbow"

NORTHERN LEOPARD FROG

California Wild Grape

Hackberry

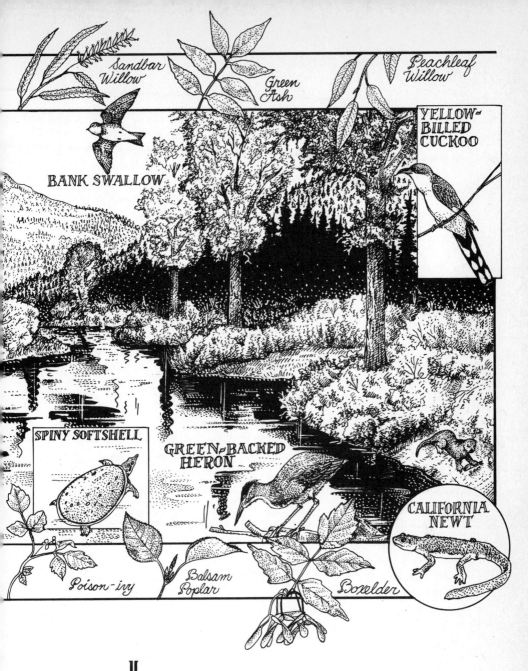

Sandbar Willow

Green Ash

Peachleaf Willow

YELLOW-BILLED CUCKOO

BANK SWALLOW

SPINY SOFTSHELL

GREEN-BACKED HERON

CALIFORNIA NEWT

Poison-ivy

Balsam Poplar

Boxelder

Lowland River Forest

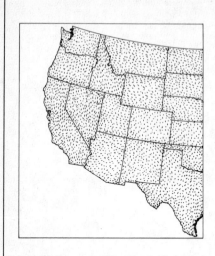

WHERE TO SEE THIS HABITAT:

Arizona: Burro Creek (Bureau of Land Management); Cibola, Havasu, and Imperial national wildlife refuges

California: Kesterson National Wildlife Refuge; Mendocino Plumas, Six Rivers, and Tahoe national forests

Colorado: Alamosa and Browns Park national wildlife refuges; Arkansas River Canyon (Bureau of Land Management); San Isabel National Forest

Idaho: Idaho Panhandle, Nez Perce, and Targhee national forests; Lower Salmon River and Snake River birds of prey areas

Kansas: Flint Hills National Wildlife Refuge

Montana: Charles M. Russell and Ul Bend national wildlife refuges; Deerlodge, Flathead, Kootenai, Lewis and Clark, and Lolo national forests

New Mexico: Bitter Lake National Wildlife Refuge

North Dakota: Little Missouri National Grassland; Upper Souris National Wildlife Refuge

Oklahoma: Salt Plains, Sequoyah, and Washita, national wildlife refuges

Oregon: Deschutes River (Bureau of Land Management)

Texas: Big Bend National Park

Utah: Canyonlands National Park; Desolation and Gray Canyons of the Green River (Bureau of Land Management); Fishlake National Forest; Glen Canyon National Recreation Area

Washington: Columbia, McNary, and Ridgefield national wildlife refuges; Colville National Forest

Wyoming: Grand Teton and Yellowstone national parks; Middle Fork of the Powder River and Upper Green and New Fork Rivers (Bureau of Land Management); Seedskadee National Wildlife Refuge; Shoshone National Forest

Lowland River Forest

BEGINNINGS

The world changes when you leave the dark needleleaf forest, the scrubby desert, or the wide, sunny grassland and step into the riverbank forest. The air is cool and shaded, the trees broad-leaved and well watered, the undergrowth lush. In a relatively narrow strip of vegetation, you may see twice the number of wildlife species you'd ordinarily see in the surrounding habitats. At the heart of it all is the crown jewel of the habitat: a flowing river.

Most rivers begin as rain or snow that falls in the uplands, gathering into a small, babbling stream that joins other streams, eventually growing wider and slower as it reaches the foothills and lowlands. Along its length, you will find vegetation that is uniquely adapted to the fertile, moist soils of the streamside and to the occasional flooding that characterizes floodplain life.

The roster of plants in the river forest shows surprising similarities no matter where you are in the West. Wetland areas in the high mountains tend to be somewhat shrubby, featuring plants such as bog willows and birches. The ubiquitous willows and cottonwoods eventually appear farther downstream, and become quite prominent along lowland rivers. Sandbar willows are pioneers, invading the newly deposited bars of sand and guarding against erosion while slowly building the soil. Cottonwoods and other species of willows eventually take root on these new shores.

The cottonwood-willow associates may differ in various locales, however. In the plains grassland region, plains cottonwood and willow are joined by green ash, American elm, hackberry, and boxelder. In the moister parts of the Pacific Northwest, you'll find gravel bars dominated by Scouler willow, and elevated flats covered with red alder giving way to Sitka spruce, bigleaf maple, and western hemlock. In the coastal region of northern

California, redwood is uniquely adapted to river habitats (see page 231). In California's Central Valley, the cottonwoods and willows are accompanied by California sycamore, California white oak, white alder, boxelder, and Oregon ash. In the Rockies, balsam poplar, quaking aspen, berry bushes, and blue spruce are the most common associates. In the arid Southwest, screwbean mesquite, Fremont cottonwood, Russian olive, tamarisk, and mesquite are found.

The common denominator in all these river communities is change. Water levels rise and fall, banks erode, sandbars form, and vegetation rearranges itself accordingly. Added now to these natural changes are human-caused changes, ones that threaten to alter the original character of streamsides past the point of no return. First, let's take a look at the natural changes.

THE RESTLESS HABITAT

A free-flowing, meandering river is constantly rearranging its bed, tearing soil and vegetation from the outside of bends and depositing them on the inside. Bends tend to grow outward this way, until the loop is 7–15 times wider than the river itself. At some point, a storm-swollen river may jump its bank and seek the straightest path between two points, thus cutting through the neck of a loop and leaving a stillwater pond (an oxbow) in the shape of a "C."

Floodplain rivers have two beds, a narrow one that they use during normal water levels, and a wide one that they use when storms or snowmelt cause them to overflow their banks. Very often, people build homes or plant crops on this wider bed, then complain about the "floods" that are actually a natural part of the river's yearly cycle.

These floods shape the landscape by depositing the heaviest sediments on ridgelike levees along the banks, then dropping finer sediments on the forest floor farther back from the river. The vegetation that grows closest to the water must be able to cope with "wet feet," especially in areas where standing water remains for several days or weeks. In order to "breathe" in waterlogged soil, they produce secondary flood roots that have large air spaces to help shuttle oxygen from the aboveground portions of the plants to the roots. Small pores in the leaves and openings in the bark also drink in oxygen to supply the plant during these waterlogged times. These plants can also practice a special kind of respiration (gas exchange) during flooding. The potentially toxic by-products of this process are not a threat; instead, the plants are adapted to use these wastes to build carbohydrates in their leaves and stems.

CHARACTERISTIC PLANTS:

Trees, Shrubs, and Vines:

American elm
American plum
Arizona alder
Arizona sycamore
Arizona walnut
Arkansas rose
balsam poplar
bigleaf maple
blackberries
black cottonwood
black hawthorn
black willow
blue elder
blue spruce
boxelder
buttonbush
California sycamore
California white oak
desert-willow
Douglas's sagebrush
eastern cottonwood
eastern redcedar
Fremont cottonwood
green ash
hackberries
hawthorns
honeysuckles
huckleberries

little walnut
mountain alder
mule fat
narrowleaf cotton-
   wood
netleaf hackberry
Oregon ash
peachleaf willow
plains cottonwood
poison-oak
quaking aspen
red alder
red-osier dogwood
redwood
Rio Grande cotton-
   wood
Rocky Mountain juni-
   per
Russian olive
sandbar willow
Scouler willow
screwbean mesquite
sitka spruce
smooth barked
   cottonwood
snowberries
southern California
   walnut
tamarisk
Texas mulberry
valley cottonwood
velvet ash
water birch
wax currant

western hemlock
white alder

Herbaceous Plants:
American licorice
bluegrasses
California wild grape
common cattail
desert saltgrass
false-boneset
foxtail barley
hairleaf water butter-
   cup
hardstem bulrush
ironweeds
marsh cinquefoil
nettles
poison hemlock
poison-ivy
pondweed
Porter's lovage
prairie cordgrass
rushes
Russian thistle
sedges
summer-cypress
sunflowers
verbenas
Virgin's bower
watercress
water plantain
western wheatgrass
wild grapes

California Wild Grape

Cottonwoods and willows have become so used to flooding that their seeds are adapted to germinate only when they are covered by water. When torn by the scouring force of a flood, they resprout vigorously from their roots, trunks, branches, and even their twigs.

AN UNNATURAL PRESSURE

Unfortunately, riversides have, in modern times, experienced changes that they are not adapted to. As soon as floods become seen as insurance liabilities instead of natural processes, we humans started inventing flood-control measures. By taming the annual swamping of streamside forests, we take away all the good things that go along with this high water. Cottonwood and willow seeds, for instance, no longer have a bath that they can germinate in. The floodplain trees no longer receive their annual "subsidy" of leaves, twigs, and nutrient-rich goop from upstream. Fish are no longer able to forage among the flooded trees, and their predators—herons, egrets, kingfishers, and bears—can no longer feast in the shallow, temporary pools.

Some stream "improvement" measures call for straightening the stream, thereby curbing the creation of oxbows, slow backwaters, and other communities that are so important to wildlife. Others call for removing the vegetation along a stream in order to increase its flow (based on an unproven theory that trees soak up too much water). Harvests of these trees often increase bank erosion, muddy the river, and remove the shade that keeps the water cool enough for certain fish.

Another continuing threat to riparian habitats is mismanaged grazing of livestock. Cattle, like people, tend to gravitate toward streamsides. Too many cattle can trample the ground and graze away all the shrubs and woody saplings, leading to a simple grass understory. When the overstory decays and dies, there are no new saplings to rebuild the community. This can be especially harmful on the Great Plains where woody areas are so rare and precious. This sort of overgrazing has also occurred in parts of the Southwest, where it has led to an explosion of an exotic plant called tamarisk. Studies show that these tamarisk groves are not as rich in wildlife as the original forests were.

Thankfully, a move is afoot to change grazing and cutting practices to protect natural cottonwood-willow ecosystems and the wildlife that depend on them. The common practice of building roads along streams is also being reexamined. Biologists have found that roadways tend to rob wildlife of habitat—not only on the strip of road, but also along both sides, where car noise keeps wildlife away.

WHAT'S IN IT FOR WILDLIFE?

In many parts of the West, a riparian area is an oasis marooned in a desert of shrubs, a sea of grasses, or a monotonous stretch of pines. The willows, cottonwoods, alders, and birches are usually the only broadleaf trees for miles. They provide shade from the hot sun, a buffer from the snow and wind, and foods that can't be found in the surrounding habitats. The various vertical layers—from tall tree to low-growing shrubs—often progress in a stairstep fashion along the edges, offering wildlife an abundance of nesting, feeding, denning, foraging, and loafing sites. Sometimes a maze of downed logs and hanging vines gives riparian zones a junglelike feel. Many more species can exist in this layered type of forest, because they can use different zones in the vegetation profile without competing with one another.

Although this oasis is narrow, it contains many "edges"—zones where two habitats come together, and the species from both can mingle. One edge occurs where the upland forest meets the riverside forest, and another is where the bank meets the water. These edges are usually the best places to watch for wildlife. The constantly changing profile of the river also creates a mosaic of subhabitats in the floodplain, including old oxbow ponds, marshy sloughs, and brushy beaver meadows. There are also a variety of age classes available; as patches of older communities are destroyed by a flood, new ones are given the opportunity to develop. The perimeters of all these subhabitats are also productive edge zones.

The climate inside a riverside forest can be different from that in a shrubland 50 yards away. Because of the influence of the running water, it's usually moister, with a higher rate of transpiration from the plants, increased air movement, and more stable temperatures. Elk, mule deer, pronghorn, and cattle are drawn to this microclimate, as are scores of smaller mammals looking for shelter, lush grasses, berries, prey species, or drinking water. Streamside mammals such as montane voles, water shrews, western jumping mice, and harvest mice provide prey for minks, weasels, foxes, bobcats, and other predators.

Streamside forests also tend to be more "buggy" than the surrounding habitats. Flying insects can breed in the swampy water, and leaf-feeding insects have acres of broad surface area on which to hide and feed. This insect wealth supports dense flocks of insect-eating songbirds such as fly-catchers, warblers, wrens, vireos, and swallows. As the songbirds return to the trees to roost, bats zigzag down to the water, using sonar to track down the rising hordes of aquatic insects. Wood-boring insects are also abundant in the large, decaying trees that finally succumb to flooding along the riverbank.

These snags harbor cavity nests of woodpeckers, owls, raccoons, squir-

ROUGHSKIN NEWT

FOOTHILL YELLOW-LEGGED FROG

NORTHERN WATER SNAKE

CALIFORNIA LEGLESS LIZARD

WESTERN HARVEST MOUSE

WILDLIFE LOCATOR CHART—LOWLAND RIVER FOREST

	Feeds from Air	Feeds in Tree Canopy	Feeds on Ground	Feeds in Water
Nests in Tree Canopy	Osprey Bald Eagle Red-shouldered Hawk Great Horned Owl Long-eared Owl Black-chinned Hummingbird Cassin's Kingbird	Yellow-billed Cuckoo Hooded Oriole Northern Oriole American Goldfinch	American Robin	Great Blue Heron, Green-backed Heron
Nests in Trunk Cavity	Lewis' Woodpecker		Bewick's Wren, Raccoon	Wood Duck, Hooded Merganser
Nests in Shrubs	Willow Flycatcher	Bushtit Bell's Vireo Black-headed Grosbeak Lazuli Bunting	Swainson's Thrush, Blue Grosbeak	
Nests on Ground			Dusky-footed Woodrat, Mule Deer, White-tailed Deer	Double-crested Cormorant
Nests Beneath Ground or Debris	Belted Kingfisher Bank Swallow		Northern Waterthrush, Virginia Opossum, Western Harvest Mouse, Deer Mouse, Montane Vole, Western Jumping Mouse, Coyote, Bobcat, Dunn's Salamander, California Legless Lizard	Water Shrew, River Otter, Snapping Turtle, Western Painted Turtle, Yellow Mud Turtle, Spiny Softshell, Checkered Garter Snake, Northern Water Snake, Western Ribbon Snake, Common Garter Snake
Nests Above Water			Beaver, Muskrat	
Nests in Water			Northwestern Salamander, Tiger Salamander, Pacific Giant Salamander, Roughskin Newt, California Newt, Northern Cricket Frog, Western Toad, Woodhouse's Toad, Canyon Treefrog, Plains Leopard Frog, Northern Leopard Frog	Foothill Yellow-legged Frog, Bullfrog

rels, Virginia opossums, wood ducks, and mergansers. In the branches of living trees, look for the colony nests of great blue herons, the bulky platforms of red-shouldered hawks, or the pendulous "purse" nests of northern and hooded orioles. The yellow-billed cuckoos that breed along river corridors in the Southwest are rarely found anywhere else in the West.

These forested corridors become wildlife highways during migration time. Elk and mule deer moving from their high-elevation summer range to their low-elevation winter range use these zones for cover while traveling across otherwise open areas. Hundreds of thousands of north-south migrating birds stop here to refuel in spring and fall, while flocks of mountain birds such as chickadees, brown creepers, nuthatches, and pine siskins may stay here all winter long. Throughout the year, when population pressures or food shortages force small mammals and birds to find new quarters, they often use these highways to disperse to new habitats.

Finally, the crown jewel of the habitat—the river—supports a large community of aquatic and semiaquatic animals. River otters slide down the muddy banks, belted kingfishers dive-bomb the shallows, and mergansers dive deep after schools of fish. Muskrats and beavers cut the glassy surface with their V-shaped wake. Herons and egrets bide their time in a frozen pose, snapping out in an eye-blink to snare a passing frog. In a typical oxbow pond, emergent plants grow half in and half out of the water, sheltering a mass of tiger salamander eggs, a canyon treefrog tadpole, a string of mallard chicks, or a prowling water snake. For more about the backwaters of the riverside forest, see Inland Marsh on page 105.

Belted Kingfisher

Imagine diving headfirst into the water from a height of 50 feet and, at the precise moment, intersecting a fish that is desperately trying to evade you. Imagine repeating this every 20 minutes from 4 A.M. to 11 P.M. Parent kingfishers are on this schedule for weeks at a time, until their young nestlings are old enough to fend for themselves. At first, the fledgling birds are not particularly eager to dive for their own food. It is only after the parents stop bringing handouts that they become interested in the river. To inspire that first headlong dive, parents will stun a fish and let it float beneath the hungry nestlings. The young birds eventually get the idea, and are soon plunging after fish of their own.

Their oversized head and neck are built to absorb the shock, and their spearlike bill is designed to get a grip on slippery prey. Kingfishers usually retire to a tree to eat, first whacking the fish on a branch, then tossing it up in the air to catch. When the fish is too long to swallow, the kingfisher simply waits, fishtail dangling from its bill, until its stomach juices reduce the prey to size.

Their bill also comes in handy when digging their 3- to 7-foot-long tunnel in the side of a cutaway bank. Kingfishers are enthusiastic diggers, kicking a flying fountain of sand behind them as they work. At the end of the upward-sloping tunnel, they carve a flattened sphere for a nest. Unlike their neighbors the bank swallows, which hang their hind end out of the holes to defecate, kingfisher young spray their excrement all over the nest. To their credit, however, they do rap the walls with their beaks, loosening dirt that soon covers the waste. By the time this rising floor begins to crowd them, they are ready for their first flight.

The belted kingfisher (*Ceryle alcyon*) is named for a female character in classical mythology. Alcyone, daughter of Aeolus, was so distraught when her husband died in a shipwreck that she threw herself into the sea. The gods took pity on the lovers and turned them into kingfishers who would forever roam the waters together. Kingfisher nesting season was said to be a time of exceptional calm at sea, to this day referred to as "halcyon days."

Look for belted kingfishers—plying the air above their stretch of river territory that may be 500 yards long or up to 5,000 during breeding season. In spring, when they are stringing "territorial fences," they make up to 90 circuits a day around the edges of their range, broadcasting their claim with loud calls. Watch when an intruding kingfisher enters the area; you'll see two slate-blue-and-white forms darting past, one "escorting" the other out of his territory. You can gauge for yourself how long the owner's territory is by watching as the bird flies up ahead of your canoe. Eventually it will reach the end of its territory and come circling back for another pass. For fishing, kingfishers prefer shallow borders and water that is clear enough to see beneath the surface.

Length: 13 inches.

Look for nest holes—3 to 4 inches in diameter, down about a foot from the top of a cutaway exposed bank, where the topsoil blends into sand. You can see two grooves at the bottom of the entrance hole where the kingfisher places its feet when leaving and entering. The nest tunnel slopes up to provide drainage and keep the nest dry. If you find a mound of fresh earth on the ground beneath the hole, the nest is probably active. Look for probe holes in the bank where kingfishers abandoned their first digging attempts. Other nest holes may belong to bank swallows or northern rough-winged swallows. Occasionally, kingfishers will nest inland, as much as a mile from water.

Look for perches—dead branches hanging out over water, where kingfishers take food to eat. Perches are usually within 100 feet of the nest, and there may be more than one in a territory.

Listen for—a "k-k-k-k-k-k-" rattle that sounds like the clicking of a fishing reel. They give these calls when flying or when perched.

River Otter

After a flying leap, a wriggling otter bellyflops on the muddy bank and slides headfirst into a deep pool. Another follows, and another after that. As they scramble from the water, they seem to race each other back to the top of the bank. Nearby, an otter juggles pebbles on its paws, while another ferries a stick across the water using its nose. They romp. They cavort. They seem to play games. Even the most objective, emotionally detached biologist has to smile; otters look like they are just plain having fun.

Biologists are beginning to take a serious look at play among animals. Through play, an animal learns to interact with its environment, to experiment with new kinds of food, and to adjust its hunting tactics in light of changing conditions. Young otters at play are rehearsing behaviors that will one day determine their success in the real life-and-death contests of later life. Perhaps the pleasure that comes from play is nature's way of getting its pupils to practice their lessons.

But not all animals play. Otters have this leisure perhaps because of their long lives, their intelligence, and the fact that their predators are few. They also work as hard as they play. Otters have a fast metabolism that burns food quickly, so they must eat up to four times a day. In the water, otters swim along the surface until they spot a fish beneath them. They arch their back, dive, and by flexing their powerful body up and down, they swiftly overtake it. Sometimes they stay beneath a fish when chasing it, as if to follow its movements silhouetted against the surface light. They also nose along the muddy bottom for crayfish, frogs, and salamanders, feeling with their long whiskers, which are anchored in large nerve pads. Onshore, they will raid bird, rabbit, and turtle nests, and even follow a muskrat into its burrow to kill it. They have been known to puncture a beaver dam, and then saunter in to collect the frogs and fish left stranded by the draining water. Humans have harnessed the angling savvy of otters for centuries. In 618 A.D., people in the Tang Dynasty trained otters to catch fish or drive them toward their nets. In some parts of Asia, otters are still being used as fishing partners.

Look for river otters—at any time of year fishing at the inflow and outflow of lakes, running rapids with their head up, eating fish on riverbanks, galloping along the shore, or swimming under the ice. They are especially active from dawn to midmorning and again in the evening. They swim with the top of their head (where their eyes are) out of the water, trailing a "V" wake behind them. Sometimes the undulating movements of 5 or 6 otters "porpoising" one behind the other looks like a giant sea serpent.

Length: Head and body, 26–30 inches. Tail, 12–17 inches.

Look for dens—under tree roots or rock ledges, in hollow logs, abandoned beaver or muskrat burrows, dense thickets along shore, or dug into the bank. They use an abovewater entrance in the summer, and an underwater one in the winter. Look for females teaching young to swim. The kits are reluctant at first, and must be ferried out to deep water on the mother's back.

Look for "haul-outs"—worn-down areas of shore where the otters habitually pull out of the water. Take one of the trails that leads away from these areas to find a patch (20 square feet) of disturbed vegetation where the otters roll to dry themselves or to mark the ground with their scent.

Look for scent stations—any prominent object, such as a rock, stump, or even a tuft of grass that the otter has twisted together. They deposit droppings and scent on these spots as a way of marking the borders of their territory. Droppings are black, mucus-filled with shells or crayfish parts, and have a strong odor. The mucus is a protective coating in their intestines that prevents punctures by sharp fish bones.

Look for belly slides—on grassy, muddy, or snow-covered hills. The slides may be as long as 25 feet, and may end in water or in a snowbank. Otters will go out of their way to bodysurf a good hill.

Look for tracks—paired prints, 3¼ inches wide, with 5 splayed toes (sometimes only the claws show), especially noticeable in mud. The inner toe of the hind paw points out to one side.

In the snow—on level ground, look for dot-dash trails consisting of a few bounding leaps, a slide, and more bounding leaps. The 5- to 15-foot-long trough looks like it was made with a toy toboggan. Don't be surprised to find these trails far from water; otters travel as many as 3 miles overland to find new territory or fishing grounds.

Listen for—a deep "huh, huh, huh" repeated rapidly. Also chuckles, chirps, purring, grunts, growls, hissing barks, and screams. A surfacing otter blows and sniffs loudly. Family members swimming together will exchange birdlike chirps.

Northern Leopard Frog

If you took biology lab in high school, chances are you may have dissected a northern leopard frog. They are widely collected for this purpose, and further reduced in some areas by toxic amounts of agricultural chemicals. Losing leopard frogs disrupts the food chain for a great many predators, including snakes, turtles, birds, weasels, fish, minks, and raccoons. Besides being a vital food source, frogs are also predators of many kind of spiders, snails, sow bugs, and insects, including those that harm farm crops.

To lure females, the males call out with a rumbling snore. They float atop the water as they call, and groups of these spread-eagle suitors can look like skydivers in formation. After breeding and laying eggs in the shallow pools, the frogs return to the waving sedges to hunt insects.

Tadpoles may transform by midsummer, or it may take as long as two years for them to lose their tail, trade their gills for lungs, grow new front legs, and lengthen their hind legs. Tadpoles also rebuild their digestive tract, shortening the long, coiled vegetarian tract into one better suited to carnivorous life. Their sense of smell, which was most efficient for detecting watery chemicals, is reorganized to detect scents in the air.

For the first year, newly metamorphosed frogs tend to stay close to the safety of the pools. When you walk along the shore, they may hop before you in a thousand directions, like kernels of corn popping. Adults wander farther away, returning to watery places when the weather gets cold. The homing instinct of frogs is keen. Even on cloudy nights, without using smell or hearing, these frogs can find their way home if displaced. Researchers think the pineal body, at the base of the brain, may come into play in this navigation.

During winter, leopard frogs pile up in groups on the bottom of ponds to hibernate, occasionally waking to swim beneath the ice. If the pond is shallow enough, it may freeze through to the bottom, depriving the frogs of oxygen and encasing them in ice. The population eventually recovers, however, freshened by the large number of eggs laid by frogs that move in from adjacent ponds. According to herpetologist Richard Vogt, a single female leopard frog can lay 6,000 eggs!

Look for northern leopard frogs—breeding in pools between March and April. Adults are in grasses and sedges throughout summer, but juveniles stick close to pond borders. When approached, they hunker down in preparation for a fast leap. When picked up, they may squirt a foul-smelling liquid.

Length: 2–5 inches.

Look for egg masses—500 to 1,000 in a clump. The eggs are dark (perhaps to absorb sunlight for solar heating), covered with jelly, and attached to submerged sticks, sedges, or grasses.

In October and November—look for groups of leopard frogs on the shores of ponds, streams, or lakes, preparing to submerge for the winter.

Listen for—a many-pulsed snoring call in March or April, beginning at dusk. Leopards have at least three types of calls: the mating snore, a croak that sounds like rubbing your finger across a balloon, and a loud chuckle that may be used to establish territory.

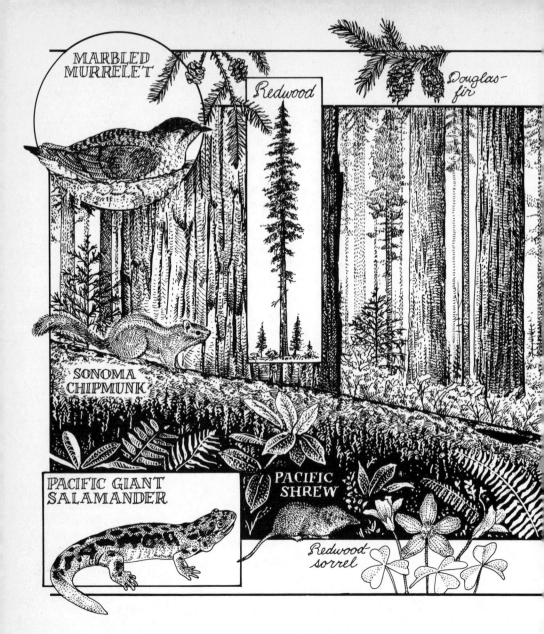

MARBLED
MURRELET

Redwood

Douglas-
fir

SONOMA
CHIPMUNK

PACIFIC GIANT
SALAMANDER

PACIFIC
SHREW

Redwood
sorrel

Red Alder

Tanoak

Pacific Madrone

VAUX'S SWIFT

STELLER'S JAY

ELK

ENSATINA

BANANA SLUG

Swordfern

Redwood Forest

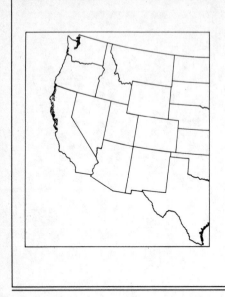

WHERE TO SEE THIS HABITAT:

California: Humboldt Redwoods State Park; Muir Woods National Monument; Redwood National Park

Redwood Forest

BEGINNINGS

The epic size and unearthly darkness of a redwood grove can disorient you at first. Your voice is swallowed by the thick, saturated air, and in the eclipsed light, your figure casts no shadow. The trees surrounding you are the tallest in the world, with tops that sway in the breeze more than 300 feet above your head (that's taller than the Statue of Liberty). A ring count in one of the 15-foot-diameter trunks would show something even more confounding. When the signers of the Declaration of Independence were blotting their ink, these trees were already founding fathers and mothers. In fact, they had been growing long before the Europeans ever imagined a New World! The oldest recorded coast redwood is 2,200 years old.

Coast redwoods are descendants of trees that circled the northern hemisphere millions of years ago when temperatures were much steamier than they are today. This era ended as mountain ranges were gradually pushed up, creating the cooler, drier conditions that now characterize the West. The redwoods are poorly equipped to handle these arid conditions. Their feathery leaves have no waxy coating, and their pores easily relinquish water vapor to the air. To make matters worse, the redwoods have never developed root hairs (the tiny projections that help trees find water in the soil). As a result, redwoods have been limited to a small strip of coastal California and southern Oregon where high humidity, moist soils, and moderate temperatures can nurture them.

This strip of redwoods is separated from the direct salt air by a 50-mile-wide buffer zone of trees such as bishop pine and shore pine that are adapted to endure the drying influence of ocean breezes. Although the salt is blocked, saturated clouds of coastal fog do reach the redwoods, wrapping their branches in a blanket of moisture. Water droplets condense on the needles and then drip to the ground, adding the equivalent of 7–12 inches of rainfall a year. Minerals are also brought in with the drops, and gradually find their way to the redwood roots.

The redwoods reach their greatest splendor on the lower slopes and river terraces in rainy northern California. The tallest trees grow right along rivers on flats that are regularly flooded and fertilized with new layers of rich, alluvial (stream-carried) sediment. Here the oldest, virgin redwoods grow in dense, parklike stands that contain the greatest amount of living material (biomass) per acre of any ecosystem on earth. Only the most shade-tolerant of plants survive beneath the canopy of these valley bottom forests.

"Second-growth" forests—those that grew in after the virgin forest was removed by logging—also acquire a parklike appearance after a few

CHARACTERISTIC PLANTS:

Trees, Shrubs, and Vines:
bigleaf maple
bishop pine
blackberries
blueblossom
California hazel
California huckleberry
California-laurel
California torreya
cascara
coyote bush
creambush oceanspray
creek dogwood
creeping wintergreen
Douglas-fir
evergreen huckleberry
golden chinkapin
grand fir
green ash
incense-cedar
Jeffrey pine
knobcone pine
lodgepole pine

Monterey pine
Oregon ash
Oregon white oak
Pacific bayberry (wax-myrtle)
Pacific dogwood
Pacific madrone
Pacific ninebark
Pacific red elder
Pacific rhododendron
Pacific yew
poison-oak
Port-Orford-cedar
red alder
red huckleberry
redwood
salal
salmonberry
Sitka spruce
snowbrush ceanothus
sugar pine
sumacs
tanoak
thimbleberry
upright snowberry

vine maple
western azalea
western hemlock
western redcedar
willows

Herbaceous Plants:
American licorice
baccharis
chainferns
checkermallow
deer fern
fireweed
fringed loosestrife
hawkweeds
Idaho fescue
needle-and-thread
northern inside-out flower
redwood-sorrel
swordfern
true forget-me-not
vanilla grass
western fescue
yerba de selva

decades, with not much of an understory at all. These deep, dark forests are occasionally interrupted by splashes of colorful wildflowers and flowering shrubs. Ferns spread their fountains of green along paths, on fallen logs, and at the bases of trees and stumps. The more common ones include sword, chain, and wood fern. Everywhere you look, mosses and lichens form a cushiony layer over branches, root tangles, and downed logs, giving the redwood forest the feeling of a cloud forest.

Away from the flats, most old-growth redwood forests have very dense shrub understories that are more than head-high. Some common shrubs and small trees include salal, Pacific bayberry, Pacific rhododendron, and evergreen huckleberry. In some places, the redwoods mix with Douglas-fir, grand fir, western hemlock, Sitka spruce, California torreya, Pacific yew, Port-Orford-cedar, or western redcedar. Among the broadleaf trees you may see are Pacific madrone and tanoak (the two most abundant), bigleaf maple, California-laurel, cascara, golden chinkapin, Oregon white oak, Pacific dogwood, red alder, vine maple, and willows.

MAKING THE BEST OF NATURAL DISASTERS

A lot can happen to a tree in 2,000 years, but not a lot that can faze the redwoods. Fires, for example, rarely kill the older trees because of their thick, moist, nonresinous bark. Reddish chemicals in their bark and wood also help them fight off insects and disease organisms that plague other trees. Even a flood can't slow them down. Redwoods are able to tolerate winter flooding, and when their roots get buried by a layer of flood-borne sediment, they simply send roots up into the new soil layer. Sometimes, the newly buried trunk sends out a whorl of new horizontal roots as well. Layer after layer of these roots are added as each new flood buries the trunk a little farther. You can recognize these oft-buried trunks because they don't have the flared base that other trees have.

When a redwood does get injured, it has an amazing capacity to recoup. If the top is blown out, it will quickly regrow a new one, thus recovering its place in the forest canopy. If the branches on one side of a tree are seared off by fire, a fresh feathery column of new growth will sprout from buds on the trunk. Sprouts can also arise from dormant buds at the base of the stems or from the stump of a tree. Look around you for mature redwoods growing in a circle; these probably originated from dormant buds that sprouted from the base when the parent tree was injured. Nourished by an already established root system, these sprouts jumped up several feet in their first year, easily outdistancing any other tree competitors. The sprouts soon put down their own roots, and eventually become independent trees forming a circle around the parent tree. If there was not enough light to make the leap upward right away, these small redwoods might have survived for hundreds of years in the shade of taller trees, never losing their ability to capitalize on an opening.

Redwoods also germinate readily from seeds, but they only survive if the right nursery conditions are available. They do not do well on a layer of needles, for instance, and usually succumb to summer drought or some form of root rot before they are well established. To be successful, the seedlings need a bare mineral seedbed, plenty of moisture, and partial shade. A fire will sometimes expose such a bed, while a flood will actually create a new one by spreading a layer of waterborne silt atop the forest floor. Redwood seedlings can also grow on fallen logs, slowly sending their roots around the log and down into the soil.

FIVE PERCENT AND COUNTING

Redwoods are opportunists, and are therefore quite adept at replacing themselves tree by tree when a disturbance creates an opening in the canopy. When humans enter, however, the disturbances can be much more sweeping, affecting every tree in a 1,200- to 2,000-year-old forest. When trees of this age are cut, they rejuvenate less readily than somewhat younger trees.

More than 95 percent of the original redwood forests have been cut over at least once, and less than 5 percent remain as they were when European ships first touched our eastern shores. Half of these remaining old-growth stands are now preserved in parks. The other half are privately owned, and have been steadily disappearing as trees are hauled out on logging skidders. From the owner's point of view, the market value of even a single redwood tree is a powerful incentive for logging. However, as John Muir once said, "These trees would make excellent lumber if put through a good sawmill, just as George Washington, in the hands of a French chef, would have made good food." Biologists warn that harvests in private areas may ultimately affect protected groves. As trees are removed in forests adjacent to parks, the runoff from rains is no longer controlled by redwood roots. This accelerates flooding to a level that even the alluvial-grown redwoods can't withstand.

WHAT'S IN IT FOR WILDLIFE?

You'll hear some comments that the redwoods are zoological "deserts." Not true! Old-growth redwoods offer acres of branch nesting and feeding opportunities, trunks that are large enough for cavity nesters, undergrowth that includes palatable browse and berries, a good collection of dead and fallen material, and a moist microclimate for amphibians and other riparian species. All told, 193 species of wildlife use redwoods for food, for cover, or to fulfill their special habitat requirements during their lives.

In the canopy above, western flycatchers sally out after insects on the wing, Steller's jays break the silence with their braggartly cries, chestnut-backed chickadees dangle upside-down from the fine foliage, and golden-crowned kinglets scour the twigs and foliage for insects. As you look up, you may be lucky enough to spot the Vaux's swift, a speedster of the redwoods that races here and there for insects. Or perhaps you'll hear a crowd of ravens harassing a roosting owl.

One of the most characteristic sounds in the redwoods (beside the sigh of wind in the branches) is the ethereal, upward spiraling song of the varied thrush. Kevin Zimmer, who wrote *The Western Bird Watcher,* said the shrill, yet organlike sound "filters up through the canopy like the sunlight in reverse." Swainson's thrush is also found in the depths of the redwoods, adding its own memorable song to the silence.

The trunks attract wildlife as well. Look for brown creepers spiraling up the trees in search of crevice insects, while pygmy nuthatches hitch down, picking out insects that their upright colleagues missed. Hairy wood-peckers peck and scale away bark, while pileateds break right through the thick tree coat, gouging large rectangular holes in dead trunks. Spotted owls, northern flying squirrels, and Douglas' squirrels will nest in these holes as soon as they are abandoned by the woodpeckers. Interestingly, the marbled murrelet, which is better known as a seagoing bird, travels all the way into the redwood forest to build its nest on the large redwood branches. Red tree voles also take up residence on the branches, building their twig-and-needle nests close to the trunk.

On the ground, blue grouse strut like chickens, pecking for fallen nuts and berries. Sonoma and Townsend's chipmunks dart in and out of un-derground burrows. Over time, the come-and-go traffic of Trowbridge's and Pacific shrews forms runways in the duff. The large hooves of elk and mule deer punch V-shaped tracks in this moist duff, showing where these large animals have come to browse the vine maples, shrubs, or grasses in the glades. Inside logs and other fallen debris, moisture-loving salamanders find snug homes, while winter wrens clamber atop the roughage, babbling to themselves as they search for insects.

The sparse undergrowth of parklike stands may not provide enough cover or browse to attract many ground or shrub species. You'd be better rewarded by watching for wildlife at the edges of these groves, especially where there is dense shrub growth around sunny fern glades or streams.

Allen's and rufous hummingbirds, Wilson's warblers, dark-eyed juncos, and purple finches all frequent these areas, searching for insects, seeds, or, in the hummingbird's case, nectar.

One of the major attractions of the redwood habitat is the abundance of moisture: some areas get more than 100 inches of rain a year (average is 60). Crawling along in the moist duff or hiding beneath logs and rocks, you might uncover any number of different salamanders, including the ensatina, California slender, clouded, Del Norte, and Olympic varieties. Banana slugs (the state invertebrate and mascot extraordinaire) also revel in the moist, cushiony litter. Trickling streams beneath the redwood boughs attract tailed frogs, redbelly newts, mountain beavers, spawning cutthroat trout and salmon, fish-eating birds, and raccoons. Aquatic insects emerging from the stream provide a varied diet for American dippers, swallows, and bats.

Vaux's Swift

The chimney swifts of the East didn't always nest inside the walls of chimneys. Long before our structures pierced the skyline, these birds nested in the hollowed-out stubs of giant eastern trees. Once these trees had been systematically removed by logging, chimneys became a handy alternative. In the West, the story is not quite so advanced. The Vaux's swift is still a bird of the forest, using burned-out or broken-off redwoods for its home.

Sometimes right before sunset, you may see a migrating flock of hundreds of Vaux's swifts circling in unison above a large, hollow redwood. They may fly in formation like this for up to an hour before one or two swifts descend into the depths of the snag. Suddenly a thin stream of swifts begins to whirl downward, unraveling from the flock like a string of black yarn. Once inside the snag, the birds cling to the walls with their strong claws. They roost clustered together in rows that overlap like shingles on a roof. In the morning, with a roar of wings, they ascend to begin their day of nonstop flying.

It is here in the air that the swifts are most completely at home. Their long, narrow, swept-back wings are the "racing model" in small bird design. The crescent shape of the wings cuts through the air with a minimum of drag, and the flight muscles are well developed both for the downstroke and, surprisingly, for the upstroke as well. Only one bird—the humming-bird—has upstroke muscles that are more developed than the swift's. In flight, swifts alternate between rapid wingbeats (too rapid for us to see) and bursts of high-speed gliding. This formula seems to work exceedingly well; in fact, the speed record for bird flight belongs to needle-tailed swifts in India, which were clocked at 172 and 218 miles per hour!

Of course, swifts are not always traveling at such breakneck speeds.

WILDLIFE LOCATOR CHART—REDWOOD FOREST

	Feeds from Air	Feeds in Tree Canopy	Feeds on Trunk	Feeds on Ground
Nests in Tree Canopy	Rufous Hummingbird Great Horned Owl	Band-tailed Pigeon Golden-crowned Kinglet Pine Siskin Red Tree Vole		Marbled Murrelet (Feeds in Water), Steller's Jay, Swainson's Thrush, American Robin, Varied Thrush
Nests in Trunk Cavity	Northern Pygmy-Owl Spotted Owl Vaux's Swift Western Flycatcher	Acorn Woodpecker Chestnut-backed Chickadee	Hairy Woodpecker Pileated Woodpecker Pygmy Nuthatch Brown Creeper	Winter Wren, Western Gray Squirrel, Douglas' Squirrel, Northern Flying Squirrel, Raccoon
Nests on Ground				Blue Grouse, Ruffed Grouse, Common Raven, Hermit Thrush, Elk, Mule Deer
Nests Beneath Ground or Debris				Pacific Shrew, Trowbridge's Shrew, Shrew-Mole, Coast Mole, Mountain Beaver, Sonoma Chipmunk, Townsend's Chipmunk, Deer Mouse, Creeping Vole, Pacific Jumping Mouse, Black Bear, Marten, Clouded Salamander, Black Salamander, California Slender Salamander, Ensatina, Del Norte Salamander, Sagebrush Lizard, Sharptail Snake, California Mountain Kingsnake
Nests in Water				Olympic Salamander, Redbelly Newt, Tailed Frog (Feeds in water)

COMMON RAVEN

WINTER WREN

CHESTNUT-BACKED CHICKADEE

GOLDEN-CROWNED KINGLET

SPOTTED OWL

VARIED THRUSH

BLUE GROUSE

Sometimes they ride the air currents in spiraling updrafts formed when (1) hot air rises from a warmed surface or (2) air is forced upward by a hill or a line of trees along a meadow. At night, some of the birds in a flock occasionally ride these updrafts out of sight, and pilots have seen them circling in flocks thousands of feet above the earth. Some researchers believe these night fliers may actually sleep on the wing, squeezing in catnaps during long glides, then waking up when they begin to lose too much altitude.

Swifts also gather all their food, nest materials, and water on the wing. The gape of their mouth is so wide it reaches behind their eyes, making it easier for them to snatch flying insects. To collect the twigs for their nests, they dive-bomb trees, breaking off twigs with their feet as they zoom past. To take a drink, they skim just above the surface of the water, dipping their bill in for an occasional sip. Sometimes they plunge just under the surface to bathe, shivering the excess water droplets off their feathers as they fly away. These birds are so aerial-oriented, in fact, that they have even been observed copulating in midair!

Look for Vaux's swifts—during the day, circling high over trees or low over lakes and rivers, chasing insects with erratic, batlike movements. On cloudy, damp days, you may find them flying closer to the ground. In the fall, just before sunset, look for flocks circling around hollow snags and then funneling into the hole. Aside from nesting and roosting, the swifts will never actually land. This constant airtime racks up many miles in their daily flight logs—516 miles/day was estimated for European swifts.

Length: 4–4½ inches.

Nests are enclosed—in hollow trees. Using their own saliva, the swifts glue twigs and conifer needles together, then attach the nest to the inside wall of the tree.

Listen for—a soft, high, insectlike call.

Pacific Shrew

As you stroll through the redwood forest, your hiking boots rock the beds of untold numbers of tiny Pacific shrews. They sleep most of the day, waking occasionally to raid their pantry of stored insects, slugs, snails, centipedes, small frogs, mice, and other foods. This meat hoard stays fresh because the prey animals are paralyzed, but not necessarily dead. Shrews usually place their numbing bite at the base of the skull, a main portal to the central nervous system. As they bite, copious amounts of saliva run down tiny grooves in their teeth, introducing a venom that is similar to a cobra's. In addition to paralyzing the prey, an enzyme in the venom also starts to digest chiton, the substance that forms the hard outer shell of insects.

Once nighttime comes, the shrews creep out onto the forest floor, hunting like small bloodhounds with their noses to the ground. At the first whiff of possible prey, they nose and dig through the litter of fallen needles, pouncing with both forefeet on anything that moves. If they hear the hum of whirring insect wings above them, they may also leap up for an attack. Whatever they can't eat on the spot they cache for daytime use. Another evolutionary trick they've learned is to reingest their own feces to get nutrients such as vitamin B and potassium they may not have absorbed the first time around.

In the hectic 16- to 18-month lifespan of a shrew, there is little time for anything besides eating and sleeping. With hearts that beat over 1,000 times a minute (compared with 10/minute for large mammals), and lungs that breathe 850 times a minute, their internal engines burn fuel faster than almost any other mammal's. At the same time, their bodies are giving off tremendous amounts of heat. Relative to their volume, they have a vast amount of skin area through which heat can escape. When the weather turns cold, they must crank up their metabolism to compensate for this heat loss. At this rate, a full gut can be dangerously empty in only three hours.

Thankfully, these shrews live in moist, damp environments that harbor millions of small food items. In many ways, they have the bounty all to themselves—small rodents such as mice and voles don't eat insects, and the larger mammals and birds can't fit into places where these insects hide. The shrew's small size enables it to exploit even very small prey such as nematodes that are only a fraction of an inch long—prey that would be uneconomical for other mammals to hunt.

Look for Pacific shrews—scurrying around logs and other fallen woody material, mostly at night but occasionally during the day. Their nose and whiskers are constantly atwitch, smelling and sensing their environment. They may also orient by echolocation, that is, sending out high-frequency sounds and "reading" the echoes that bounce back from objects in their path (similar to our sonar). The bobbing head motions of shrews in a new environment may be part of this reading process. Shrews also tend to memorize their surroundings, and then operate via automatic pilot, occasionally falling into researchers' traps that they didn't count on.

Length: Head and body, 3⅓ inches. Tail, 2–2¾ inches.

Look for nests—stuffed under logs, made of vegetation such as grasses, mosses, lichens, or leaves. The shrew burrows into the pile of material and shapes a small chamber. Sleeping shrews curl up nose to rump with their feet resting on their shoulders, presumably for warmth.

Look for runways—tiny matted-down trails or grass-covered tunnels around the bases of grass and sedge plants. Shrews may also dig pencil-sized burrows, leading with their flexible, sensitive snout. Watch as they emerge with an insect seized in their jaws.

Listen for—constant twittering as they forage.

Ensatina

In its egg, this salamander breathes with a set of large gills, vestiges from a time when its ancestors lived in water. By the time it hatches, these gills have disappeared, but no landlubbing lungs have formed to take their place. Instead, the ensatina must absorb oxygen through its skin or through tissues in its mouth lining. The oxygen must first be dissolved in a layer of water that surrounds the salamander like a life-support suit. For this reason, you rarely see these salamanders on the surface after the ground begins to dry up in early summer. They retreat to the moist burrows of other animals, to the root channels of dead trees, and under damp logs, leaves, and rocks. When the first drenching rains of autumn and winter saturate the ground, the ensatinas surface, drinking in water with their skin and tapping their nose to the rain-spattered ground to "smell" the odors of possible prey.

February and March are active breeding months, when the usually solitary ensatinas come together in a strange and elaborate mating ceremony. Instead of direct male-to-female insemination, all salamander males plant a jelly-capped stalk called a spermatophore on the ground, and the female picks this up with her cloacal lips (the cloaca is a vent on the undersurface of the body). In ensatinas, the ceremony begins when the male slowly sidles up to the female and rubs scent from his head and neck glands along her face, throat, and head. He eventually walks ahead of her, and she follows, straddling his tail and lower back in a "tail walk" that may go on for several hours. Finally, the male stops and begins to rock from side to side, lowering his vent to the surface and depositing a spermatophore. They again "tail walk" until the female is directly over the stalk. As she picks it up, he throws his tail over her back, moving it back and forth vigorously. This ceremony, with a few twists, is common to all the salamanders in this family.

Look for ensatinas—under a blanket of leaf litter and downed logs that hold in moisture and buffer temperatures. Their prey species—insects, spiders, crustaceans, and earthworms—are also attracted by this damp blanket. Ensatinas are most common in areas where there is a mixture of redwoods and oaks. The redwoods give them moisture and shade during the summer, allowing them to stay aboveground longer. In the winter, the bare oaks let in light that keeps the floor warm enough for foraging. They spend dry periods underground in the burrows of other animals, in rotted logs, or under redwood slabs, rocks, or other objects. Their defensive display is very similar to that of the arboreal salamander, described on page 187.

They stand stiff-legged and swaybacked, with tail waving to tempt the predator. When the predator strikes, this tail will break off and allow the harassed ensatina to make a quick getaway. Before too long, a new tail grows, hopefully before another predator strikes.

Length: 3–5⅞ inches.

Eggs are underground—in hollows under the surface litter, beneath the bark of logs, and in the burrows of other animals. Eggs are laid in spring or early summer in grapelike clusters of 12–14, and faithfully attended by one of the parents, usually the female. She guards against predators and keeps the eggs moist with her skin secretions and urine, presumably to prevent mold and spoilage.

Listen for—a squeaking or terse scream when the salamander is picked up. Though it has no real voice, it produces this sound by contracting its throat and forcing air through its jaws or nostrils.

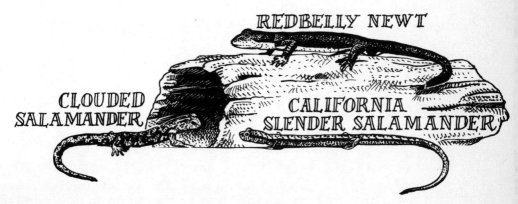

REDBELLY NEWT

CLOUDED SALAMANDER

CALIFORNIA SLENDER SALAMANDER

Ponderosa Pine

Douglas-fir

WHITE-HEADED WOODPECKER

ABERT'S SQUIRREL

Needle-and-thread

MILK SNAKE

Deer Brush

Birchleaf Spirea

Big Sagebrush

Kinnikinnik

VIOLET~GREEN SWALLOW

FLAMMULATED OWL

PYGMY NUTHATCH

YELLOW~PINE CHIPMUNK

GOPHER SNAKE

Antelope Bitterbrush

Curlleaf Cercocarpus

Ponderosa Pine Forest

WHERE TO SEE THIS HABITAT:

Arizona: Apache-Sitgreaves, Coconino, Kaibab, and Tonto national forests

California: Eldorado, Inyo, Klamath, Lassen, Mendocino, Plumas, Shasta-Trinity, Sierra, Six Rivers, Stanislaus, and Tahoe national forests; Kings Canyon, Sequoia, and Yosemite national parks

Colorado: Arapaho, Gunnison, and Pike national forests; Rocky Mountain National Park

Idaho: Boise, Caribou, Challis, Clearwater, Idaho Panhandle, Nez Perce, Payette, Salmon, Sawtooth, and Targhee national forests

Montana: Beaverhead, Bitterroot, and Custer national forests; Glacier National Park

New Mexico: Carson, Cibola, Gila, Lincoln, and Santa Fe national forests

Oregon: Malheur, Ochoco, Umatilla, Wallowa-Whitman, and Winema national forests

Utah: Ashley, Fishlake, and Manti-La Sal national forests

Washington: Okanogan National Forest

Wyoming: Bridger-Teton, Medicine Bow, and Shoshone national forests; Middle Fork of Powder River (Bureau of Land Management)

Ponderosa Pine Forest

BEGINNINGS

Ponderosa pines are the first tall forest trees you encounter as you climb the foothills. To reach them, you may have to pass through grasslands, sagebrush, chaparral, oak woodlands, or pinyon-juniper woodlands, depending on where you're hiking. Once past the ponderosa zone, you may still see fingers of these pines colonizing burned areas, or toughing it out on sites that are too dry, hot, and sunny for other trees. If they can find the right niche, the "can-do" ponderosas will even venture up as far as the subalpine zone of spruce and fir.

No other major western tree can defy altitudinal boundaries this way. Nor is any tree as widely distributed. One reason for the ponderosa's versatility is its extraordinary resistance to drought. Its main weapon is a root system that snakes down as far as 36 feet and sprawls out as far as 100 feet on either side of the trunk. Instead of tapering into fine, hairy rootlets the way most trees' do, ponderosa roots are boldly and simply branched. This gives the tree enough root surface to absorb moisture when it is abundant, but prevents the tree from pumping the soil layer dry when moisture is scarce.

Aboveground, the evergreen needle has a thick skin and breathing pores that are sunken out of the wind. This allows the tree to greatly reduce its loss of water. On the other hand, when soil water is abundant, the tree is able to exhale water vapor at a rapid rate—a quality that helps it keep cool on those sizzling, south-facing slopes. Most surprisingly, the ponderosa can drink in traces of water through its leaves and transport them to its roots! By reversing this normal process of water intake, the ponderosa is able to take advantage of the night dew and foggy weather.

The open, parklike look of an old ponderosa pine forest is a direct result of centuries of drought and fire. The trees are widely spaced so that

CHARACTERISTIC PLANTS:

Trees, Shrubs, and Vines:

antelope bitterbrush
Apache pine
Arizona pine
big cone Douglas-fir
bigleaf maple
big sagebrush
birchleaf spirea
bitter cherry
blue spruce
buckbrush
California black oak
California buckthorn
California-laurel
California red fir
California white fir
canyon live oak
cercocarpuses (mountain mahogany)
Chihuahua pine
chokecherry
Colorado barberry
common juniper
Coulter pine

creambush oceanspray
deer brush
Digger pine
Douglas-fir
Fendler ceanothus
Gambel oak
gooseberries
grand fir
greenleaf manzanita
Hooker's townsendia
incense-cedar
Jeffrey pine
kinnikinnik
knobcone pine
limber pine
lodgepole pine
mountain-misery
mountain ninebark
Oregon white oak
Pacific dogwood
Pacific madrone
pin cherry
pinyon pine
poison-oak
ponderosa pine
quaking aspen

ribes (currant)
Rocky Mountain juniper
roses
rubber rabbitbrush
Sierra currant
Sierra gooseberry
snowberries
snowbrush ceanothus
southwestern white pine
sugar pine
tanoak
thimbleberry
wax currant
western juniper
western larch
western serviceberry
western starflower
western white pine
whitebark pine
white fir
willows
Wood's rose
yellowleaf silktassel

Antelope Bitterbrush

each one has its own helping of moisture and nutrients. Competing plants in the understory are pruned back by regular lightning fires. For eons, this formula worked well for the pines, and enabled them to spread throughout the West. In a few short years of "progress," we have managed to alter that formula, triggering a series of changes that will affect the forests for decades to come.

Herbaceous Plants:
Arizona fescue
bedstraws
blanket-flower
bluebunch wheatgrass
blue grama
bluegrasses
bottlebrush squirrel-
   tail
bracken fern
cheatgrass brome
common wild gera-
   nium
creeping Oregon grape
curlycup gumweed
fescues
forest clarkia
goosefoot violet
green penstemon
groundsels
hairy dropseed
hawkweeds
Idaho fescue
larkspurs
lupines
milkwort
miner's candle
mountain bladderpod
mountain brome
mountain muhly
muhly
muttongrass
needle-and-thread
oatgrasses
one-sided penstemon
pasque flower
pipsissewa
prairie junegrass
prairie spiderwort
purple nightshade
reedgrass
sand lily
Sierra iris
Simpson's hedgehog
   cactus
spike fescue
splendid gilia
sulphur buckwheat
threeawn
trailplant
western needlegrass
western wallflower
western wheatgrass
wheatgrasses
whiskbroom parsley
wild strawberry
wooly mule's ears
yarrow

Curlleaf
Cercocarpus

THE PRICE OF PROXIMITY

When the gold rush descended on California in 1859, ponderosa pine forests were the most convenient sources of softwood lumber. They were stripped for their timber, then cleared to give cattle and sheep more forageland.

   When the cattle boom ended in the 1930s, a series of good growing years happened to coincide with a series of good ponderosa cone crops. Winters were warm and springs were cool. There were no longer as many cattle to graze the young seedlings, nor were the overgrazed grasses vigorous enough to exclude the pines. All across their range, seedlings grew into dense thickets that scarcely resembled the traditional forests of open, park-like graciousness. Natural fires that might have helped thin these forests were squelched by crews of professional fire fighters. As a result, the ponderosa forests from this era are still dense and shady, with an understory dominated by shade-tolerant plants.

What's missing in the understory is the next generation of ponderosas. Seedlings of ponderosa pine can't get a good start in the shade of their densely packed parents. Shade-tolerant species such as Douglas-fir thrive here, however, forming a solid underlayer that looks like a forest within a forest. As the old ponderosas fall prey to insects and disease, these successors are ready and waiting to fill in the gap. In the Sierra Nevada, the heir-apparents are incense-cedar and white fir. In ponderosa forests here and throughout the West, this changing of the guard is taking place silently but surely, altering the character of the land for generations to come.

WHAT'S IN IT FOR WILDLIFE?

Ponderosa pine forests have a hundred different faces: from the spacious savannas of the foothills, to the shady second-growth thickets, to the wild mixtures of quaking aspen, cottonwoods, ponderosa, and other needleleaf trees. Wildlife can find cover, shelter, and food not only in these forested sections, but also in the scattered, dry meadows that are so closely tied to the pine forests.

The more open the pine stands are, the more lush their undergrowth, and the more varied their wildlife clientele. The grasses, sedges, forbs, and shrubs beneath the trees provide nutritious forage for grazers such as mule deer. Because these forests grow at elevations that are cool enough to get precipitation, and their soils are deep enough to store it, there is moisture to support green growth for much of the season. In the very hot months of late summer, when downslope grasslands have dried up and turned brown, the forage beneath the ponderosas is still green and beckoning. In the spring, elk stop by on their way up to cooler summer heights, and in the fall, they return on their way down to winter ranges.

Other species look to ponderosa pines for what their canopies can offer. Watch for flocks of American crows and black-billed magpies heading out to the meadows at dawn, and trickling back to roost in the branches at dusk. Wild turkeys prefer old trees because of the open crowns.

Birds and mammals that live here in the winter rely on food sources that remain above the snow—namely, insects in the bark and seeds clustered in cones. Good cone crops come only once every 3–5 years, and populations of red crossbills and Abert's squirrels fluctuate yearly in response to this food supply. Some small rodents cache an emergency larder of ponderosa seeds for the winter. The caches that are forgotten will sprout into clumps of tender seedlings, which in turn attract mice, rabbits, chipmunks, and ground squirrels. Northern pocket gophers will head underground to dine on the seedlings' roots. Mule deer and elk may also depend on ponderosa for twigs and buds in the winter, when other food sources are scarce. For porcupines, the inner bark is a good meal at any time of year. Even dwarf mistletoe, a parasitic plant that buries its roots under the bark of ponderosa branches, does not go to waste. Tree squirrels feed on its leafless twigs, and birds eat the berries, unwittingly helping to transport the seeds to healthy trees.

In addition to dwarf mistletoe, root rots and stem rusts may also weaken ponderosas and hasten their death, much to the delight of cavity-drilling birds such as northern flickers and white-headed, Lewis', and hairy woodpeckers. Once abandoned, these cavities are used by such species as northern pygmy- and flammulated owls, American kestrels, western bluebirds, and violet-green swallows. Brown creepers simply tuck their nests into the space behind the loosening bark. Inside the snag, demolition crews of wood-chewing insects are having a field day, and their spiraling numbers are supporting an extra-large army of insect-eating birds. These snags may remain standing for up to 30 years, depending on how they were killed. Those struck by lightning, mountain pine beetles, or fire stand the longest because of the "embalming" resin that remains in their trunk. Diseased trees evidently lose much of this resin and break down sooner. Living trees that have been partially damaged by lightning, wind, or mistletoe infection may begin serving the wildlife community even before they die. Forests that are older than 160 years are most likely to have a good supply of both dead and "living snags," and thus a good supply of snag-dependent species for you to watch.

Pygmy Nuthatch

Pygmy nuthatches are the all-terrain vehicles of the ponderosa treetops. They can hitch up tree trunks the way woodpeckers can, then turn around and head down the trunk just as easily. These smallest and lightest members of the nuthatch family are also the most agile. They're the ones you see hopping out to the most remote cones and hanging upside down with their back to the ground. Their thin, needle-sharp bill is perfect for poking into crevices and picking moths and spiders from leaf surfaces. Their favorite

WILD TURKEY — CASSIN'S FINCH — LEWIS' WOODPECKER — WESTERN BLUEBIRD — MOUNTAIN BLUEBIRD — WESTERN TANAGER — MOUNTAIN CHICKADEE

WILDLIFE LOCATOR CHART—PONDEROSA PINE FOREST

	Feeds from Air	Feeds in Upper Canopy	Feeds in Lower Canopy	Feeds on Trunk	Feeds on Ground
Nests in Tree Canopy	Bald Eagle Cooper's Hawk Red-tailed Hawk Golden Eagle Long-eared Owl Black-chinned Hummingbird Anna's Hummingbird Olive-sided Flycatcher Western Wood-Pewee Hammond's Flycatcher American Redstart Hoary Bat	Clark's Nutcracker Hermit Warbler Grace's Warbler Western Tanager Purple Finch Red Crossbill Pine Siskin Evening Grosbeak	Band-tailed Pigeon Golden-crowned Kinglet Ruby-crowned Kinglet Solitary Vireo Yellow-rumped Warbler Black-throated Gray Warbler American Goldfinch		Mourning Dove, Steller's Jay, Black-billed Magpie, American Crow, American Robin, Varied Thrush, Chipping Sparrow, Cassin's Finch, Abert's Squirrel, Kaibab Squirrel
Nests in Trunk Cavity	American Kestrel Flammulated Owl Great Horned Owl Northern Pygmy-Owl Northern Saw-whet Owl Lewis' Woodpecker Western Flycatcher Violet-green Swallow	Acorn Woodpecker	Ash-throated Flycatcher Black-capped Chickadee Mexican Chickadee Mountain Chickadee Chestnut-backed Chickadee House Wren Western Bluebird	Yellow-bellied Sapsucker Williamson's Sapsucker Hairy Woodpecker White-headed Woodpecker Black-backed Woodpecker Pileated Woodpecker Red-breasted Nuthatch White-breasted Nuthatch Pygmy Nuthatch Brown Creeper	Bewick's Wren, Mountain Bluebird
Nests in Shrubs		Black-headed Grosbeak			Blue Grosbeak, Black-chinned Sparrow
Nests on Ground	Townsend's Solitaire				Blue Grouse, Wild Turkey, Hermit Thrush, Dark-eyed Junco
Nests Beneath Ground or Debris	Bank Swallow Western Small-footed Myotis				Yellow-pine Chipmunk, Colorado Chipmunk, Uinta Chipmunk, Northern Pocket Gopher, Deer Mouse, Mexican Woodrat, Western Rattlesnake, Milk Snake, California Mountain Kingsnake, Gopher Snake

foods include wasps, ants, beetles, moths, caterpillars, grasshoppers, spiders, spittlebugs (which form masses of white frothy bundles between the needles), and pine seeds.

Pygmies head down the trunk in a series of "drops," using their long strong toes and sharp, curved claws like grappling hooks on the long, rectangular blocks of bark. Most of the time, they move with their body at an angle across the trunk, rather than straight up and down. At rest, they may point their head and body straight down, but they keep their back foot turned sideways to keep a good grip on the bark. Their other foot is kept below them to brace their weight. From this head-down position, the nuthatches are able to look for insects in all the crevices that their right-side-up colleagues missed.

Usually your ears lead you to pygmy nuthatches before your eyes pick them out. They drift through the pines in highly social flocks, calling incessantly to one another in a high-pitched, excited "ti-di, ti-di, ti-di, ti-di." Other birds such as yellow-rumped warblers, plain titmice, and mountain chickadees join the nuthatches, taking advantage of the fact that birds that forage in flocks find more food than those going solo. Pygmy nuthatches are also gregarious when roosting at night. One ponderosa pine cavity in Colorado was home to 100 birds. While the company may help them conserve heat on cool evenings, the warmth is not without cost. Researchers investigating these group homes found that the bottom layer of birds often suffocate before morning!

Look for pygmy nuthatches—in the upper canopy of open-grown ponderosa pines, foraging in small family groups or mixed flocks. Pygmy nuthatches don't migrate, but they may drift down the mountain to lower elevations in the winter. Flock numbers are greatest at this time. They are most active during the day, hopping with staccato movements on the twigs, branches, and trunks, or flying in an undulating, bouncing-ball flight. They do most of their foraging in the outermost twigs and pine needle tufts. They may even flutter in the air in front of the foliage to catch insects.

Length: 3³/₄–4¹/₂ inches.

Look for nest holes—6 to 60 feet up (typically more than 25) in well-

UINTA CHIPMUNK

253

rotted wood near the top of a large, dead pine or on the underside of a branch. The hole is roughly circular, up to 2 inches wide, and leads to an 8- to 9-inch-deep cavity pecked out by the bird's small bill. When they can find it, they may also use an abandoned woodpecker nest, lining it with pinecone scales, bark shreds, moss, leaves, fur, and feathers.

Listen for—"ti-di, ti-di" uttered repeatedly.

Abert's Squirrel

These tassel-eared squirrels look like they belong in an enchanted forest. White fur covers their underside, frosts their tail, and rings their eyes, while tall, reddish tufts sprout from their ears in an exclamation of surprise. Their lustrous coats are gray with a rusty band along the back, in perfect harmony with the orange and gray bark of the ponderosa pines. In some places, you can go for days without seeing one of these sprites, and then you'll see a treeful of seven or eight scurrying in a whirlwind.

The breeding season brings them together in day-long "mating bouts." Up to eight males will surround the base of a tree where a female is casually eating or preening. When she moves to another tree, the entourage follows her. Eventually, one dominant male will ascend the tree and claim it as his own. He then spends most of his time warning and chasing off the other males that try to get close to the female. These hair-raising chases may include 8-foot leaps between trees or crashing drops through the branches. In freefall jumps of more than 50 feet, the squirrels spread their limbs to make a sail of themselves, presumably waving their tail for balance. With a bounce they land on their chest and abdomen, seemingly unharmed. For his trouble, the male earns the right to mate with the female and pass on his genes.

Few mammals are as loyal to a particular species of tree as the Abert's squirrel. With the exception of the roots, the squirrels make use of every part of the ponderosa pine for nesting, shelter, and food. They favor the seeds above all, and in a single summer day, a squirrel may raid 75 cones. Ponderosas don't bear good cone crops every year, however, so squirrels have had to find alternate sources of nourishment.

One of their most important foods is the inner bark of twigs—the thin "cambium" layer that grows between the outer bark and the inner wood. This cambium is composed of vessels that transport freshly manufactured sugars to all parts of the tree. White, succulent, and sweet, the cambium is available at all times of year, becoming especially important to the squirrels in winter. The outermost branch tips are most prized. After breaking off the twig, the squirrel trims off the terminal tuft, then rotates the twig in its forefeet., using its teeth to strip the bark like a blade on a lathe. Squirrels "twig" certain trees repeatedly, presumably favoring those with more nutritive value and better taste (which may be a function of the lower amount of essential oils in the tree).

To supplement their winter diet of cambium, the squirrels will methodically comb the branches for succulent buds. They pull the buds toward them, then peel off the coarse outer bracts to get to the softer tissues within. In early May, they eat the blossoming flowers whole. Later in the season, as the petals dry, they concentrate on the yellow pollen, often carrying a faceful around in their fur.

Many experts believe that Abert's squirrel populations roller-coaster in synch with the cone crop cycle of the pines. A heavy seed crop usually drains the tree of nutrients, and the cambium layer is therefore not as rich the following year. Over the next 3–4 years, cone crops will be sparse, but the cambium layer will grow richer as the tree restocks its stores. After feasting on this cambium buildup all winter, the squirrels are usually in good breeding condition come spring, and wind up having larger, more successful broods. For the tree, the buildup culminates in another large seed crop. The surplus of squirrels live high on the hog for one summer, and then must face another couple of years of slim cambium pickings. At this point, the roller-coaster dives, and the squirrel numbers are once again reduced.

Look for Abert's squirrels—dashing up tree trunks or around to the back side of branches as you approach. They sit on perches in the tree to gnaw twigs, and can often be seen climbing out to the outermost branches for flowers, buds, or cones. In October or November, when seeds are being shed from cones, they may forage on the ground for individual seeds. They also enjoy mushrooms that grow in the litter layer beneath the tree, and are apparently unharmed by species of mushrooms that would poison humans. They are most active during the day, and can be seen out in all but the most inclement weather. On the north rim of the Grand Canyon, you may see a subspecies called kaibab squirrel that has dark underparts and an all-white tail.

Length: Head and body, 11–12 inches. Tail, 8–9 inches.

Look for nests—typically a 1½-foot-wide ball of pine twigs placed in a fork on the south side of a tree or where a large limb branches. The average nest is placed 30–50 feet off the ground in a tree with a trunk diameter of about 17 inches. The squirrels seem to prefer uneven-aged, open forests with trees spaced in small, even-aged clumps throughout. They may also build nests in "witches' brooms" (the bunched-up branches found in trees infected with dwarf mistletoe). They weave twigs up to a half inch wide and 6–24 inches long to form the frame, then line the inside with shredded grass, juniper bark, pine bark, cloth, string, cotton, and newspapers. There may be as many as three openings in the nest. When the young are between 3 and 6 days old, they are moved to a larger nest, where the entrance is higher above the bottom, perhaps to make sure the young don't accidentally fall out. These nests are used for resting as well, and in the summer, the squirrels may remove the roof for an air-conditioned effect. Look for a thick layer of droppings on branches just outside the nest.

Look for feeding debris—barkless twigs, shreds of pine bark, bracts of buds, and discarded tufts of pine needles clipped from the ends of twigs. Researchers actually count the fallen needle tufts after a snowstorm to get an approximate population count. They figure a single squirrel will strip 45 twigs/day.

Look for tracks—foreprints are round, 1 inch long, while hindprints are twice as long and more triangular. When bounding, the hindprints might register ahead of foreprints, leaving tracks that look like exclamation points (!!).

Listen for—clucks, growls, barks, screeches, and squeals, especially during confrontations between vying males. Visual signals such as tail fluffing, foot thumping, and tail flicking often accompany these calls.

Gopher Snake

The gopher snake is one of great sound but little real fury. Its hiss has one of the highest decibel levels heard in snakes, thanks to some fancy "amplifiers" in its throat. Behind the opening in its vocal cords, two portions of the trachea balloon with air. In front of them, a fin of cartilage stands in the airstream acting like a reed in a horn, creating even more sound as air is expelled. The hiss is part of a sophisticated ruse in which the gopher snake imitates the far more dangerous western rattlesnake, and thus makes predators think twice before approaching. To begin its act, the snake coils, bobbing its upper body up and down and spreading its triangular head to make itself look larger than it really is. At first glance, the blotches on its back are surprisingly similar to the diamonds on a rattler's skin. As a final touch, it vibrates its tail rapidly in dry vegetation, convincingly imitating the sound of rattles.

In reality, the gopher snake has neither rattles nor venom to back up its threatening display. When it comes time to subdue its prey, it uses a patient, steady grip instead of a strike. After looping around a mouse, ground squirrel, or bird, it holds the grip just tight enough to keep the animal from taking a breath. This slow suffocation, rather than crushing, is practiced by all "constrictor" snakes.

Its namesake, the pocket gopher, is one of the snake's favorite prey selections. Using its head like a spade, the snake digs into the tough bulkhead of a gopher mound, piling the dirt onto a loop of its body and tossing it backward. Once inside, it sinuously wends its way down into the bedroom of its quarry. In areas with plenty of eligible prey, the snake need not wander far. In fact, it may spend months or even years within an area of only a few hundred feet to a mile in diameter.

If a road is anywhere in its domain, the snake may frequently stretch out there to bask, especially in the spring when it has just emerged from hibernation. Unfortunately, its rattlesnake imitation works too well on human beings. Many of these innocent, nonvenomous snakes are badly beaten by drivers who mistake them for rattlesnakes (and then presume they have the "right" to kill a venomous snake). The loss of gopher snakes puts a sharp dent in the ecosystem; ask any farmer who once depended on these snakes to help keep rodent populations under control.

Look for gopher snakes—during the day, stalking prey on the ground or, occasionally, up in a tree or bush in search of bird eggs. They seek refuge in rodent burrows and under objects such as stones, logs, and boards.

Length: 2½–6 feet.

Eggs are underground—in shallow cavities or under logs and other debris. The 3–24 eggs incubate in 70 days; the emerging young are 12–18 inches long.

Look for fighting males—locked in a combat dance that looks like the entwined snakes of the physician's symbol. These battles are mostly pushing contests (like arm wrestling) and may go on for over an hour. When waged in a prone position, the object is to force the opponent to roll over. The snakes corkscrew slowly ahead for several yards in this manner. Eventually, the loser becomes exhausted and slithers away, leaving the victorious snake with a patch of ground on which he can court a female. It may be that females are attracted to winners of these contests, perhaps by a distinctive smell they acquire.

WESTERN RATTLESNAKE

SPOTTED OWL

Douglas-fir

Grand Fir

Western Hemlock

RED TREE VOLE

"snag"

Spotted Owl nest

PILEATED WOODPECKER

PACIFIC TREEFROG

Salal

Pacific Rhododendron

Bigleaf Maple

Western Redcedar

"witches' broom"

Western White Pine

NORTHERN FLYING SQUIRREL

WINTER WREN

CLOUDED SALAMANDER

Vine Maple

Creambush Oceanspray

Common Pipsissewa

Old-Growth Douglas-Fir Forest

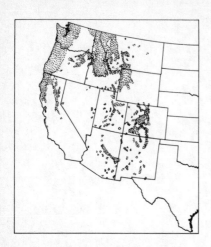

WHERE TO SEE THIS HABITAT:

California: Klamath and Six Rivers national forests
Idaho: Boise, Clearwater, Idaho Panhandle, Nez Perce, Salmon, and Sawtooth national forests
Montana: Beaverhead, Bitterroot, Helena, Kootenai, Lewis and Clark, and Lolo national forests
Oregon: Malheur, Mount Hood, Rogue River, Siskiyou, Siuslaw, Umpqua, and Willamette national forests; Valley of the Giants Natural Area
Washington: Colville, Gifford Pinchot, Okanogan, and Olympic national forests; North Cascades and Olympic national parks
Wyoming: Grand Teton National Park

Old-Growth Douglas-Fir

Forest

BEGINNINGS

Douglas-fir plays different roles in the forest depending on where it grows. In the Rockies, for instance, interior Douglas-fir is a "climax" species on midelevation slopes, taking over after pioneers such as lodgepole pine, quaking aspen, western larch, or ponderosa pine have prepared the site. In these cold and often arid sites, a 100-foot Douglas-fir would be considered large.

In the moist, majestic forests of the Pacific Northwest, however, coastal Douglas-fir is a giant, reaching heights of 165–295 feet and diameters of 3–6 feet. Here, the Douglas-fir acts as a pioneer tree, preparing the ground for western hemlock and western redcedar, the true "climax" trees of the region. This takeover usually requires a good 400–600 years without a major disturbance such as a catastrophic fire or insect outbreak. Because such tranquil periods are rare in nature, the hemlocks and redcedars have not had a chance to take over completely. Many of the Pacific Northwest forests are still dominated by Douglas-fir.

In this moister region, forests don't start developing "old-growth" characteristics until the trees are 175–250 years old.

By this time, many of the ancient trees have begun to succumb to insects and diseases. Large and leafless, these snags often remain standing for more than a century. Those that have fallen create a mossy obstacle course on the forest floor. Streams in old-growth forests are also littered with huge logs. Besides these obvious signs, there is a ponderous "feel" to an old-growth forest that is difficult to describe, yet unmistakable.

Old-growth Douglas-fir trees have crowns that are shaped like bottle brushes and filled with up to 60 million needles, exposing 30,000 square feet of food-making surface area to the sun. Each tree has its own peculiar shape, fashioned over centuries by genetics, weather, insects, animals, and fire. Many times, the top will have broken off, and side branches will have begun to grow upward. Scores of different kinds of lichens and mosses grow atop the branches. These lichens convert atmospheric nitrogen into a plant nutrient which then becomes available to the whole forest through leaching, litter fall, and decomposition. After years and years, the layers of lichen begin to form a sort of organic "soil" atop the branches, sometimes several centimeters thick.

Unfortunately, many of the forests in this region will never live to see this ripe old age. Timber producers usually want to harvest trees as soon as their growth rate slows. In fact, most rotations (cutting cycles) in the

CHARACTERISTIC PLANTS:

Trees, Shrubs, and Vines:

bigleaf maple
California red fir
chokecherry
common juniper
creambush oceanspray
Douglas-fir
Engelmann spruce
golden chinkapin
grand fir
Greene Mountain-ash
incense-cedar
kinnikinnik
lodgepole pine
mountain hemlock
mountain-lover

mountain ninebark
noble fir
Oregon white oak
Pacific madrone
Pacific silver fir
ponderosa pine
Port-Orford-cedar
quaking aspen
red alder
red huckleberry
red raspberry
redwood
Rocky Mountain juniper
Rocky Mountain maple
roses
salal
salmonberry
Scouler willow

Sitka spruce
subalpine fir
sugar pine
tanoak
thimbleberry
vine maple
western hemlock
western larch
western redcedar
western white pine
whitebark pine
white fir

Herbaceous Plants:

cliff bush
heartleaf arnica
pipsissewa
swordfern

Pacific Rhododendron

Pacific Northwest are only 45–145 years long—not nearly long enough for a forest to develop old-growth characteristics.

At the same time, our last remaining examples of truly ancient forests are being slowly but surely removed. The incentives for harvesting old-growth forests are powerful; in 1975, 100 acres of this timber sold for about $1.6 million. As the private holdings of old-growth Douglas-firs dwindle, the last remaining stands on public lands grow more and more valuable, especially to wildlife.

AN ACTIVE AFTERLIFE

When a Douglas-fir dies, it may remain standing 75–125 years, rotting in stages from the top down. Because it doesn't immediately lose its bark, you may not recognize the dead trees (snags) in an old-growth forest until you look up. You can be sure that wildlife recognize them, however. Researchers have identified at least 53 species (39 birds and 14 mammals) that nest in these cavities, relying on the thick bark to insulate them from extremes of heat and cold. Besides nesting, snags are used for foraging, food storage, hunting perches, branch nests, roosting, courtship displays, and overwintering.

Once a snag falls to the ground, it begins to serve a whole new community of plants and animals, offering a habitat that is moist, protected from predators, and long-lasting. A 30-inch-diameter log may take 480–580 years to decompose. During this time, the log may be the only element of the habitat that survives a disturbance (such as logging, windthrow, etc), thus providing its clients with some continuity during times of change.

These logs are also vital to the new forests that seed into the disturbed openings. The logs attract small mammals that scatter their droppings throughout the opening. The droppings often contain spores of "helper" fungi (mycorrhiza) that the mammals have eaten. These helper fungi grow in association with the roots of needleleaf trees, helping them to extract nutrients from the soil. By "lacing" the disturbed opening with these root fungi, the mammals inadvertently help tree seedlings to get established.

The logs themselves may also serve as nurseries for small tree seedlings. Logs absorb water like sponges, and are full of nutrients from the decaying wood. The seeds that fall on such a bed quickly germinate into a row of tiny seedlings. As they grow, they send their roots down on either side of the log, traveling as much as 10 feet to reach the ground below really huge logs. When the log finally rots away, the mature trees are left perched on their prop roots with the log-space now open beneath them. It almost looks as if they are trying to escape their earthly bounds!

VAUX'S SWIFT

DEER MOUSE

When a log falls into a stream, it provides an equally vital service, Water backed up behind the log is soon coated with a "scum" of organic matter—fallen needles, leaves, etc. Insects and decay organisms break this litter into smaller food particles that other organisms can eat. Material flowing over the log may plunge down to a similar pool, where it is decomposed further. This stepped stream profile also dissipates the energy that would normally cut a stream channel and erode the banks. In addition, the log dams, pools, and gravel bars form a mosaic of habitats for various stream organisms (see Mountain Stream, page 93.)

WHAT'S IN IT FOR WILDLIFE?

Old-growth forests are unique in their diversity and their wide range of habitat niches. Lush, multilayered understories of herbs, shrubs, and small trees occur in patches where sunlight breaks through the canopy. Other shade-tolerant ferns, bushes, and vines flourish in the darker sections. This greenery provides an ideal curtain of protection as well as a source of food for a variety of birds and mammals.

Wildlife living in the canopy of an old-growth tree are shielded from enemies, high winds, and drought. The densely needled branches hold 264,000 gallons of water per acre, equivalent to 1¼ inches of precipitation. In addition to collecting rain, the needles "comb" condensed moisture from the fog. The airborne dust in this bit of moisture is enough to support the aerial gardens of lichen on the branches, where 1,500 different invertebrates (including insects) make their homes. The red tree vole may spend a lifetime aloft in the branches, rarely coming down. The spotted owl and the northern flying squirrel also use old-growth canopies for protection and nesting.

The larger the tree, the better it is for cavity nesters; a tree that is "ripe" for nesting will be at least 15 inches in diameter, adorned with shelflike fungal conks, rotting dead branch stubs, or woodpecker cavities. Woodpeckers often drill many more cavities than they need in a season,

HERMIT THRUSH

DOUGLAS' SQUIRREL

BLACK SALAMANDER

MULE DEER

HAMMOND'S FLYCATCHER

WILDLIFE LOCATOR CHART—OLD-GROWTH DOUGLAS-FIR FOREST

	Feeds from Air	Feeds in Upper Canopy	Feeds in Lower Canopy	Feeds on Trunk	Feeds on Ground
Nests in Tree Canopy	Osprey, Bald Eagle, Sharp-shinned Hawk, Northern Goshawk, Rufous Hummingbird, Olive-sided Flycatcher, Hammond's Flycatcher	Townsend's Warbler, Hermit Warbler, Western Tanager, Red Crossbill, Pine Siskin, Evening Grosbeak	Golden-crowned Kinglet, Ruby-crowned Kinglet, Yellow-rumped Warbler	Yellow-bellied Sapsucker, Williamson's Sapsucker, Acorn Woodpecker, Hairy Woodpecker, White-headed Woodpecker, Black-backed Woodpecker, Pileated Woodpecker, Red-breasted Nuthatch, White-breasted Nuthatch, Brown Creeper, Shasta Salamander	Steller's Jay, Hermit Thrush, Varied Thrush, Chipping Sparrow, Cassin's Finch
Nests in Trunk Cavity	Great Horned Owl, Spotted Owl, Northern Saw-whet Owl, Western Flycatcher, Vaux's Swift		Mountain Chickadee, Chestnut-backed Chickadee		Winter Wren, Mountain Bluebird, Northern Flying Squirrel, Douglas' Squirrel, Raccoon
Nests in Shrubs					Swainson's Thrush
Nests on Ground		Townsend's Solitaire	Red Tree Vole		Spruce Grouse, Blue Grouse, Ruffed Grouse, Dark-eyed Junco, Elk, Mule Deer
Nests Beneath Ground or Debris					Trowbridge's Shrew, Deer Mouse, Southern Red-backed Vole, Porcupine, Black Bear, Clouded Salamander, Black Salamander, Oregon Slender Salamander, Ensatina, Western Whiptail, Western Skink, Short-horned Lizard, Rubber Boa, Sharptail Snake, Western Rattlesnake
Nests in Water					Tiger Salamander, Pacific Treefrog

and these excess cavities are then used by other cavity nesters such as small owls, raptors, raccoons, porcupines, and northern flying squirrels. Temperatures are buffered by the thick woody walls, making it snug for roosting, breeding, and overwintering. In the rotted or fire-scarred base of a tree, you may find a larger den used by black bears.

Look for the platform nests of ospreys and bald eagles on the broken-off tops of snags. When the snag's bark finally starts to loosen, brown creepers and bats can tuck their nests in the envelope between the trunk and the loose bark. Branches may also hold nests, or may be used as hunting and perching sites by owls, daytime birds of prey, and flycatchers.

Snags are usually full of insects, and have three different layers that insect hunters can explore. Brown creepers, white-breasted nuthatches, and white-headed woodpeckers pick adult bark beetles, spiders, and ants from the outside surface of the bark. Hairy woodpeckers and sapsuckers dig to the layer just beneath to excavate beetle larvae and pupae from their maze-like "galleries." Pileated woodpeckers strike all the way into the heartwood of the snag, digging large rectangular holes in their hunt for carpenter ants. Acorn woodpeckers drill a collection of tiny holes, then plug them with acorns that will sustain them throughout the winter (see page 184).

Once a snag topples, it makes an ideal stomping ground for moisture-craving salamanders and frogs. The Pacific treefrog escapes extreme temperatures and the eyes of hungry owls by hiding between the loose bark and the wood. Protected areas under the log may harbor a grouse and her eggs or a chilled snowshoe hare. The root wad is used by flycatchers for perching and by juncos for nesting. Limbs that now stick up in the air are used as perches and, if hollow, as nest cavities. The fallen trunk provides a food source for woodpeckers such as the pileated. Elevated areas of the log are used as lookouts and as feeding platforms. The hollow insides may harbor weasels, fishers, raccoons, and a variety of other small mammals. When the snag finally begins to crumble into the earth, the powdery wood becomes a cache site for squirrels, a daybed for elk, a dusting bath for grouse, and a tunneling track for deer mice.

Spotted Owl

The spotted owl has become a biological mascot for organizations wishing to preserve the last remaining tracts of old-growth forests in the Pacific Northwest. Spotted owls clearly prefer forests with old-growth characteristics. If these traditional nesting grounds are destroyed by logging or development, the birds will not renest unless similar, unoccupied tracts are available.

Unfortunately, many of the remaining old-growth forests are still being felled; only isolated islands will remain by the year 2000. In urging public land managers to preserve extensive areas of old-growth, biologist Eric Forsman reasons this way: it's better to err on the conservative side and find out we've preserved too much than to cut now and find out later that our forests are fragmented beyond usefulness. After all, he reminds us, once it's logged, it's extremely unlikely that old-growth will ever be regenerated.

The owls themselves are well adapted for foraging in the low-light conditions of dense forests. Their eyes are huge (almost as large as ours) and have oversized pupils able to take in lots of light. An extra supply of "rods," minute visual cells that are extremely sensitive to movement, allow them to detect prey in 1/100 of the light that we would need.

The eyes of spotted owls are also placed close together on the front of their face, so that the right and left fields of vision overlap somewhat, giving them stereoscopic, binocular vision. This three-dimensional sight covers a 70-degree arc, which is ten times wider than the three-dimensional range of most birds. In this range, their vision has depth; prey objects stand out from a matching background so their position is easier to compute for an accurate strike. These well-adapted eyes are tubular, rather than disk-shaped as in other birds, and so can't be rotated in their sockets. To compensate, owls' necks are remarkably flexible, enabling them to turn their head 270 degrees so they can look directly behind them.

Even without their sight, spotted owls would usually be able to locate their prey by sound alone. Their large ear openings are placed far apart on either side of a wide face. One ear opening is shaped differently and positioned slightly higher on the head than the other. These asymmetries cause sounds to register sooner or be a little louder in one ear than the other. By taking these two "readings" and triangulating, the owl is able to pinpoint the source of sound, even as it scurries under a thick clump of foliage.

To carry them from their perch to their target, spotted owls have a wingspan of over 3 feet. When you consider that their body weighs only 22–28 ounces, you can see why they are such agile fliers, able to turn and twist with ease through the dense maze of tree limbs. Their feathers are softer than those of most other birds and frayed on the leading edges to deflect air smoothly and silently. Unsuspecting prey literally never hear what's coming until the squeeze of powerful talons is upon them. After immobilizing their prey with talons, the owls crush the base of the cranium with their beak. Like many other birds of prey, they eat the head of their quarry first. If they kill an animal that is too large to eat in one meal, they cache the uneaten portion and then return to it later.

Look for spotted owls—during the day, roosting on limbs near the trunk. If it is hot, look in the shady understory trees; in cold weather, they roost higher in the canopy, closer to the sun. Although there is very little movement during the day, the owls will occasionally wake up to hunt if an opportunity scurries by them. They become truly active shortly before sunset and continue through the night until shortly before sunrise. You may be able to attract this owl during the day or night by making squeaking noises (resembling a mouse or squirrel in distress). They are fairly tame and will allow people to get within a few feet.

Length: 16½–19 inches.

Look for nests—in cavities that form when the tops of large old trees break off or when limbs are ripped loose. The treetop cavities are shaped like stovepipes, with walls formed by the hardened shell of the broken trunk. Live secondary crowns that overtop the broken trunks shield the nest cavities from rain and sun. Owls also nest on platforms in "witches' brooms" (bunching of branches caused by dwarf mistletoe) or on accumulations of debris (twigs, needles, cones, lichens) entrapped by limbs. They will also use nests constructed by other species such as goshawks, Cooper's hawks, red-tailed hawks, woodrats, or squirrels.

Look for juvenile owls—that sometimes fall to the ground after trying to fledge too early. They are fairly good climbers, ascending the trunk with their wings flapping and their talons grasping the rough bark. They may also use their beak to grasp limbs and pull themselves up. When tired, they wrap their wings around the trunk for a rest. If you find a juvenile on the ground, leave it alone unless it is obviously injured. It is quite normal for young spotted owls to roost for several days on or near the ground after they leave the nest.

Look for pellets—large, compact balls of "indigestibles"—fur, feathers, and bones—on the ground beneath roosts. Owls cough these up after they digest their meal. The pellets keep sharp bones from cutting their digestive tract, and they also scrape away bacteria in the owl's throat as

they come up. Pick apart dried pellets (wear gloves!) to find whole skulls and other remnants of the owl's prey.

Look for feeding debris—owls disembowel squirrels and other larger prey before eating them. You may also find their cache of uneaten or partially eaten prey beside logs, trees, or large rocks. A pair of spotted owls and their young can consume up to 500 northern flying squirrels a year.

Listen for—a high-pitched "hoo—hoo-hoo—hoo." A higher-pitched barking call has been compared with the baying of a dog. Also listen for a variety of whistling and shrieking calls. Spotted owls are vocal beginning with the courting season in February and March and continuing through summer.

Northern Flying Squirrel

Just as most of us are returning home from a day of hiking, the curtain rises on one of the most fascinating performances in the forest. In the gray wash of twilight, the branches come alive with tiny squirrels, crouched for their first flight of the night. Their eyes are huge and liquid, and as their heads bob up, down, and side to side, their eyes take a series of readings from which they calculate their route. Suddenly one springs from a branch and spreads its arms and legs as far as they will go. A cape of flesh and fur vibrates against the air, slowing the squirrel's glide to that of a fluttering leaf. By dropping its right arm and leg and adjusting its tail, it takes a hard right-hand turn in the air. Inches from landing, it raises its tail and brakes with its cape, alighting with a soft "tick" on the lower trunk of a tree. Within seconds it is up in the branches and airborne again, gliding from tree to tree with the greatest of ease.

Flying squirrels rely on a rhythmic kind of muscle memory to guide them through the woods. They move at astonishing speeds, faster than any other kind of squirrel. Their secret is a cape of skin that extends from wrist to ankle on each side of their body. Stretched out spread-eagle, the squirrel looks like a living airfoil, with 50 square inches of sail area. They are capable of 150-foot glides, although most are 20–60 feet long.

At rest, flying squirrels can pucker in their fleshy parachute with a muscle, allowing them to be nimble on their feet. Watch as one ventures out on a branch, using its hind legs like grappling hooks and freeing its front paws to grab lichens, seeds, flowers, fruits, berries, and tender buds. At night, these arboreal acrobats eagerly descend to earth to dig for one of their favorite delicacies—the subterranean truffle.

Truffles, which look like tiny potatoes, are the fruiting bodies of various fungi that grow in association with the roots of needleleaf trees. The arrangment is a compatible one for all parties: host tree, fungi, and the bacteria that live inside the fungi. The trees manufacture sugars for the fungi; the fungi feed the bacteria and transfer water, minerals, and nutrients to the tree roots; and the bacteria convert airborne nitrogen into a form that both tree and fungi can use. The final piece of the puzzle is provided by the flying squirrel. By eating and excreting the remains of the truffles, the flying squirrel transfers their spores to various places in the forest, thus spreading this helpful fungi.

Look for northern flying squirrels—in branches, in midair, or on the lower trunks of trees at any time of year. They become active at nightfall, and have peaks of activity during the first two hours after sundown and the few hours before sunrise. To spot squirrels around your camp, put a red cellophane covering over your flashlight so squirrels can't see your light. Or try illuminating your own backyard feeder. After a while, squirrels become used to even white light and will come in for food while you watch.

Length: Head and body, 5½–6⅖ inches. Tail, 4⅓–5½ inches.

Look for nests—in cavities at the top of dead stumps (6–20 feet high), in mature trees, or in hollow limbs. They often adopt old woodpecker cavities, lining them with shredded bark, lichens, moss, feathers, or leaves. In the summer, flying squirrels may nest on the branches, using abandoned red squirrel nests or the many-branched "witches' brooms" common to diseased trees.

In the snow—look under the umbrella of needleleaf trees or on snow-shoe hare trails for bounding tracks connected by lines from the cape of skin. Their 4-point landings leave "stizmarks," while more gradual descents leave a drag mark of 1½ feet. Although the squirrels don't hibernate, they do seem to congregate in nests for warmth, allowing them to be active down to −11 degrees F.

Listen for—a low, birdlike chirp or a chucking or chuckling sound when disturbed.

Clouded Salamander

This salamander has bronze or rusty blotches that float like clouds upon the darker brown surface of its skin. When light and temperatures change, these clouds can seem to disappear as the entire salamander turns a dark color. This rapid change of color occurs when cells that contain melanin, a dark pigment, suddenly spread out under the skin surface. Because dark colors absorb sunlight better than light colors, the salamanders use this color change to regulate their own body temperature. Besides acting as a solar collector, the dark pigment also protects the salamander's inner tissues from the ultraviolet rays of the sun.

Naturalists have found that the best place to find clouded salamanders is in a well-lighted opening in a mature forest where sawed-off or wind-snapped stumps, snags, and downed logs are prevalent. Most are found in cracks in the logs, under leaf mats on stumps, or in the space between the bark and the rotting heartwood of the tree. Here, these lungless salamanders find the dampness that they need to help them breathe and drink through their skin. As a bonus, they find a community of juicy prey items such as ants, carabid beetles, centipedes, millipedes, crickets, earthworms, or slugs that are also attracted to the rotting Douglas-firs.

The salamander's main hunting device—its tongue—is worth studying. Instead of being attached at the back, it is free at the back and sides, and attached at the front of the mouth, on the lower half. When clouded salamanders crawl by a likely dinner, they flip out their tongue, rather like a switchblade flipping from its sheath. The sticky "flypaper" saliva snags the struggling insect so it can be carried back to the mouth.

Look for clouded salamanders—in cracks and under the bark of rotting Douglas-fir logs and standing trees in open clearings. They may also be in Port-Orford-cedar and in other trees. Don't forget to look up as well; these salamanders are agile climbers and have been known to establish a home base as far as 20 feet up in a dead tree. Their toes have expanded tips that help them cling to vertical surfaces.

Length: 3–5¼ inches.

Eggs are enclosed—under bark and in hollows in rotting logs. Each egg is covered with a milky, yellowish gelatinous covering that narrows into a stalk connecting the egg to the ceiling of the chamber. The strands of the other eggs are also attached here, usually twisted about and adhering to each other. Females lay their eggs in late spring or summer, and then guard them until they hatch in late summer or fall.

WESTERN TANAGER

SHARP-SHINNED HAWK

Subalpine Fir

Oregon Boxwood

PORCUPINE

WILLIAMSON'S SAPSUCKER

MOUNTAIN CHICKADEE

WESTERN SKINK

Canada Buffaloberry

Heartleaf Arnica

Lodgepole Pine Forest

WHERE TO SEE THIS HABITAT:

California: Eldorado, Inyo, Klamath, Lassen, Mendocino, Plumas, Shasta-Trinity, Sierra, Stanislaus, and Tahoe national forests; Kings Canyon, Sequoia, and Yosemite national parks

Colorado: Arapaho, Gunnison, Pike, Rio Grande, Roosevelt, Routt, and San Isabel national forests; Rocky Mountain National Park

Idaho: Boise, Caribou, Challis, Clearwater, Idaho Panhandle, Nez Perce, Salmon, and Sawtooth national forests

Montana: Beaverhead, Bitterroot, Flathead, Gallatin, Helena, Kootenai, Lewis and Clark, and Lolo national forests; Glacier National Park

Oregon: Fremont, Malheur, Ochoco, Umpqua, Wallowa-Whitman, and Winema national forests

Utah: Ashley National Forest

Washington: Wenatchee National Forest

Wyoming: Bridger-Teton, Medicine Bow, and Shoshone national forests; Grand Teton and Yellowstone national parks

Lodgepole Pine Forest

BEGINNINGS

Lodgepole pine is the third most abundant western tree behind Douglas-fir and ponderosa pine. It covers 80 percent of the forested land in the northern and central Rockies, showing up most commonly in the lower fringes of the subalpine zone and in the Douglas-fir zone directly below. Pure stands of lodgepole that seeded in after fires have monopolized the landscape in some areas.

These forests are distinguished by their almost painful-looking density. Trees are sardined so close together that each one can manage only a very slim trunk, too slim it seems, to support its great height. The shade in these "dog-hair" stands is so great that lower branches die out, leaving a Christmas tree atop a telephone pole. Although this may seem to us to be an inefficient way for a forest to grow, it is actually ingenious, from an ecological point of view.

Before technology allowed us to snuff out most forest fires, they burned in dense lodgepole forests throughout July and August, sometimes blackening large expanses before the cool rains of September would put them out. This natural harvest would clear a seedbed that was free of litter, rich with nutrients from the charred vegetation, and open to the sun—perfect conditions for pine seedlings. To ensure that their seeds would be available no matter when the fire struck, the lodgepole evolved two kinds of cones: one that distributes seeds every 1–3 years, and one that remains on the tree, closed up and sealed with resin. When a fire heats up to 140 degrees, the resin melts, releasing a bumper crop of seeds onto a perfectly prepared seedbed. This is how the "dog-hair" thickets begin.

Take a walk inside an older stand, and you'll learn something else about lodgepole ecology. In the understory, you'll see the seedlings of Douglas-fir, Engelmann spruce, or subalpine fir. These trees are tolerant of shade, and come in after lodgepole has blanketed the soil with a layer of organic material. As long as there are no fires, these climax trees will eventually take over as the "nurse" lodgepoles die out.

As in all of nature, there are always exceptions to the rule. In some areas, lodgepoles have dominated the scene for many generations. Rather than surrender to shade-tolerant species, they simply replace fallen lodgepoles with new lodgepoles, using seeds from the cones that mature every 1–3 years. Experts believe that lodgepoles may persist because seed sources from other trees are not available, or because the site is too dry, too moist, too frost-prone, too steep, or too fire-prone for the other trees.

HEYDAY FOR THE MOUNTAIN PINE BEETLE

Lodgepole pines and all the organisms associated with them are used to fires; in fact, they've evolved for millions of years in a fire-driven ecosystem. For the past 80 years, land managers on public lands have been suppressing these fires before they can get rolling. The result is a region-wide aging of trees that normally would have been removed by flames. One organism, the mountain pine beetle, must feel like it has found paradise.

When it's time to lay their eggs, female mountain pine beetles go looking for large-diameter pines, usually those over 8 inches. Experts believe the beetles use not only visual clues to find the big trees, but also chemical clues, namely a pungent "terpene" compound that big trees produce. These large trees are preferred because they have a thick phloem—the sleeve of food-conducting tissue under the bark—which will nourish the beetles' offspring as they grow.

The flying females, no bigger than a matchhead, land on the lower portions of the trunk and begin to gnaw their way in. As they cut through resin ducts, the tree exudes pitch, sometimes in quantities large enough to drown the females and pitch them back out. You can find the 1-inch-diameter tubes of pitch on trees that have successfully "pitched out" the females. To overcome the tree's defenses, the beetles produce a pheromone, a chemical messenger that attracts other beetles to the tree. If the assembled crowd is large enough, the tree can't produce enough resin to pitch them all out, and the beetles can get the upper hand.

On special structures in their mouth, they carry a partner-in-crime— the blue stain fungus. As the beetles lay their eggs, they also lace the tree with the fungus' spores. The blue stain clogs the water vessels, keeping the nursery area moist, but cutting off the water supply to the rest of the tree. The beetle eggs hatch into hungry, grublike larvae that eat their way around the tree, girdling its food supply lines. The one-two punch of the fungus and the larvae is usually enough to kill the tree.

For us humans, a hillside of rusty red lodgepole crowns may look like a natural disaster, but for the rest of the community, it may be a blessing. By periodically removing the largest lodgepoles, the mountain pine beetles are able to speed succession, returning older wood fiber to the soil and giving the understory trees a chance to shoot up in the sun. In the northern Rockies today, however, an unnaturally large percentage of lodgepole stands are older and stagnant. By "protecting" these forests from beneficial fires, we have created an all-you-can-eat invitation for mountain pine beetles. Heavy infestations in these forests can spread to younger trees in nearby stands. As acres of these trees die, they become ripe for catastrophic fires, fueled by 80 years of combustible growth.

CHARACTERISTIC PLANTS:

Trees, Shrubs, and Vines:
alders
alpine prickly currant
balsam poplar
blueberries
California red fir
Canada buffaloberry
common juniper
creambush oceanspray
creeping Oregon grape
curlleaf cercocarpus
currants
Douglas-fir
Engelmann spruce
grand fir
grouse huckleberry (whortleberry)
Jeffrey pine

kinnikinnik
lodgepole pine
manzanitas
mountain hemlock
one-sided wintergreen
ponderosa pine
quaking aspen
red alder
Rocky Mountain Douglas-fir
roses
snowberries
snowbrush ceanothus
subalpine fir
thimbleberry
western hemlock
western larch
western redcedar

western serviceberry
western white pine
white spruce
Wood's rose

Herbaceous Plants:
heartleaf arnica
lupines
narrow goldenrod
Oregon boxwood
pendant-pod locoweed
pinegrass
pink wintergreen
reedgrass
sickletop
twinflower
willow-herbs
woodlands pinedrops
Wyoming paintbrush

Heartleaf Arnica

WHAT'S IN IT FOR WILDLIFE?

Though we may mourn the death of lodgepoles around our camp or mountain home, a community of wildlife species are cashing in on the spoils. When you see a lodgepole with boring dust at its base and great sheets of its bark ripped off, you know it has been recently visited by the pine beetles, which in turn attracted woodpeckers. The beetle activity tends to loosen the bark from the trunk, making it easy for three-toed and black-backed woodpeckers to peel sheets back and expose the mapwork of larval galleries. A snag may stand for 20 years or more, providing hunting perches for flycatchers and hawks and, if large enough, cavities for owls, wood-peckers, chickadees, and squirrels. Once down, the decomposing trunks and crowns are a haven for small animals such as southern red-backed voles, moisture-dependent toads and salamanders, and reptiles such as west-ern skinks, garter snakes, and rubber boas. Atop the debris, look for the energetic winter wren, flipping its tail at you as it searches for insect prey. Fallen logs also give the blue grouse a platform for its hooting display.

In live lodgepole stands, the majority of birds belong to the guild that feeds on insects found in the foliage or on the bark. Foliage insects are combed off the needles by yellow-rumped warblers, ruby-crowned kinglets, and black-capped and mountain chickadees. Bark insects are teased out of crevices by brown creepers and by red- and white-breasted nuthatches. Insects that burrow deeper are uncovered by northern three-toed and black-backed woodpeckers.

On the ground, look for hermit and varied thrushes, Townsend's sol-itaires, and western and mountain bluebirds searching for insects. Some of these same birds take to lower shrubs in search of berries and other fruits. The western wood-pewee, Hammond's flycatcher, and violet-green swallow snatch their insects straight out of the air.

Another source of nourishment is lodgepole seeds, relished by pine siskins, Clark's nutcrackers, Cassin's finches, evening and pine grosbeaks, gray jays, and dark-eyed juncos. Red crossbills are specially adapted to pry the seeds out of needleleaf cones. The top and bottom halves of their bill overlap to form an "X," so that when the bird closes its bill, the cone scales are forced open. The beautiful blue grouse can actually digest the resin-soaked needles of the lodgepole, enabling it to spend winters in these forests.

The lichen that hangs from the branches is coveted by mule deer, especially in winter, when their diet is lacking in nutrients. When a wind-storm scatters hoary branches upon the ground, you'll find deer feeding on them the next day. Farther down on the trunks, look for patches of bark that have been gnawed off by porcupines, bears, or even elk, all hungry for the sweet inner layer called cambium. Another sought-after lodgepole product is its sap, mined by brushy-tongued, yellow-bellied, and Williamson's sapsuckers.

Come spring, northern goshawks and red-tailed hawks may build large stick nests near the top of the largest trees. Cavity nesters have to search for large-diameter trees, which may be rare in the dense stands of post-fire lodgepole. Look for their holes in more open-grown stands where the trees are well-spaced enough to put on a little girth. Also in more open-grown stands, a curtain of branches can extend farther down the trunk, and understory shrubs can provide cover for showshoe hares and other mammals. Running above them in the canopy, you'll find fishers, martens, and red squirrels. At twilight, northern flying squirrels spread their capes and flutter like leaves to the ground.

Elk and mule deer may retreat to shady lodgepole stands to escape the summer heat. Elk especially like stands that are close to meadows where they can graze on grasses with the security of a hiding place nearby. These openings are also important foraging grounds for bullsnakes, milk snakes, red-tailed hawks, ermines, long-tailed weasels, foxes, and other rodent-eating predators. The blue grouse puffs up its neck sacs, spreads its tail, and struts in these openings as part of its breeding ceremony.

Black-Backed Woodpecker

The death of a lodgepole pine forest is the beginning of the good life for the zealous black-backed woodpecker. Even before the tree's needles turn orange, these woodpeckers are busy chiseling, hammering, and hauling out the fat, juicy grubs (larvae) of wood-boring beetles. When the bounty is rich, the blackbacks may be so absorbed in their feeding that they'll tolerate the gawking of a binoculared fan. This gives you plenty of time to study their unique adaptations.

Their stout bill makes a handy crowbar for prying loose sheets of bark, exposing the road map of beetle galleries underneath. Their sticky, barbed tongue collects scores of the grubs tucked in the cul-de-sacs of these galleries. To reach the wood borers farther inside the tree, the blackback leans its body back onto its stiff tail and swings forward, pounding through the wood like a jackhammer. Because blackbacks don't have a fourth toe like other woodpeckers, they can rotate their heel out of the way and lean even farther back to gain more momentum. As they swing forward, they rotate the heels inward to deliver an extra push going into the tree.

An average day in the woodpecker's life may include 8,000–12,000 blows on a hard surface. Luckily, their brain is encased in air, and their neck muscles and skull are fortified. They even have bristlelike feathers to cover their nostrils so that sawdust won't enter their lungs.

STELLER'S JAY

YELLOW-RUMPED WARBLER

DARK-EYED JUNCO

RED CROSSBILL

PINE SISKIN

RUBY-CROWNED KINGLET

RED SQUIRREL

WILDLIFE LOCATOR CHART—LODGEPOLE PINE FOREST

	Feeds from Air	Feeds in Upper Canopy	Feeds in Lower Canopy	Feeds on Trunk	Feeds on Ground
Nests in Tree Canopy	Northern Goshawk Red-tailed Hawk Golden Eagle Black-chinned Hummingbird Western Wood-Pewee Hammond's Flycatcher Dusky Flycatcher (Nests in Shrubs) American Redstart	Gray Jay Clark's Nutcracker Bohemian Waxwing Hermit Warbler Western Tanager Pine Grosbeak Red Crossbill Pine Siskin Evening Grosbeak	Band-tailed Pigeon Golden-crowned Kinglet Ruby-crowned Kinglet Yellow-rumped Warbler Black-throated Gray Warbler		Steller's Jay, American Robin, Varied Thrush, Chipping Sparrow, Cassin's Finch
Nests in Trunk Cavity	American Kestrel Western Flycatcher Violet-green Swallow		Black-capped Chickadee Mountain Chickadee Boreal Chickadee Western Bluebird	Yellow-bellied Sapsucker, Williamson's Sapsucker, Hairy Woodpecker, Three-toed Woodpecker, Black-backed Woodpecker, Red-breasted Nuthatch, White-breasted Nuthatch, Brown Creeper	Winter Wren, Mountain Bluebird, Red Squirrel, Northern Flying Squirrel
Nests on Ground	Black Swift Townsend's Solitaire				Spruce Grouse, Blue Grouse, Common Raven, Hermit Thrush, Fox Sparrow, Dark-eyed Junco, Snowshoe Hare, Mule Deer, Elk
Nests Beneath Ground or Debris					Lodgepole Chipmunk, Deer Mouse, Northern Pocket Gopher, Bushy-tailed Woodrat, Heather Vole, Long-tailed Vole, Porcupine, Coyote, Red Fox, Black Bear, Marten, Fisher, Ermine, Long-tailed Weasel, Black Salamander, Western Whiptail, Western Skink, Rubber Boa, Sonoran Mountain Kingsnake, Milk Snake, Bullsnake

Once inside the beetle-riddled tree, the woodpecker's amazingly long tongue snakes into crevices where the bill won't reach. Where does a woodpecker store such a long tongue? If you could peer inside its head, you'd see that the base of the tongue forks into two horny structures that curve up over the back of the skull, down around the forehead, finally rooting in or near the nostrils. These structures reel the tongue in and out, allowing the woodpecker to spear grubs that are deep inside labyrinthian tunnels. The backward-pointing barbs on the tip of the tongue help pluck the grubs from their snug homes.

Other organisms in the lodgepole forest also benefit from the hole digging. Blackbacks are a "pathfinder" species; that is, they open up cavities in trees that birds with weaker bills could not have made. Once abandoned, these holes become nests and feeding sites for many other birds and mammals. Blackbacks also speed the process of tree decay. As they rip off sheets of bark and tear out pieces of rotted wood, they "lift up the tent" for fungi and insects that will break down the wood. By-products of this decay enrich the soil for a whole new crop of herbs and trees.

Look for black-backed woodpeckers—in rather open stands of dead or dying trees. They tend to work low on the tree trunks, as well as on fallen logs and branches. They are relatively tame and singleminded, and will allow you to approach closely. Like other woodpeckers, they communicate with each other by means of a complicated language of visual and auditory signals. In encounters with their mates or with other birds such as northern flickers, hairy woodpeckers, or tree swallows, watch for ritualized gestures such as raising their crest, pointing their bill downward, spreading their wings, shaking their head back and forth, or bobbing their head up and down.

Length: 8–10 inches.

Look for nest holes—1½ to 2 inches in diameter, 2 to 15 feet up a dead stub or tree, usually on the side that received the first sunbeams of the day (south or east). The bark is characteristically peeled away around the entrance, leaving a bare ring that may discourage predators or leave nest-hole pirates without a perch to stand on. The bottom of the nest "doorway" is beveled, and is used as a pausing place while entering or leaving the nest. If you're close to a nest, you can often hear the nestlings mewing for food.

Look for peeled trees—where the woodpecker has pried off large sheets of bark. Favored drumming sites near the nest are usually heavily pockmarked.

Listen for—loud hammering starting at 18 beats a second (males) and speeding up in tempo throughout the burst. Each burst lasts less than 2 seconds on the average. These woodpeckers hammer when an intruder (including you) enters their territory or when their mate arrives at the nest. Also listen for their call—a fast, double-clicking note that marks encounters between birds. Aggressive encounters may incite the "scream-rattle-snarl," a call performed with the back hunched and the wings spread.

Porcupine

Some people are surprised to find a porcupine riding the top of a tall lodgepole pine. Some may want to rescue it, thinking it has been driven up there by a dog. But porcupines don't need our protection, thank you, even from a pack of dogs. There are 30,000 good reasons not to fool with porkies, and any dog that has taken even one quill in the nose has learned to give porkies a wide berth.

Porkies climb trees on their own, and are as well equipped as tree surgeons to do it. Their paws are clawed, padded, and knobby, and their muscled, viselike legs have all-over spurs (downward-pointing quills) to help keep them in place. For them, a treetop is a seat at the best restaurant in town. Porcupines eat the buds, leaves, twigs, and inner bark of trees. Their 21-foot gut takes up 75 percent of their body cavity, and is inhabited by an army of microbes that break down woody matter into digestible energy.

The trees, for their part, seem to defend themselves from being the object of the porcupine's desires. Aspens, for instance, cluster their most nutritious parts on the outermost tips of branches, where the footing becomes too fragile to support a porcupine. Porkies counter with a neat trick of twig-nipping. They simply cut the twig close to them and bring the buds and leaves within reach, discarding the stripped twig like a well-picked bone.

As the leaves mature later in the summer, they accumulate tannin, an acidic compound that blocks the flushing of potassium out of the porkie's liver. Without flushing, potassium could build up and become a toxin. So

ERMINE   MARTEN

BLACK SALAMANDER

when trees accumulate too much tannin, or are otherwise too high in acid, the porcupine simply ambles to another, more palatable tree.

The high potassium in their diet leads to another nutritional dilemma. As their liver flushes potassium, porcupines also lose what little salt they have in their system. This results in the porcupine's legendary passion for salt, which is all too familiar to resort owners in porkie country. Salty human perspiration on ax handles, canoe paddles, wooden porches, and even road salt on tires can entice porcupines to gnaw, often causing much damage.

Most folks aren't willing to tussle with a porcupine over a canoe paddle, though. Those 30,000 bristling quills are a handy deterrent, foiling all but the fisher, an arch foe that can flip a porcupine neatly to get at its quill-less underbelly. Contrary to popular myth, porcupines don't shoot their quills or throw them like darts. They simply deliver a bouquet of quills by swatting their victim with their tail. The barbed spears are only loosely anchored in the porcupine's skin and therefore come out easily when caught in the victim's skin. The center of the quill is spongy. As it absorbs moisture, it swells, flanging out the backward-pointing barbules, and making it very painful to pull a quill out of skin. Once embedded, quills are drawn deeper into the tissue each time the victim's muscles contract. A porcupine researcher who had a quill accidentally submerged in his upper arm was able to record its downward progress. By the time the quill finally emerged from his forearm, it had traveled an inch a day. Talk about occupational hazards!

Look for porcupines—hunched in a ball or draped on an upper branch, either chewing on succulent leaves or dozing in the sun. They spend much of their time in trees, but may be seen on the ground as well, gnawing on bark, nibbling on herbs, or waddling from den to feeding tree. Their only speedy move is when they pivot to display their tail full of quills. They are more active by night than by day.

Length: Head and body, 18–22 inches. Tail, 7–9 inches.

Look for dens—in a deep rock crevice, a hole under a stump, an abandoned beaver burrow or fox den, a hollow log, or a cave. Brown, jelly bean-shaped droppings may pile up so high inside the den that they spill out, evicting their owners along with them. Young porcupines are called porcupettes.

Look for feeding debris—discarded twigs in sprays on the ground beneath porcupine's feeding perch. Look for a diagonal cut on the end of the twig and tiny parallel bites on the bark.

Look for gnaw marks—on anything made of wood, from saplings to buildings. Trunk scars with neatly gnawed edges and tooth marks are the result of the porkie's habit of tearing off the bark to get at the sweet inner bark. Look for bark shavings on the ground.

In the winter—porcupines will den together in crevices or caves. Hunger sends them out for food, and you'll usually find them feasting in the top of trees.

Look for tracks—pigeon-toed, with a waddling stride of 5–6 inches, and a straddle up to 9 inches wide. The hindprint is more than 3 inches long, with 5 claw marks ahead of an oval-shaped pad. The quills may leave a broom-swept look on snow or soil.

Smell for—a strong urine odor near their dens, favorite feeding trees, or along the trails in between. The urine is a scent signature that is "read" by other porcupines.

Listen for—an insistent sniffing as the porcupine tracks down food or senses danger. Mating includes a high-falsetto wooing song, a circle dance, nose rubbing, and face touching. Listen for a low-pitched meow during mating. They snort, bark, cry, whine, and chatter their teeth and quills when they are afraid.

Western Skink

The western skink moves at speeds that are hard for the eye to follow and almost impossible for the hand to catch. Unlike other lizards that pause for a split second of surprise when first exposed, western skinks immediately disappear beneath a rock or log. If the soil is loose, they may slither into it, pinning their arms to their sides and using their snout as a plow.

The sporty western skink comes standard with a blue tail (brighter in juveniles than in adults) and body scales that glisten as if varnished. The bright tail baits the predator, and diverts the strike away from the more vulnerable torso and head. When touched, the tail breaks off and thrashes wildly, keeping the predator busy while the skink shimmies out of reach.

These fragile tails are built to break off. A wall of cartilage passes through each vertebrae, creating a weak point where muscles and blood sinuses are also modified to allow for an easy break. If in danger, a skink may even break off its own tail by pressing against something, thus leaving its pursuer with a wriggling calling card.

Losing a tail is a trick that only works once, and there are definite ecological costs associated with it. The new tail grows in slowly, for instance, and is never as long or as colorful as the last tail. Nor does it have fracture planes to allow it to break off again. Losing a tail means losing some stored fat that might have gotten the skink through a food shortage, especially in winter or during drought. And, of course, it takes energy to grow a new tail, energy that must be borrowed from breeding or feeding activities. When a pregnant female loses her tail, her eggs may be smaller, and thus have less chance of surviving. Besides, a skink that loses the use of its tail, even for a short time, is not as well equipped to run, swim, balance, or climb. Nevertheless, after millions of years of evolution, skinks still go tailless occasionally, suggesting that the benefits of losing a tail must outweigh the costs.

Look for western skinks—during the day by turning over rocks, leaves, and rotting logs, where they dive for cover as soon as they see you coming. Unless you remain absolutely still, you'll rarely see them on the surface. To get a better look at this getaway artist, try hunting late in the fall or early in the morning, when air temperatures are cool and the skinks are stiff. Skinks, like all reptiles, need an external source of heat (the sun) to warm them before they can be active. Try peeling away the dead bark of trees to find them curled and sluggish among the centipedes and ants. When the sun is shining, look for them in the sunnier parts of clearings in the lodgepoles. A reddish tinge around the head, chin, and tail tip is the badge of a breeding male.

Length: $6^1/_2$–$9^5/_{16}$ inches.

Nests are underground—in 10- to 15-inch-long burrows that the females dig under rocks. The nest cavity at the end of the burrow is flask-shaped and 2–3 inches in diameter. Here, the female remains curled around her 4–6 eggs, leaving only occasionally to bask or feed. If the nest is disturbed in any way, she quickly repairs it. The female will urinate on the eggs to keep them from drying out, and will turn them frequently to prevent molding. This tending behavior is unique to skinks; most other lizards simply bury their eggs and leave them.

Listen for—the sound of rustling in dry leaves, as skinks forage for moths, beetles, crickets, grasshoppers, and leafhoppers. As they hunt, they flick their forked tongue over the surface, picking up chemical clues that they analyze in special scent receptors called "Jacobson organs."

FISHER

Bristlecone Pine

Foxtail Pine

RED SQUIRREL

MARTEN

"krummholz"

WESTERN RATTLESNAKE

CLARK'S NUTCRACKER

Mountain Hemlock

Whitebark Pine

Limber Pine

Engelmann
Spruce

Subalpine
Fir

"flag tree"

"candelabra tree"

CASSIN'S
FINCH

GRIZZLY
BEAR

Beargrass

RUBBER
BOA

Twinflower

White
Rhododendron

Subalpine Forest

WHERE TO SEE THIS HABITAT:

California: Kings Canyon, Sequoia, and Yosemite national parks; Klamath, Plumas, Stanislaus, and Tahoe national forests
Colorado: Arapaho, Gunnison, Pike, Rio Grande, Roosevelt, Routt, and San Isabel national forests; Rocky Mountain National Park
Idaho: Caribou, Challis, Clearwater, Idaho Panhandle, Nez Perce, Salmon, and Targhee national forests
Montana: Beaverhead, Bitterroot, Helena, Kootenai, Lewis and Clark, and Lolo national forests; Glacier National Park
Oregon: Mount Hood, Wallowa-Whitman, Willamette national forests
Utah: Fishlake, Manti-La Sal, and Uinta national forests
Washington: Mount Baker-Snoqualmie and Wenatchee national forests; Mount Ranier, North Cascades, and Olympic national parks
Wyoming: Bridger-Teton and Shoshone national forests; Grand Teton and Yellowstone national parks

Subalpine Forest

BEGINNINGS

As you hike closer to the summit, the alpine sun grows more intense, the grade steepens, the air thins, and air temperatures may take a headlong plunge. The tall, densely packed conifers that have surrounded you begin to thin out and diminish in size. Finally, when the trees can no longer stand erect against the harsh temper of the summit, they sprawl into gnarled, shrubby shapes, pruned like bonsai by the wind and weather. This marks the upper limit of the subalpine forest, a zone that begins in dense forest and ends in prone shrubland. Beyond this, the treeless alpine tundra begins.

The trees you will find in the subalpine zone may vary from place to place in the West. In the Pacific Northwest, mountain hemlock and subalpine fir are among the important players. Farther south, the pair splits up, and mountain hemlock joins whitebark, lodgepole, and foxtail pine in the the Sierra Nevada and Klamath Mountains. Firs are especially important in the Sierras, where there are no spruces. To the east, the Great Basin mountaintops sport the legendary "Methuselah" pines: bristlecone and limber. The Rockies, north to south, have a fairly consistent subalpine forest of Engelmann spruce and subalpine fir. Despite their regional differences, these forests do share many of the same associate species.

They also share a common heritage. In the ice age, glaciers spreading southward from the Arctic pushed cold air down into the United States. The boreal tree species that could survive this climate traveled along the ridges of mountains. When the climate cooled even further, glaciers began to form on these mountaintops, forcing the boreal species downslope and into the basins between mountains. When the climate warmed and the glaciers melted, sagebrush took over the dry basins, and the boreal species were forced back up the slopes. Here they have remained, glacial relics that are bred to handle the demanding conditions of the subalpine zone.

CHARACTERISTIC PLANTS:

**Trees, Shrubs, and
 Vines:**
Alaska-cedar
alpine prickly currant
American mountain-
 ash
balsam poplar
big huckleberry
birchleaf spirea
black spruce
blueberries
blue spruce
bristlecone pine
California red fir
Canada buffaloberry
Colorado currant
common juniper
common snowberry
corkbark fir
creeping Oregon
 grape
Douglas-fir
dwarf huckleberry
Engelmann spruce
European red elder
fool's huckleberry
fool's skunkbush
foxtail pine
grand fir
grouse huckleberry
 (whortleberry)
highbush cranberry
Jeffrey pine

limber pine
lodgepole pine
mountain gooseberry
mountain hemlock
mountain-lover
mountain snowberry
noble fir
Pacific silver fir
paper birch
quaking aspen
Rocky Mountain
 Douglas-fir
Rocky Mountain
 maple
Rocky Mountain
 whortleberry
shrubby cinquefoil
subalpine fir
subalpine larch
swamp currant
trapper's tea
western hemlock
western larch
western redcedar

Beargrass

western white pine
whitebark pine
white fir
white rhododendron
white spruce
Wood's rose

Herbaceous Plants:
Arizona peavine
beargrass
blue columbine
bluejoint reedgrass
elk sedge
fairy slipper
fireweed
heartleaf arnica
heartleaved bittercress
Jacob's ladder
lesser wintergreen
mountain bluebell
mudwort
muttongrass
orange sneezeweed
Oregon boxwood
pinegrass
pipsissewa
queen's cup beadlily
red columbine
sedges
smooth woodrush
sweetscented bedstraw
twinflower
woodnymph

IT'S TOUGH AT THE TOP

One of the worst things about life on a mountaintop is the schedule. Winter rages for 9–10 months and spring may not arrive until July. That leaves only two frost-free months for growing new shoots, distributing seed, and getting seedlings under way. New growth must "harden" before the temperatures dip again, and the sap must thicken with its natural antifreeze. In this challenging land, the long march to maturity comes in very small steps. The tiny shrub you dislodge with your boot may have taken 40 years to grow to its full height of 6 inches!

The winter wind is a harsh gardener, pruning exposed branches and stripping bark with an abrasive blast of ice pellets and snow crystals. In concert with the strong sun, winter wind can create a virtual desert as it sucks moisture from needles at a time when soil water is frozen and unavailable.

Snow in quantities of up to 550 inches (Cascade Range) can be either a blessing or a curse. At the right depth, it can be a lifesaving quilt, keeping ground temperatures constant and providing trees with a guaranteed watering come spring. But where it is too deep, it may not melt in time for plants to meet their already hectic growing cycle. In the meantime, a fungus that grows in snow may glue the branches together with a brown sticky growth. Heavy snow may sometimes break branches or sweep away entire swathes of forest with a single avalanche. Where the snow is too shallow, it may melt too soon, exposing the dormant plants to hot sun and drying winds.

SIGNS OF THE STRUGGLE

Now that you know what goes on when the mountain roads are snowed in, you'll understand why some subalpine trees adopt contorted postures, depending on how exposed they are to the weather. In the lower subalpine forest, the summer ground is moist with meltwater, and trees can grow in dense packs and reach a good size. Upslope, the trees that are spaced farther apart begin to show signs of wear.

Flag trees have branches that stream out to one side like banners in the wind; the shoots that try to grow into the wind are quickly dried out or damaged by ice blasting. *Candelabra trees* have fully foliated lower branches but peter out to ragged ends on top, where they stick out above the snowpack. Once one of these trees makes a stand, others may hunker in its windshadow, forming a clump or a *tree island* that points upslope. The trees on the windward edge of this island are constantly assaulted by ice and winds. Those protected on the leeward side can advance by "layering;" that is, when a lower branch touches the ground, it takes root, and sends up a vertical stem. After decades of leeward layering and windward dieback, the island slowly begins to migrate downwind. Sometimes you'll see an island straddling a trail in its journey.

In areas where large drifts of snow accumulate behind the islands, leeward branches are killed in addition to the windward ones. This leaves seedlings on the sides as the only advance guard. These eventually create *ribbon forests* that run in thin horizontal bands across the slope.

Even farther up, near timberline, elfin trees called *krummholz* (meaning "crooked wood") may creep along the ground in twisted shapes, reaching heights of 18 inches or less, depending on the depth of the snowpack. Winds here are so intense that branches extending above the pack are automatically pruned, forcing the trees to grow horizontally. The clumps are so tightly hedged that they can actually bear the weight of heavy objects.

Among the most famous alpine trees are the bristlecone pines. Examine one in light of what you know about alpine conditions. The buffeting storms and ice damage may have bleached the branches and twisted them into tortured shapes. The bark and cambium (inner bark) on the windward side may be scoured away, leaving only a small strip of cambium on the leeward side to transport food and water. Though they may look dead, these gnarled sculptures are very much alive, and have been growing longer than any other trees on earth. The Methuselah tree in Bristlecone Pine National Monument is 4,600 years old!

While natural hardship does not seem to deter the subalpine forests, human-caused disturbances may. Fires, logging, or even firewood collecting can undo thousands of years of growth. In the lower realms, spruce and fir may be unseated for a generation or two as aspen, lodgepole, western white pine, Douglas-fir, or other pioneers take over. Eventually, spruce and fir will reappear in the understory, dominating again.

WHAT'S IN IT FOR WILDLIFE?

In a habitat where thunderstorms can brew in an hour and blizzards can rage for days, cover is a precious commodity. The densely packed conifers of the lower subalpine zone act as a natural screen—slowing winds, modifying temperatures, and capturing blowing snow in drifts. In the summer, mule deer, elk, mountain sheep, mountain goats, coyotes, and foxes head here to wait out the storms. In the winter, blue grouse roost in the treetops, while mice, voles, northern pocket gophers, and shrews tunnel in the snug world of the snowpack.

Besides cover, the evergreens of the deep forest provide food for birds, mammals, and insects. Seeds from pines, firs, and spruces are relished by many animals including pine grosbeak, red crossbill, Clark's nutcracker, northern flying squirrel, red squirrel, lodgepole chipmunk, golden-mantled ground squirrel, and bushy-tailed woodrat. Grizzlies and black bears let the squirrels do their work for them; they will often run across a cache of whitebark pinecones in their foraging, hungrily devouring every one. Insects that infest the pines provide an additional menu item for woodpeckers and other insect eaters. The needles, twigs, and buds of the conifers are less popular food items, but some animals do turn to them in winter. Grouse eat the buds and twigs, and porcupines feed on the sweet inner bark.

Because many of these forests are too remote for logging and too moist for fires, they have enjoyed relative peace for hundreds of years. The aged forests often have a tangled profusion of snags and downed logs. This is good news for the cavity dwellers here, most of which aren't able to penetrate the dense wood of living spruce trees (only three-toed woodpeckers can). They must rely instead on the soft wood of snags or, to some extent, on the softer fir trees. In areas with plenty of downed logs, search around for moisture-loving salamanders and secretive rubber boas and kingsnakes.

As the dark, brooding forest thins into a parkland, mule deer and elk find plenty of succulent forage between the scattered trees. Grizzlies find roots, mushrooms, fruits, and herbs of the parkland to their liking. In the fall, they raid berry patches to build up a layer of fat that will see them through the winter.

Scattered throughout this parkland are sunny subalpine meadows, a favorite with humans as well as wildlife. These meadows are a mecca in the springtime, providing the first snow-free patches of green herbs to a winter-weary community. Western rattlesnakes, still groggy from months of hibernating, may be seen sunning themselves in open places. Later in the summer, when grazing ranges downslope have begun to brown up and die, green grass and berries such as snowberries and gooseberries are still in season in the meadows. Many birds establish headquarters at the edge of the meadows, enjoying the best of both worlds: the security of forests for their nests, and a convenient banquet of meadow plants and the insects that are drawn to them. Rufous, calliope, or broad-tailed hummingbirds insert their long bills into the tubular blossoms found here.

A whole new dimension opens up when you peer beneath the ground of a subalpine meadow. Burrowing animals such as gophers, badgers, voles, skunks, chipmunks, and ground squirrels carve miles of tunnels beneath the surface. Look for the volcano-shaped craters of moles, the off-center entrance holes of pocket gophers, and the well-hidden 3-inch entrances of chipmunks.

Top illustration labels: SPRUCE GROUSE, TOWNSEND'S SOLITAIRE, MOUNTAIN CHICKADEE, HERMIT THRUSH, GOLDEN-CROWNED KINGLET, GOLDEN-MANTLED GROUND SQUIRREL, GRAY JAY

WILDLIFE LOCATOR CHART—SUBALPINE FOREST

	Feeds from Air	Feeds in Upper Canopy	Feeds in Lower Canopy	Feeds on Trunk	Feeds on Ground
Nests in Tree Canopy	Red-tailed Hawk Golden Eagle Calliope Hummingbird Broad-tailed Hummingbird Rufous Hummingbird Olive-sided Flycatcher Western Wood-Pewee Hammond's Flycatcher American Redstart	Gray Jay Clark's Nutcracker Townsend's Warbler Western Tanager Pine Grosbeak Red Crossbill Pine Siskin Evening Grosbeak	Band-tailed Pigeon Golden-crowned Kinglet Ruby-crowned Kinglet Yellow-rumped Warbler Black-throated Gray Warbler		Steller's Jay, American Robin, Varied Thrush, Chipping Sparrow, Cassin's Finch
Nests in Trunk Cavity	American Kestrel Northern Saw-whet Owl Western Flycatcher		Black-capped Chickadee Mountain Chickadee Chestnut-backed Chickadee	Yellow-bellied Sapsucker Williamson's Sapsucker Hairy Woodpecker White-headed Woodpecker Black-backed Woodpecker Pileated Woodpecker Red-breasted Nuthatch White-breasted Nuthatch Brown Creeper	Winter Wren, Mountain Bluebird, Red Squirrel, Northern Flying Squirrel
Nests on Shrubs			White-crowned Sparrow		Swainson's Thrush
Nests on Ground	Black Swift Townsend's Solitaire				Spruce Grouse, Blue Grouse, Ruffed Grouse, Hermit Thrush, Dark-eyed Junco, Snowshoe Hare, Elk, Mule Deer, Mountain Goat, Mountain Sheep
Nests Beneath Ground or Debris					Masked Shrew, Pika, Least Chipmunk, Uinta Chipmunk, Hoary Marmot, Yellow-bellied Marmot, Golden-mantled Ground Squirrel, Northern Pocket Gopher, Bushy-tailed Woodrat, Southern Red-backed Vole, Western Jumping Mouse, Porcupine, Coyote, Grizzly Bear, Black Bear, Marten, Long-tailed Weasel, Black Salamander, Sacramento Mountain Salamander, Western Whiptail, Rubber Boa, Western Rattlesnake, Sonoran Mountain Kingsnake
Nests in Water					Tiger Salamander

Talus slopes and boulder fields are also characteristic of subalpine zones, providing cover and nest sites for pikas, marmots, and bushy-tailed wood-rats. Watch for the long-tailed weasel slipping in and around their crevice homes in search of a plump, furry meal.

Clark's Nutcracker

It's the steepest part of your hike; the wind grows brisk and the trees begin to stoop and thin out. Ahead you hear the guttural "kra-aa kraaa-a" of the Clark's nutcracker, a sign that the timberline is just up the trail. Twenty-five to 100 birds may flock in the limber and whitebark pines of the timberline, perching on the top of cones or dangling beneath them. If a cone is too small to hang on to, they may twist it off and take it to a horizontal feeding perch. Holding the cone down with one foot, they pry the scales apart with their long, sharp pickax of a bill.

Each seed is evaluated before the nutcracker will swallow it. First they weigh the seed in their bill, then open and close their bill a few times in order to rattle it. Evidently, they can tell by its weight and consistency whether or not it is diseased or aborted. Sometimes, even the good seeds don't get swallowed on the spot. Instead, nutcrackers store them in a pouch on the floor of their mouth, and then, once they've packed away as many as 70 seeds, they fly to communal storage areas where they bury them in the ground. These seeds become their winter staple, enabling the birds to avoid the hazards of migrating south in order to find food.

The caching areas are usually on steep, south-facing slopes—areas where the snow will melt early or the wind will sweep it away. Patient observers who have watched the storing process report that a single nut-cracker can store 32,000 whitebark pine seeds in a harvesting season, and later find up to 70 percent of them, sometimes digging through as much as 8 inches of snow. Nutcrackers bury enough seeds to feed not only themselves, but also their nestlings. A well-stocked pantry allows them to start breeding much earlier than other birds, thus giving them an ecological advantage.

When it comes time for nesting, nutcrackers look for a site that is quite different from their cache site. Instead of a windswept area, the nutcrackers' primary concern is to find a nest tree that is well sheltered from the wind. Even though they nest in February, they don't seem to mind a cold side of a hill where snow accumulates to great depths—as long as it's out of the wind. They build their nests with extra-thick walls to keep the cold out and the heat in. In addition, the male as well as the female develops a brood patch—a bald patch on the underside of their body that swells with increased blood vessels and thickens just before the eggs are laid. When on the nest, the parents place this "heating pad" in close contact with the eggs in order to keep them warm. In most species of birds, only the female develops this patch.

Look for Clark's nutcrackers—picking at pinecones or walking along the ground like crows. In the spring, before seeds ripen, they scour the ground for beetles, ants, grasshoppers, crickets, snails, carrion, and acorns. They even fly after butterflies and other insects in the air, or pick berries and wild fruit from the vine. They will also hammer trunks for grubs or steal the eggs and young of small birds. Nutcrackers are renowned for their curiosity and boldness around campsites. You can sometimes get them to come around by imitating the call of a northern pygmy- or great horned owl. If this doesn't work, start fixing dinner, and wait until a hungry nutcracker swoops down for tidbits of your food.

Length: 12–13 inches.

Look for nests—nestled on a protected branch or bushy top of a pine or juniper. Nest trees are usually on a steep hill that is socked in with snow but well protected from the wind. The nest is a foot-wide bowl of twigs and bark, heavily lined with grass, bark, pine needles, and even some soil.

Look for shelled seeds—on the ground, indicating a possible caching area. Nutcrackers poke in the ground (often through snow), uncover a small cache of seeds, then eat them on the spot. The small pile of discarded shells might help them recognize used sites so they don't waste time digging for seeds there. Also look for split and pried-apart pinecones.

Listen for—a squawking "chaar, char-r-r, chur-r-r, kra-a-a, or kar-r-ack." Also a musical call that sounds like a toy tin trumpet.

Marten

The long, slender marten puts both paws on top of a leaning trunk and peers over it. There, in the tangle of windthrown logs, a faint rustling has piqued the marten's curiosity. Defying physics, it snakes its body through the tightly laced roots and branches, until, sure enough, it flushes a red squirrel from the other end of the brush. In a moment both animals are racing up a tree trunk in a wild chase that will send them diving from branch to branch and leaping out over open space between trees. In the final round, the marten wraps its long, sinuous body around the cornered squirrel and, with surgical precision, applies a clean, killing bite to its neck.

With the exception of the closely related fisher, the marten is the only animal that can beat the squirrel at its own treetop game. Two of its adaptations to treetop living include a set of sharp, curved claws for traction and a long, bottle-brush tail for balance on tightwire branches. Despite its arboreal prowess, the marten takes to the trees only to supplement its diet. Most of its time is spent on the ground hunting for mice, voles, chipmunks, snowshoe hares, shrews, reptiles, amphibians, insects, and berries.

A marten may travel several kilometers in a night of hunting to collect its required 80 kilocalories a day (equivalent to 3 mice). Its favorite hunting grounds seem to be mature forests that have at least a 30–50 percent canopy cover and lush shrub and forb vegetation to support rodent prey. For resting cover and denning sites, martens also need dead and dying trees, and plenty of stumps and fallen trunks. Slopes that are in the path of prevailing winds (east- and north-facing) are particularly popular because they often have high numbers of crisscrossed windfallen trees. These areas must also have live tree cover, however, because martens are reluctant to cross areas that are too open. A cutover area, for instance, is of little value to a marten for at least 15 years. It's important, therefore, that corridors of mature forest be preserved to keep travel lanes open for secretive animals like the marten.

Look for martens—combing their territories on foot, often crossing and recrossing their own tracks to investigate stumps, holes, and brush piles that may contain food. They often use fallen trees as walkways. They are active at night, but you can also see them in early morning and evening. During the day they rest in tree cavities, hollow logs, stumps, ground burrows, rock crevices, old root holes, active squirrel middens, and "witches' brooms" (bunched-up branches in trees infected with dwarf mistletoe). The same curiosity that makes them vulnerable to trapping may help you glimpse your first marten. If you sit quietly enough in a marten's home range, it might sneak up to investigate you!

Length: Head and body, 14–17 inches. Tail, 7–9 inches.

Look for nests—in hollow trees or logs or in rocky crevices. Young are usually born in tree dens and later moved down to ground level.

In the winter—they tunnel into the snow, digging down next to logs or stumps. Their relatively large foot size allows them to walk across soft snow without falling in. During the winter, their paw pad becomes heavily furred. Winter is a good time to see tracks.

Look for droppings—dark, twisted, and sometimes segmented, up to 6 inches long, deposited repeatedly at scat stations. You can distinguish them from mink and weasel droppings because they include berries and nuts in season.

Look for tracks—1½ to 1⅞ inches wide, with a stride (males) of 6 inches (doubles when running) and a straddle up to 3 inches. A leaping marten leaves a full-body impression in the snow under a tree.

Listen for—huffs, pants, chuckles, growls, screams, whines, and "eeps." When the female wants to mate, she first marks the area with her scent glands (dragging her belly over objects) and then starts a low clucking guaranteed to attract a male. Females with young may coo or utter a soft, purrlike grunt. Martens make the loudest sounds when they are cornered. Most of the time they are rather silent.

Rubber Boa

When you say "constrictor," most people think of the thick-bodied jungle snakes they see wrapped around alligators on TV. Few would believe that a genuine boa constrictor lives in many of our cool, moist mountain forests. These North American boas are only 2 feet long, and are among the slowest and gentlest snakes in the woods. Even when picked up, rubber boas rarely bite. In fact, they are more likely to coil up into a protective ball, with their head well tucked beneath their body.

Rather than fighting, which can be risky business in the natural world, natural selection has encouraged an elaborate bluff as a means of defense for the boa. To authenticate its bluff, the rubber boa's tail has evolved to look exactly like its head. From its coiled crouch, the snake lifts this false head and waves it at the predator, with motions that resemble actual strikes. If the predator attacks, it winds up injuring only the tail, while the protected head looks for a crevice, a hole, or another means of escape. The effectiveness of this ruse can be gauged by the high proportion of snakes that have scars on their tail, but are still alive and well.

When hunting its own prey—lizards, birds, small rodents, even small rattlesnakes—the boa seizes the animal with its open mouth, then throws a coil of its body around it. It holds the prey just tightly enough to keep it from taking a breath, thus killing it by suffocation, not by crushing. It then carefully swallows the prey headfirst so that wings and legs won't snag going down. To swallow something larger than its own head, it simply unlocks its flexible jaws and "chokes up" on the prey bit by bit until it engulfs it. (For more about swallowing prey, see Prairie Rattlesnake on page 144.)

Look for rubber boas—under rocks, boards, pieces of bark, rotting logs, and other debris in moist forests and adjoining mountain meadows. They readily burrow in loose soil, and have also been known to climb trees with sinuous "caterpillar" motions. Although most of their activity is at night, as well as at dusk and dawn, they can be seen out during cloudy days. Because they can survive cool temperatures that would immobilize other snakes, boas occupy a wide range, including upper elevations and northern states.

Length: 14–33 inches.

Look for young snakes—3 or 4 young boas hatch inside their mother's body and are then born alive in late July and August.

Resources for the Curious

GETTING INVOLVED

There are a number of ways you can help wildlife prosper in your area. Becoming a member of the following organizations will put you in touch with local chapters that are making provisions (through politics, research, and education) to keep wildlife habitats whole. These groups often meet to hear invited speakers or to take field trips to see wildlife. For a more complete listing of organizations, state and federal agencies, and universities involved in wildlife conservation, try the *Conservation Directory,* available through the National Wildlife Federation and many libraries.

National Audubon Society
950 Third Avenue
New York, NY 10022
Publications: *Audubon, American Birds, Audubon Wildlife Report, Audubon Adventures, Audubon Activist*
(212) 832-3200

National Wildlife Federation
1412 16th Street NW
Washington, DC 20036-2266
Publications: *National Wildlife, International Wildlife*
(202) 797-6800

Sierra Club
730 Polk Street
San Francisco, CA 94109
Publications: *Sierra, National News Report*
(415) 981-8634

The Nature Conservancy
Suite 800
1800 N. Kent Street
Arlington, VA 22209
Publication: *The Nature Conservancy News*
(703) 841-5300

The Wilderness Society
1400 I Street NW, 10th Floor
Washington, DC 20005
Publication: *Wilderness*
(202) 842-3400

World Wildlife Fund—U.S.
1250 24th Street NW
Washington, DC 20037
Publication: *Focus*
(202) 293-4800

Here are some other ways to get involved:

1. Participate in local censuses (studies that estimate numbers and locations of wildlife).
2. Volunteer to be part of a research project.
3. Take a class or teach one.
4. Keep a wildlife observation journal and share it with other wildlife watchers.
5. Write to your local representatives about the need to protect habitats in your area.
6. Manage your own land for wildlife—be it backyard or back forty.

GETTING OUTSIDE

Next time you're dreaming about a vacation, envision yourself in wildlife habitats. How many do you think you could explore on your next outing? Could you see all 18 on an extended trip through the West? For vacation-planning maps and a world of wildlife information, contact the following land management agencies (the lands they manage are in parentheses):

U.S. Forest Service (National Forests)
United States Department of Agriculture
P.O. Box 2417
Washington, DC 20013
(202) 447-3957

U.S. Fish and Wildlife Service (National Wildlife Refuges)
United States Department of the Interior
Washington, DC 20240
(202) 343-4131

National Park Service (National Parks)
United States Department of the Interior
Interior Building
P.O. Box 37127
Washington, DC 20013-7127
(202) 343-6843

Your city, county, or state land management agencies (city, county, and state parks and forests). These agencies have different names depending on where you live. Begin by calling the capitol and asking for one of the following: Department of Natural Resources, Forestry Department, Fish and Game Commission, or Conservation Department. Direct specific wildlife questions to the Non-Game Specialist.

Your State University's Cooperative Extension Service. This is a good place to get advice about managing your own land for wildlife. The Extension Service is usually connected with an agricultural or forestry college.

RECOMMENDED READING

Natural history literature, ranging from the scientific to the poetic, can be found in back-pocket guides or lavish coffee-table books. I heartily recommend reading as a great way to explore habitats when you're cabin-bound and to better appreciate habitats when you're outside. I've included mostly area-wide books, but don't forget about local guides to birds, mammals, reptiles, and amphibians. Many states have their own, as do some of the larger parks. Visitor centers and sporting goods stores are a good place to find these local guides.

Habitats

Angel, Heather, and Pat Wolseley. 1982. *The Water Naturalist.* Facts on File, NY, 192 pp.

Arno, Stephen F., and Ramona Hammerly. 1977. *Northwest Trees.* The Mountaineers, Seattle, WA, 161 pp.

Attenborough, David. 1984. *The Living Planet.* Little, Brown, & Company, Boston, 320 pp.

Bakker, Elna S. 1971. *An Island Called California: An Ecological Introduction to Its Natural Communities.* University of California Press, Berkeley, 484 pp.

Barbour, Michael G., and Jack Major. 1977. *Terrestrial Vegetation of California.* John Wiley & Sons, NY, 1002 pp.

Barrett, John W. 1980. *Regional Silviculture of the United States.* 2nd edition. John Wiley & Sons, NY, 551 pp.

Bender, G. L., ed. 1982. *Reference Handbook on the Deserts of North America.* Greenwood Press, Westport, CT, 594 pp.

Bishop, Owen N. 1973. *Natural Communities.* John Murray, London, 181 pp.

Blackford, John L. 1956. *Western Wonderlands.* Vantage Press, NY, 120 pp.

Brown, Lauren. 1985. *The Audubon Society Nature Guides. Grasslands.* Alfred A. Knopf, NY, 606 pp.

Burgis, Mary J., and Pat Morris. 1987. *The Natural History of Lakes.* Cambridge University Press, Cambridge, Great Britain, 218 pp.

Caduto, Michael J. 1985. *Pond & Brook: A Guide to Nature Study in Freshwater Environments.* Prentice-Hall, Englewood Cliffs, NJ, 276 pp.

Carefoot, Thomas. 1977. *Pacific Seashores: A Guide to Intertidal Ecology.* University of Washington Press, Seattle, WA, 208 pp.

Carson, Rachel. 1955. *The Edge of the Sea.* Houghton Mifflin, Boston, 276 pp.

Costello, David. 1969. *The Prairie World.* University of Minnesota Press, Minneapolis, MN, 244 pp.

Curry-Lindahl, Kai. 1981. *Wildlife of the Prairies and Plains.* Harry N. Abrams, NY, 232 pp.

Daubenmire, R.F., and Jean B. Daubenmire. 1968. *Forest Vegetation of Eastern Washington and Northern Idaho.* Washington Agricultural Experiment Station Technical Bulletin 60, 104 pp.

DeGraff, Richard M., ed. 1980. *Management of Western Forests and Grasslands for Nongame Birds.* Workshop Proceedings. USDA, Intermountain Forest and Range Experiment Station and Rocky Mountain Forest and Range Experiment Station, Odgen, UT, 535 pp.

Durrell, Gerald. 1984. *The Amateur Naturalist.* Alfred A. Knopf, NY, 320 pp.

Eyre, F. H., ed. 1980. *Forest Cover Types of the United States and Canada*. Society of American Foresters, Washington, DC, 148 pp.

Farb, Peter. 1963. *Face of North America: The Natural History of a Continent*. Harper & Row, NY, 316 pp.

Franklin, Jerry F., and C.T. Dyrness. 1973. *Natural Vegetation of Oregon and Washington*. USDA Forest Service General Technical Report PNW-8, Portland, OR, 417 pp.

Garrison, George A., et al. 1977. *Vegetation and Environmental Features of Forest and Range Ecosystems*. USDA Forest Service, Agricultural Handbook No. 475, Washington, DC, 68 pp.

Gleason, Henry A., and Arthur Cronquist. 1964. *The Natural Geography of Plants*. Columbia University Press, NY, 420 pp.

Grasslands and Tundra. 1985. Planet Earth Series. Time-Life Books, Alexandria, VA, 175 pp.

Hoover, Robert L., and Dale L. Wills, eds. 1984. *Managing Forested Lands for Wildlife*. Colorado Division of Wildlife, Denver, CO, 459 pp.

Hylander, Clarence J. 1966. *Wildlife Communities from the Tundra to the Tropics in North America*. Houghton Mifflin, Boston, 342 pp.

Jaeger, Edmund C., and Arthur C. Smith. 1966. *Introduction to the Natural History of Southern California*. University of California Press, Berkeley, CA, 104 pp.

Johnston, Verna. 1970. *Sierra Nevada*. Houghton Mifflin, Boston, 281 pp.

Karstad, Aleta. 1979. *Wild Habitats*. Charles Scribner's Sons, NY, 144 pp.

Kelly, Don Greame. 1972. *The Edge of the Continent: The Pacific Coast from Alaska to Baja*. American West Publishing Company, NY, 288 pp.

Kirk, Ruth. 1973. *Desert: The American Southwest*. Houghton Mifflin, Boston, 361 pp.

Kozloff, Eugene N. 1976. *Plants and Animals of the Pacific Northwest: An Illustrated Guide to the Natural History of Western Oregon, Washington, and British Columbia*. University of Washington Press, Seattle, WA, 280 pp.

MacMahon, James A. 1985. *The Audubon Society Nature Guides. Deserts*. Alfred A. Knopf, NY, 638 pp.

Madson, John. 1982. *Where the Sky Began: Land of the Tallgrass Prairie*. Houghton Mifflin, Boston, 321 pp.

Mayer, K. E., and F. W. Laudenslayer, eds. In press. *A Guide to Wildlife Habitats of California*. California Department of Forestry, Sacramento, CA.

McConnaughey, Bayard H., and Evelyn McConnaughey. 1985. *The Audubon Society Nature Guides. Pacific Coast*. Alfred A. Knopf, NY, 633 pp.

Mutel, Cornelia Fleisher, and John Emerick. 1984. *From Grassland to Glacier: The Natural History of Colorado*. Johnson Books, Boulder, CO, 238 pp.

Neiring, William. 1985. *The Audubon Society Nature Guides. Wetlands*. Alfred A. Knopf, NY, 638 pp.

Page, Jake. 1983. *Planet Earth Series. Forest*. Time-Life Books, Alexandria, VA, 176 pp.

Platt, Rutherford. 1965. *The Great American Forest*. Prentice-Hall, Englewood Cliffs, NJ, 271 pp.

Rabkin, Richard, and Jacob Rabkin. 1981. *Nature in the West: A Handbook of Habitats*. Holt, Rinehart, & Winston, NY, 248 pp.

Sackett, Russell. 1983. *The Edge of the Sea*. Time-Life Books, Alexandria, VA, 176 pp.

Sanderson, Ivan. 1961. *The Continent We Live On*. Random House, NY, 299 pp.

Schwartz, Susan. 1983. *Nature in the Northwest*. Prentice-Hall, Englewood Cliffs, NJ, 256 pp.

Shelford, Victor E. 1963. *The Ecology of North America*. University of Illinois Press, Urbana, IL, 610 pp.

Shreve, F., and I.L. Wiggins. 1964. *Vegetation and Flora of the Sonoran Desert*. Vol. I & II. Stanford University Press, Stanford, CA, 1740 pp.

Smith, Dixie R., ed. 1975. *Proceedings of the Symposium on the Management of Forest and Range Habitats for Nongame Birds.* USDA Forest Service General Technical Report WO-1, Washington, DC, 343 pp.

Society of American Foresters. 1981. *Choices in Silviculture for American Forests.* Society of American Foresters, Washington, DC, 80 pp.

Stokes, Donald W. 1981. *The Natural History of Wild Shrubs and Vines.* Harper & Row, NY, 246 pp.

USDA Forest Service. 1973. *Silvicultural Systems for Major Forest Types of the United States.* Agricultural Handbook No. 445, Washington, DC, 124 pp.

Vankat, John. 1979. *The Natural Vegetation of North America.* John Wiley & Sons, NY, 255 pp.

Wagner, Frederic H. 1980. *Wildlife of the Deserts.* Harry N. Abrams, NY, 231 pp.

Walker, L. C. 1984. *Trees: An Introduction to Trees and Forest Ecology for the Amateur Naturalist.* Prentice-Hall, Englewood Cliffs, NJ, 306 pp.

Watts, May T. 1957. *Reading the Landscape: An Adventure in Ecology.* Macmillan, NY, 230 pp.

Whitney, Stephen. 1979. *Sierra Club Naturalist's Guide to the Sierra Nevada.* Sierra Club Books, San Francisco, 526 pp.

Whitney, Stephen. 1985. *The Audubon Society Nature Guides. Western Forests.* Alfred A. Knopf, NY, 671 pp.

Whittaker, R. H. 1970. *Communities & Ecosystems.* Macmillan, NY, 158 pp.

Zwinger, Ann. 1986. *Wind in the Rock: A Naturalist Explores the Canyon Country of the Southwest.* University of Arizona Press, Tucson, AZ, 258 pp.

Wildlife
Birds

Behler, John L. 1979. *The Audubon Society Field Guide to North American Reptiles and Amphibians.* Alfred A. Knopf, NY, 718 pp.

Bent, Arthur C., et al. 1919–1968. *Life Histories of North American Birds.* 23 Volumes (various publishers).

Burton, Robert. 1985. *Bird Behavior,* Alfred A. Knopf, NY, 224 pp.

Ehrlich, Paul R., et al. 1988. *The Birder's Handbook: A Field Guide to the Natural History of North American Birds.* Simon and Schuster, NY, 785 pp.

Haley, Delphine, ed. 1984. *Seabirds of the Eastern North Pacific and Arctic Waters.* Pacific Search Press, Seattle, WA, 214 pp.

Harrison, Hal H. 1979. *A Field Guide to Western Birds' Nests.* Houghton Mifflin, Boston, 279 pp.

Perrins, Christopher M., and Alex L.A. Middleton. 1985. *The Encyclopedia of Birds.* Facts on File, NY, 447 pp.

Savage, Candace. 1985. *Wings of the North.* University of Minnesota Press, Minneapolis, MN, 211 pp.

Stokes, Donald W. 1979 and 1983. *A Guide to Bird Behavior.* 2 Volumes. Little, Brown & Company, Boston, 336 pp each.

Terres, John K. 1980. *Audubon Society Encyclopedia of North American Birds.* Alfred A. Knopf, NY, 1109 pp.

Welty, J. C. 1975. *The Life of Birds.* 2nd edition. Saunders, Philadelphia, 623 pp.

Mammals

Cahalane, Victor H. 1961. *Mammals of North America.* Macmillan, NY, 682 pp.

Forsyth, Adrian. 1985. *Mammals of the American North.* Camden House Publishing, Ltd., Camden East, Ontario, 351 pp.

Haley, Delphine, ed. 1986. *Marine Mammals of the Eastern North Pacific and Arctic Waters.* Pacific Search Press, Seattle, WA, 295 pp.

MacDonald, David. 1984. *The Encyclopedia of Mammals.* Facts on File, NY, 895 pp.

Maser, Chris, et al. 1981. *Natural History of Oregon Coast Mammals.* USDA Forest Service, Pacific Northwest Forest and Range Experiment Station, General Technical Report PNW-133. Portland, OR, 496 pp.

Nowak, R. M., and J. L. Paradise. 1983. *Walker's Mammals of the World.* 2 Volumes. 4th edition. The Johns Hopkins University Press, Baltimore, MD, 1362 pp.

Savage, Arthur, and Candace Savage. 1981. *Wild Mammals of Northwest America.* The Johns Hopkins University Press, Baltimore, MD, 209 pp.

Whitaker, John O., Jr. 1988. *The Audubon Society Field Guide to North American Mammals.* Alfred A. Knopf, NY, 744 pp.

Reptiles and Amphibians

Ernst, Carl H., and Roger W. Barbour. 1972. *Turtles of the United States.* The University Press of Kentucky, Lexington, KY, 347 pp.

Halliday, Tim R., and Kraig Adler. 1986. *The Encyclopedia of Reptiles and Amphibians.* Facts on File, NY, 143 pp.

Obst, Fritz Jurgen. 1986. *Turtles, Tortoises, and Terrapins.* St. Martin's Press, NY, 231 pp.

Parker, H. W. 1977. *Snakes: A Natural History.* 2nd edition. British Museum of Natural History. Cornell University Press, Ithaca, NY, 108 pp.

Shaw, Charles E., and Sheldon Campbell. 1974. *Snakes of the American West.* Alfred A. Knopf, NY, 328 pp.

Stebbins, Robert C. 1985. *A Field Guide to Western Reptiles and Amphibians.* Houghton Mifflin, Boston, 336 pp.

General

Grzimeks, B. 1972. *Animal Life Encyclopedia.* 13 Volumes. Van Nostrand Reinhold, NY.

Martin, Alexander C., Herbert S. Zim, and Arnold L. Nelson. 1961 reprint of 1951 edition. *American Wildlife and Plants: A Guide to Wildlife Food Habits.* Dover Publications, NY, 500 pp.

Ways of Seeing: Wildlife Watching

Brown, Vinson. 1972. *Reading the Outdoors at Night.* Stackpole Books, Harrisburg, PA, 191 pp.

Brown, Vinson. 1969. *Reading the Woods.* Collier Books, NY, 160 pp.

Durrell, Gerald M., with Lee Durrell. 1983. *The Amateur Naturalist.* Alfred A. Knopf, NY, 320 pp.

Farrand, John, Jr. 1988. *How to Identify Birds.* McGraw-Hill Book Company, NY, 320 pp.

Heintzelman, Donald S. 1979. *A Manual for Bird Watching in the Americas.* Universe Books, NY, 255 pp.

Kress, Stephen W. 1981. *The Audubon Society Handbook for Birders.* Charles Scribner's Sons, NY, 322 pp.

Leahy, Christopher. 1982. *The Birdwatcher's Dictionary: An Encyclopedic Handbook of North American Birdlife.* Bonanza Books, NY, 917 pp.

McElroy, Thomas P., Jr. 1974. *The Habitat Guide to Birding.* Alfred A. Knopf, NY, 257 pp.

Murie, Olaus J. 1974. *A Field Guide to Animal Tracks.* Houghton Mifflin, Boston, 375 pp.

Pettingill, Olin S., Jr. 1953. *A Guide to Bird Finding West of the Mississippi.* 2nd edition. Oxford University Press, NY, 709 pp.

Riley, W. 1979. *Guide to National Wildlife Refuges.* Anchor Press, Garden City, NY, 653 pp.

Roth, Charles E. 1982. *The Wildlife Observer's Guidebook.* Prentice-Hall, Englewood Cliffs, NJ, 239 pp.

Stokes, Donald, and Lillian Stokes. 1986. *A Guide to Animal Tracking and Behavior.* Little, Brown & Company, Boston, 418 pp.

Thinking About Wildlife

Dillard, Annie. 1978 reprint of 1974 edition. *Pilgrim at Tinker Creek.* Bantam Books, NY, 279 pp.

Ehrlich, Paul R., and Anne Ehrlich. 1981. *Extinction.* Random House, NY, 305 pp.

Leopold, Aldo. 1966 reprint of 1949 edition. *A Sand County Almanac with Essays on Conservation from Round River.* Ballantine Books, NY, 295 pp.

Tributsch, H. 1982. *How Life Learned to Live: Adaptation in Nature.* MIT Press, Cambridge, MA, 218 pp.

Common and Scientific Names of Plants

(Page numbers refer to Characteristic Plants Charts for each habitat.)

Common Name *Scientific Name*

Acacia, Whitethorn *Acacia constricta* 166

Alaska-cedar *Chamaecyparis nootkatensis* 290

Alder, Arizona *Alnus oblongifolia* 221

Alder, Mountain *Alnus tenuifolia* 96, 221

Alder, Red *Alnus rubra* 221, 234, 262, 277

Alder, White *Alnus rhombifolia* 96, 221

Alders *Alnus* spp. 207, 277

Algae *Trientepholia* spp. 53

Algae, Corraline *Corallina* spp. 53

Algae, Enteromorpha Green *Enteromorpha* spp. 53

Algae, Green *Cladophora* spp. 53

Amaranth, Redroot *Amaranthus retroflexus* 135

Angelica, Giant *Angelica ampla* 96

Arnica, Heartleaf *Arnica cordifolia* 262, 277, 290

Arnica, Meadow *Arnica chamissonis* spp. *foliosa* 81

Arrowgrass, Seaside *Triglochin maritimum* 66

Arrowhead, Common *Sagittaria latifolia* 81, 108, 207

Ash, Green *Fraxinus pennsylvanica* 221, 234

Ash, Oregon *Fraxinus latifolia* 96, 221, 234

Ash, Velvet *Fraxinus velutina* 221

Aspen, Quaking *Populus tremuloides* 96, 207, 221, 248, 262, 277, 290

Aster, Hairy Golden *Heterotheca villosa* 135, 166, 193

Aster, Leafy *Aster foliaceus* 135

Common name *Scientific name*

Aster, Siskiyou *Aster hesperius* 96

Asters *Aster* spp. 96, 135

Avens, Large-leaved *Geum macrophyllum* 135

Azalea, Western *Rhododendron occidentale* 96, 120, 234

Baccharis *Baccharis* spp. 234

Balsamroot, Arrowleaf *Balsamorhiza sagittata* 166, 193

Baneberry, Red *Actaea rubra*

Banner, Golden *Thermopsis divaricarpa*

Barberry, Colorado *Berberis fendleri* 248

Barley, Foxtail *Hordeum jubatum* 81, 135, 166, 221

Barley, Meadow *Hordeum brachyantherum* 66

Bayberry, Pacific (Waxmyrtle) *Myrica californica* 234

Beadlily, Queen's Cup *Clintonia uniflora* 290

Beak, Marsh Bird's *Cordylanthus maritimus* 66

Beak, Soft Bird's *Cordylanthus mollis* 66

Bean, Buck *Menyanthes trifoliata* 81

Beargrass *Xerophyllum tenax* 290

Bedstraw, Small *Galium trifidum* 120

Bedstraw, Sweetscented *Galium triflorum* 207, 290

Bedstraws *Galium* spp. 249

Birch, Bog *Betula glandulosa* 96

Birch, Paper *Betula papyrifera* 207, 290

Birch, River *Betula fontinalis* 96

Birch, Water *Betula occidentalis* 81, 96, 221

Biscuitroots *Lomatium* spp.

Bistort, American *Polygonum bistortoides* 81, 120

Bitterbrush, Antelope *Purshia tridentata* 166, 193, 207, 248

Bittercress, Heartleaved *Cardamine cordifolia* 81, 96, 290

Blackberries *Rubus* spp. 221, 234

Blackbrush *Coleogyne ramosissima* 166, 193

Bladderpod, Mountain *Lesquerella montana* 135, 249

Bladderpods *Lesquerella* spp. 151

Bladderwort, Common *Utricularia vulgaris* 108

Blanket-flower *Gaillardia aristata* 166, 249

Blazing-star, Dotted *Liatris punctuata* 135

Bluebell, Mountain *Mertensia ciliata* 96, 120, 290

Bluebells *Mertensia* spp. 81, 135

Blueberries (Huckleberries) *Vaccinium* spp. 277, 290

Blueblossom *Ceanothus thyrsiflorus* 234

Bluegrass, Alpine *Poa alpina* 120

Bluegrass, Cusick *Poa cusickii* 120

Bluegrass, Fowl *Poa palustris* 96, 120

Bluegrass, Kentucky *Poa pratensis* 135

Bluegrass, Nevada *Poa nevadensis* 166

Bluegrass, Nodding *Poa reflexa* 96, 120

Bluegrass, Secunda *Poa sandbergii* 135, 166, 193

Bluegrasses *Poa* spp. 96, 207, 221, 249

Bluestem, Big *Andropogon gerardii* 135

Bluestem, Little *Andropogon scoparius* 135

Bluestem, Sand *Andropogon hallii* 135

Boa, Feather *Egregia menziesii* 53

Boas *Egregia* spp. 53

Bower, Virgin's *Clematis* spp. 135, 221

Boxelder *Acer negundo* 221

Boxwood, Oregon *Pachistima myrsinites* 277, 290

Brome, Cheatgrass *Bromus tectorum* 135, 166, 193, 249

Brome, Mountain *Bromus carinatus* 249

Bromegrasses *Bromus* spp. 180, 207

Brookgrass *Catabrosa aquatica* 120

Brush, Deer *Ceanothus integerrimus* 248

Brush, Nail *Endocladia muricata* 53

Buckbrush *Ceanothus fendleri* 180, 248

Buckeye, California *Aesculus californica* 180

Buckthorn, California *Rhamnus californica* 180, 248

Buckthorn, Hollyleaf *Rhamnus crocea* 180

Buckwheats *Eriogonum* spp. 166, 193

Buckwheat, Sulfur *Eriogonum umbellatum* 249

Buffaloberry, Canada *Shepherdia canadensis* 207, 277, 290

Bulrush, Great *Scirpus validus* 108

Bulrush, Hardstem *Scirpus acutus* 81, 96, 108, 221

Bulrush, Low *Scirpus cernuus* 66

Bulrush, Panicled *Scirpus microcarpus* 96

Bulrush, Saltmarsh *Scirpus robustus* 66

Bulrush, Seacoast *Scirpus maritimus*

Bulrush, Three-square *Scirpus americanus* 66

Bulrushes *Scirpus* spp. 108

Bur-reed, Narrowleaf *Sparganium angustifolium* 81, 108

Bush, Brittle *Encelia farinosa* 151

Bush, Cliff *Jamesia americana* 262

Bush, Coyote *Baccharis pilularis* 66, 234

Bush, Creosote *Larrea tridentata* 151

Bush, Iodine *Allenrolfea occidentalis* 166

Buttercup, Hairleaf Water *Ranunculus aquatilis* 221

Buttercup, Rocky Mountain *Ranunculus cymbalaria*

Buttercup, Yellow Water *Ranunculus flabellaris* 81, 108

Buttercups *Ranunculus* spp. 81

Buttonbush *Cephalanthus occidentalis* 221

Buttons, Brass *Cotula corenopifolia* 66

Cabbage, Yellow Skunk *Lysichitum americanum* 81, 108

Cactus, Barrel *Ferocactus acanthodes* 151

Cactus, Beavertail *Opuntia basilaris* 151

Cactus, Candelabra *Cylindropuntia imbricata* 135, 193

Cactus, Desert Christmas *Opuntia leptocaulis* 151

Cactus, Fishhook *Mammilaria microcarpa* 151

Cactus, Fishhook Barrel *Ferocactus wislizenii* 151

Cactus, Hedgehog *Echinocereus engelmannii* 151

Cactus, Organ Pipe *Cereus thurberi* 151

Common and Scientific Names of Birds, Mammals, Amphibians, and Reptiles

(Page numbers refer to Wildlife Locator Charts for each habitat.)

INDEX

(Page numbers in *italics* refer to illustrations. Page numbers in **boldface** refer to life history profiles. This is an index to the narrative portions of the text.)